Poverty and inequality
in Common Market countries

Poverty and inequality in Common Market countries

Edited by
Vic George
Professor of Social Policy and Administration,
University of Kent

and
Roger Lawson
Lecturer in Social Policy and Administration,
University of Southampton

Routledge & Kegan Paul

London, Boston and Henley

First published in 1980
by Routledge & Kegan Paul Ltd

39 Store Street,
London WC1E 7DD,

Broadway House,
Newtown Road,
Henley-on-Thames,
Oxon RG9 1EN and

9 Park Street,
Boston, Mass. 02108, USA

Set in IBM Press Roman by
Hope Services, Abingdon
and printed in Great Britain by
Lowe & Brydone Ltd, Thetford, Norfolk

British Library Cataloguing in Publication Data

Poverty and inequality in Common Market countries.

   1. Income distribution — European Economic
Community countries
   2. European Economic Community countries — Economic
conditions
   I. George, Victor II. Lawson, Roger
   339.2'094   HC240.9.15   79-41590

   ISBN 0 7100 0424 9
   ISBN 0 7100 0517 2 Pbk

Contents

Tables

France

Ireland

Italy

West Germany

EEC Countries

Introduction

When we embarked on this study, we planned to provide answers to three main questions: (a) How is poverty defined in the various EEC countries and what government policies are there to deal with the problem? (b) How extensive is inequality in income and wealth in the various EEC countries? (c) What trends can be established in the understanding, treatment and prevalence of poverty and inequality? We decided that the emphasis in the study should be on conditions and trends within the individual states of the EEC and we should not attempt to examine the activities of the European Commission or other Community institutions in the field. As students of social policy we were anxious to discuss poverty and inequality in terms of the other social services and particularly of social security; and to take account, as far as possible, of the various social divisions in society – class, sex, ethnicity, urban/rural, age and so on.

Though we provided the authors of each chapter with guidelines, we also allowed them enough freedom to write their chapters in such a way as to bring out the national flavour of policies, debates, trends, and so on. We anticipated that there would be difficulties in terms of the nature of data needed to write each chapter: unreliable data, noncomparable data, or even total absence of data. And we were not proved wrong! Indeed, we underestimated the difficulties; and this is shown by the fact that we have not been able to include chapters on Denmark, the Netherlands and Luxemburg. Our final chapter shows some of these difficulties, for we have not been able to make strict and detailed comparisons among the various countries along all the dimensions we originally planned. In spite of these difficulties and inadequacies, we hope the book will be of some use to students of social policy and to government administrators.

Our sincere thanks to all our contributors, without whose perseverance the book would not have been completed. We are also grateful to Margaret Joyce for generous secretarial work. As editors, we accept the responsibility for errors and inadequacies, inevitable in such a study.

It is a sad reflection that after twenty-five years of unprecedented economic growth and massive government expenditure in social security, poverty is still prevalent in all EEC countries. Economic growth and increased public expenditure do not by themselves reduce inequalities or abolish poverty. Governments need to implement explicitly designed policies to achieve such ends.

Vic George, University of Kent
Roger Lawson, University of Southampton

1 Explanations of poverty and inequality

Vic George

There is no shortage of attempts to explain inequality and poverty. Indeed so many theories have been put forward that a summary of them will be a lengthy task in itself. A more serious difficulty is the lack of any sustained effort to group such theories into those which attempt to explain why there is inequality and poverty and those which attempt to explain which individuals are likely to be the low paid and the poor. Such an attempt is made in this chapter, which distinguishes between macro-theories which deal with the causes of inequality and poverty and micro-theories which are concerned with the distribution of inequality and poverty. Before discussing these theories, it is necessary to distinguish between inequality and poverty.

Definitions

Inequality is used to refer to the unequal distribution of income and wealth as well as of status and power. It is a feature of all contemporary societies irrespective of economic development, political system or anything else. There may be legitimate debate about the extent of inequality in different societies but not about its existence. While acknowledging the importance of status and power in society, this chapter is concerned with inequalities of income and wealth only. An attempt to explain these inequalities, however, will throw some light on the former, for the two are related.

Poverty is not so easily defined; or rather there is not the same consensus of opinion as to its meaning as there is with regard to inequality. If it is confined to income and wealth, two main types of definition have been used so far. The first definition is an 'absolute' standard which does not change much over time or across countries. Rowntree's work in Britain at the end of the last century was the first serious attempt to define poverty in absolute terms. His work has been extremely influential on subsequent studies and on social policy both in Britain and in other countries. According to Rowntree, a family is in poverty if its 'total earnings are insufficient to obtain the minimum necessaries for the maintenance of merely physical efficiency.'[1] The 'minimum necessaries' were food, clothing, housing, heating, lighting and utensils for cooking and washing—all purchased at the lowest prices and in quantities necessary for physical subsistence only. Once the standard has been 'scientifically' decided, all that is needed is to update it to take into account the rise in prices of the basic necessities.

Experience since Rowntree has shown that an absolute definition of poverty is impossible to sustain over a long period of time during which the general standard of living has risen substantially. Rowntree himself partly acknowledged this in his second study in 1936 when his poverty line was 40 per cent higher than his former one, after taking into account the rise in prices. The improvement, however, was much less substantial when the two poverty lines were compared with the prevailing level of wages.[2] The main reason is, of course, the very obvious fact that what are considered basic necessities as well as the acceptable amount and quality of basic necessities change over time. It is possible, however, to maintain an absolute definition of poverty over a short period of time. The official poverty line in the USA, for example, is adjusted annually according to changes in prices but not in wages. Thus the poverty line for a family of four constituted 55 per cent of the median income in 1959 and 38 per cent in 1972. As a recent OECD report observed, it is not surprising that the extent of poverty declined during these thirteen years because 'economic growth is likely to eliminate much of it without any special income maintenance programmes'.[3]

The second definition views poverty in relative terms. It is based on the notion that needs are not physiologically based but culturally determined. It has a long theoretical tradition with such diverse exponents as Hegel, Adam Smith and Marx. 'By necessities I understand,' wrote Adam Smith, 'not only the commodities which are indispensably necessary for the support of life, but whatever the custom of the country renders it indecent for creditable people, even of the lowest order, to be without.'[4] This view of poverty remained dormant and had little influence on social science thinking and on social policy until the 1960s when poverty was 'rediscovered' in the USA and in Britain. Its influence, however, has been greater on academic thinking than on actual government policy. Nevertheless, several industrially advanced countries began in the late 1960s to raise their poverty line annually to keep pace with the rise in wages. This enabled the poor, or rather those who relied on social security benefits, to gain from rising national economic prosperity. Thus a relative concept of poverty was grafted on an absolute standard—producing an absolute muddle, as we shall see in the next chapter. No serious work has been done to determine the exact criteria to be used in estimating the level of the relative poverty line. With all its imperfections, the subsistence poverty line of Rowntree was based on some survey work within a conceptual framework. Townsend's recent work in rigorously defining relative poverty is a welcome advance but it needs to be put to the test of applied research.[5]

A general acceptance of the relative view of poverty and a general rejection of the absolute standard, however, can lead to incongruous conclusions in comparative studies. It can, for example, lead to the conclusion that the extent of poverty in India is not too different from that in West Germany; that in underdeveloped countries the extent of poverty, using a relative standard, is lower than using an absolute yardstick; and vice versa the extent of poverty in affluent societies is higher if based on a relative rather than an absolute definition. It is thus important to keep the absolute definition of poverty in mind when one is discussing conditions in underdeveloped countries. It is only in industrially advanced and affluent societies that the absolute definition of poverty has lost most of its usefulness. Even in such societies it is useful to keep the notion in mind and perhaps use the term destitution to refer to it to avoid confusion with poverty used in relative terms.[6]

Relative poverty is not the same as inequality. It is only the tail end of inequality that prevails at any one time. Where relative poverty begins on the ladder of inequality is a political issue decided in the political arena of a country. The higher up it is, however, the greater its effect on the income distribution of the country. An acceptance of a relative definition of poverty does not necessarily mean that poverty will always exist, because it is quite possible for governments to ensure that no one has an income below whatever the relative poverty line happens to be at any one time. Clearly, too, abolition of relative poverty does not mean abolition of inequality though it does mean a reduction of it. Indeed, governments of many industrially advanced countries have proclaimed their intention of abolishing relative poverty but certainly not inequality. In spite of the fact that relative poverty is the tail-end of inequality, it is viewed differently both morally and politically. In Marshall's words, 'Poverty is a tumour which should be cut out and theoretically could be; inequality is a vital organ which is functioning badly.'[7] A less emotive and a more correct way of expressing this is to say that moderate inequality is acceptable but excessive inequality is not.

For purposes of explanation, poverty is best seen as part of inequality. To explain inequality is to explain both wealth and poverty, for the two are the extreme positions of income distribution in society.

Macro-theories of inequality and poverty

The two main schools of thought attempting to explain the causes of inequality and poverty are the functional and conflict explanations of social stratification. The functional school is the more coherent of the two and it is to be found in the work of Talcot Parsons, Kingsley Davis and Wilbert Moore. The conflict school has no generally acknowledged leaders, largely because there is no generally agreed conflict theory. All conflict theory writers of social stratification, however, adopt, in varying degrees, a Marxist perspective, and it is a composite semi-Marxist conflict explanation that this chapter will examine as a rival to the functional view.

Functional theories of social stratification

The functional explanation of stratification encompasses income inequality and hence poverty, though it does not specifically refer to poverty. The Davis-Moore seminal paper in 1945 is the most systematic presentation of the functional view of social stratification. All societies are stratified even though the forms that stratification takes may differ. Inequality of income, status and prestige is therefore a universal phenomenon. The fundamental reason for this is that in every society there are certain positions which are more functional to the survival of that society than other positions. Society must, therefore, ensure both that the most able fill those positions and that once so filled the proper incentives are provided for their adequate functioning. At a more general level, society must place the 'proper' people into the 'proper' positions and then provide them with adequate incentives to fulfil the duties related to those positions as well as possible. The incentives required are economic, aesthetic and symbolic. These rewards go with the job, so to speak, and the occupants of the job are therefore the rightful owners. Since the rewards that go with different jobs must be unequal, then the whole society must be stratified. 'The rewards and their distribution become a part of the social order and thus give rise to stratification. Social inequality is thus an unconsciously evolved device by which societies insure that the most important positions are conscientiously filled by the most qualified persons.'[8] Thus social stratification and hence income inequality and poverty are universal, necessary and inevitable. Inequality benefits all in society including the poor. Poverty must exist if society is to function adequately and efficiently.

At the heart of the Davis-Moore thesis is the varying functionality of different positions in society. Davis and Moore suggested two criteria for the functionality of any position: the uniqueness of a position and the number of other positions that are dependent on it. It may be possible to demonstrate that within the same organisation some positions are more functional than others. Thus it can be argued that the position of a Vice-Chancellor in a university is more functional than the position of a lecturer since it is more central to the university as an institution and more positions within the university depend on the Vice-Chancellor than on a lecturer. On the other hand, however, students can be influenced more by the quality of an individual lecturer than by the quality of the Vice-Chancellor. If comparisons between positions in the same organisation are difficult and involve a great deal of tautological argument and implicit value assumptions, comparison between positions in different organisations is well nigh impossible. Is the position of the Vice-Chancellor more functional than the position of a headmaster of a primary school, or of an airline pilot? The vagueness of the concept of functional importance is more fully demonstrated when it is applied to the occupational hierarchy of contemporary advanced industrial societies. In such societies, professional and administrative occupations are top, followed by white collar workers, skilled workers and unskilled manual workers. In what ways are accountants more important to the survival of society than miners? Or how are farm workers less important than salesmen? The suggestion by some sociologists that functional importance could be determined not by the Davis-Moore criteria but by public opinion is not very useful. What type of criteria will the public use to assess functional importance? Will people's opinions correspond to reality or will they merely echo prevailing ideology with regard to the ranking of positions in the social hierarchy?

Davis and Moore, however, argued that the functional importance of a position is not the sole criterion for its ranking. The scarcity of the right persons to fill positions is the other. Positions which require substantial training or high intellectual abilities will have to provide greater rewards in order to attract the right people. Davis and Moore do not elaborate on the inter-relationships between functional importance and scarcity of personnel. Positions which possess both criteria will rank high but will positions where one or the other criterion exist rank equally? Are the two criteria of equal weight or do they differ? If they do, is their difference constant or does it vary according to circumstances? If it is the latter, then it needs to be defined clearly for empirical assessment.

The scarcity of personnel argument rests on two assumptions: that talent is limited and that long training needs to be rewarded. In advanced industrial societies, however, where the cost of training is borne mostly by the state, it can be argued that the individuals concerned make no great sacrifice and hence have no great claim to greater rewards. The pool of talent argument is too crude as presented by Davis and Moore. Not only are the talents and abilities needed by different positions different and not necessarily differential, but there is no evidence that the number of people with high abilities *vis-à-vis* the numbers of the most important jobs is limited.

Indeed, as Tumin has argued, the more rigidly stratified a society is, the more it thwarts the discovery and development of talent. Stratification is thus dysfunctional rather than functional to the well-being of society.[9]

The motivational assumptions of the Davis-Moore hypothesis have also been criticised by Tumin and particularly by the Polish sociologist W. Wesolowski. The implicit view of man in the Davis-Moore thesis is that he is lazy, selfish and materialistic. Thus, the rewards which are offered for positions of authority are correspondingly designed. There is no reason to believe, however, that it is not possible to induce people to occupy positions of authority by equal rewards in societies culturally different from western European societies.[10] Davis and Moore have, as a result, confined their thesis to mainly competitive, achievement-oriented societies.

Even with this restriction, however, the functional thesis is ideologically conservative. It assumes that the people who today occupy the better paid and more prestigious positions have done so because of their superior talent and their longer training. It ignores substantial empirical evidence which indicates that family background is a prime factor. The importance of family background is even greater with regard to the persistence of social inequality across generations. Buckley's criticism that Davis and Moore confuse social differentiation, (i.e. social inequality in any one generation) and social stratification (i.e. social inequality from generation to generation) is clearly valid. Family background is important to both but crucial to the second.[11] It is totally unrealistic to maintain that people do not use the privileges and wealth which they may possess in order to further their own and their descendants' position. Such an implicit assertion flies in the face of everyday reality.

The Davis-Moore thesis emphasises the functional necessity of inequality and makes no mention of the dysfunction of inequality. Tawney, among others, argued that extreme inequalities and power lead to a denial of equality of opportunity for all, they accentuate conflict and strife in society and they do not make the best use of the country's resources, since the rich squander money on frivolities.[12] Forty years later, Gans made similar points about the dysfunction of inequality in American society.[13] Extreme inequality and poverty are not only not beneficial, but they are definitely harmful to the well-being and integration of society. They promote social and industrial conflict and they undermine industrial efficiency and productivity, social stability and order. In brief, while there may be an element of truth in the Davis-Moore thesis that some jobs may be more important to society's survival and economic advancement than others, the theory is too vague and crude to explain the existing pattern and extent of inequality in advanced industrial societies.

Conflict theories of social stratification

If functional explanations stress consensus and functionalism, conflict explanations stress conflict and power in society. While functional explanations assume general consensus in society as regards values and interests, conflict explanations see conflict at both the social class level and the group level as a general prevalent feature of society. If the unequal functional importance of different positions is the key concept of functional explanations, the unequal possession of power by social classes and groups is the corresponding concept of conflict explanations.

The concept of power raises as many problems as the concept of functionality. What exactly is power, how do we ascertain its existence, and how do we measure it? Clearly, the definition of power one uses will influence and it may even predetermine the outcome of research designed to ascertain and measure it. The pluralist model of power advanced by Dahl defines power like this: 'A has power over B to the extent that he can get B to do something that B would not otherwise do.'[14] It is a situation-based view of power. One must study concrete situations of decision-making in order to find out who influences whom in direct and indirect ways. Thus in his study of community decision-making, Dahl set out to[15]

> determine for each decision which participants had initiated alternatives that were finally adopted, had vetoed alternatives initiated by others, or had proposed alternatives that were turned down.
> These actions were then tabulated as individual 'successes' or 'defeats'. The participants with the greatest proportion of successes out of the total number of successes were then considered to be the most influential.

The main objection to the pluralist model is not concerned so much with what it covers but with what it leaves out. Thus Bachrach and Baratz refer to the two faces of power. The pluralist model covers only one – decision-making – and leaves out the equally, if not more important, face of power i.e. non-decision making. The pluralist approach to power, they write, 'takes no account of the fact that power may be, and often is, exercised by confining the scope of decision-making to relatively "safe" issues.'[16] They are concerned not only with the actual exercise of power round the conference table but also with the source of power in society which can ensure that vital issues are left out of public debate. The source of power in society can be found in the economic and value structure of society which benefits the *status quo*.

Lukes extends the Bachrach-Baratz two-dimensional view of power into a three-dimensional concept. The two-dimensional view of power holds that the 'non-decision-making face of power' only exists when the researcher can uncover genuine grievances and conflicts of interest in a

8   Vic George

specific issue. Thus Bachrach and Baratz argue that 'if there is no conflict, overt or covert, the presumption must be that there is consensus
on the prevailing allocation of values, in which case, non-decision
making is impossible.'[17] In other words, if there is general public agreement on a specific issue it is impossible 'to determine empirically whether the consensus is genuine or instead has been enforced through
non-decision making.'[18] Bachrach and Baratz do not say that in such
situations non-decision making does not operate; simply that we cannot
tell whether it does or not.

This creates difficulties in the analysis of power. Does the fact that
bus drivers do not overtly or covertly ask for wages equal to those of
solicitors mean that they are genuinely agreed on this or that they have
been socialised to accept this as right and proper? Lukes points out
that, 'To assume that the absence of grievance equals genuine consensus is simply to rule out the possibility of false or manipulated consensus by definitional fact.'[19] But equally dangerous is to assume that
false consciousness accounts for all situations where there is no grievance.
Lukes's attempts to resolve this dilemma by postulating the notion of
'latent conflict'. A conflict is latent 'in the sense that it is assumed that
there would be a conflict of wants or preferences between those exercising power and those subject to it, were the latter to become aware of
their interests.'[20] He maintains that it is possible to ascertain empirically
the existence of latent conflicts by examining the ways in which the
political system operates. In the last analysis, however, the researcher
would have to make certain assumptions as to what the real interests of
those subjected to power are. Thus Lukes refers approvingly to Crenson's study of the air-pollution issue in American cities, where Crenson
shows that in a city where strong business interests prevailed the issue
of pollution was prevented from becoming a political issue for a long
time, and when it emerged as a political issue it was resolved in ways
that took into account the interests of US Steel, the company that
dominated the city. The relevant point for our discussion is that the
ordinary man's real interests were served by anti-pollution measures
on the assumption that 'other things being equal, people would rather
not be poisoned (assuming in particular that pollution control does not
necessarily mean unemployment) even where they may not even articu-
late this preference.'[21]

The differences between the two- and three-dimensional views of
power may not be all that great for research purposes. They both
acknowledge the difficulties involved in the analysis of issues where
covert conflict is not evident, but they attempt to deal with these
difficulties from different perspectives. Fundamentally, however, they
both see power as concentrated in the hands of the small population
group that owns the country's wealth. This group has dominated not

only the country's economic system but its dominant value system as well, with the result that it has succeeded in exercising an unduly great influence on the country's political system and its decisions on fundamental issues. They see the economic and political élites as inter-related in a variety of ways to their mutual benefit. Referring to the situation in this country, Worsley epitomises the general conclusion of this school of thought: 'The uninterrupted, albeit modified, dominance of the property-owning classes, in a society which has long been the most highly "proletarianised" in the world, is surely one of the most striking phenomena of modern times.'[22]

Inequality and poverty are seen as the inevitable result of the maldistribution of power. They are not an unconscious device benefiting all in society but an 'enforced condition',[23] benefiting the powerful. They perform a number of functions, all of which benefit the wealthy sections of society. Gans lists fifteen such functions – 4 economic, 3 political and 8 socio-cultural. They ensure that 'dirty' work is done; that some types of work are done cheaply; the poor serve as the battleground for politicians anxious to promote policies that do not necessarily serve the poor; poverty acts as a reminder to those who may feel like not conforming to the work ethos; the poor act as scapegoats; and so on.[24] Thus, while a functional explanation accepts the legitimacy of the existing economic order, a conflict explanation sees it as illegitimate.

In a later section we shall discuss which are the less powerful groups in society and how they lose out in the struggle for the distribution of economic rewards. We conclude this section by saying that the conflict explanation of inequality makes better sense than the functional explanation in contemporary industrial societies, where power so obviously determines the resolution of everyday conflicts in economic and social issues. The conflict explanation is more adequate, perhaps, in explaining why inequality persists rather than how it originated. The functional explanation, however, is even more inadequate in explaining either the origins or the continuation of inequality.

Micro-theories of inequality and poverty

Whether the main cause of poverty in advanced capitalist industrial societies is the functional utility of different positions in society, or the exploitative power of different groups in society, there still remains the problem of explaining the distribution of poverty; i.e., which individual or group characteristics decide who is going to be poor. There have been a number of explanations which can be grouped under three headings: those which offer individual characteristics; those which put forward sub-cultural factors; and those which consider structural reasons. These characteristics or factors will decide which people will occupy the low-paid positions in society. The first two approaches are in line with the functional theory, while the structural approach is in line with the conflict theory of inequality and poverty.

Individual characteristics

Intelligence and education are the two main individual characteristics which have been extensively discussed by psychologists, sociologists, economists and others as being responsible for income inequalities and particularly inequalities in earnings from employment. These two characteristics have been used both jointly as well as individually as explanations of inequality. The most extreme claim for the importance of these two factors rests on a series of four inter-related hypotheses: intelligence can be defined, measured and is largely due to genetic factors; intelligence, so defined, is substantially correlated with educational standard; intelligence and educational standard are strongly correlated with occupational status; and, finally, intelligence, educational standard and occupational status are strongly correlated with income inequality.

Intelligence is a confused concept. It has been variously defined as capacity to learn, ability to reason abstractly, speed of assimilating new information, and so on. There is no agreed definition. Psychologists have also been divided as to whether intelligence is one general factor that affects an individual's performance in a variety of situations, or whether it is a group of special factors each of which affects one aspect of an individual's performance, or whether it is a combination of a general factor and a number of special factors. The general consensus nowadays is that intelligence consists of a general factor (g) and a number of special factors (s) such as verbal ability, numerical ability, spatial ability, memory, reasoning, etc. Disagreement still exists, however, as to the relative importance of each special factor, of the inter-relationships between special factors, and of the extent of correlation between the general factors and each of the special factors.

Whatever intelligence may be, it is measured by standardised IQ tests. An individual's score in an IQ test says something about his intelligence in relation to others in the same age-group. IQ tests, to be fair, must not discriminate against any one group in society; and a great deal of work has been put into the construction and validation of fair tests. Nevertheless, IQ tests still discriminate against working-class respondents in varying degrees. This is partly because some of the questions included in IQ tests reflect scholastic knowledge, a fact which favours middle-class respondents. It is also because the questions, diagrams and problems included in the IQ tests reflect more the experience of middle-class society than working-class life. In general

Ryan's conclusion that it is 'probably impossible to standardise a test perfectly and without bias' is justified.[25]

Bearing in mind the problems in defining intelligence and the biases involved in its measurement, how much of an individual's IQ score is due to heredity and how much to environment? This is an important issue for the extent to which measured intelligence is due to environmental factors; to that extent it is a consequence and not a possible cause of inequality. There is no agreement on this issue. At one extreme Halsey maintains that 'distribution of innate intelligence among different social classes is approximately random and that the mean differences found in tested intelligence between different social classes are due, not to genetic constitution but solely to environment.'[26] At the other extreme, Eysenck claims that 'the best available estimates suggest a ratio of 4 to 1 for the relative importance of the contributions of heredity and environment.'[27] Between these two extremes there is considerable variety of estimates, and it does not seem that there is likely to be any more agreement in the near future.[28] Jencks, who adopts a middle position in the heredity versus environment controversy, concluded that innate intelligence (i.e. that part of a person's IQ score due to hereditary factors) had very little to do with income distribution in the USA. He estimated that if innate intelligence was the same for the entire American population, it would reduce income inequalities by only 3 per cent.[29] Similarly, Bowles and Nelson, reviewing the American literature, concluded that 'the genetic inheritance of IQ is a relatively minor mechanism for the inter-generational transmission of economic social status.'[30] Though the literature is sparse and is confined to the USA, it suggests that innate intelligence has little to do with inequality. Poverty is no more due to low intelligence than wealth is due to genius.

There seems to be more support for the crude effects of educational standards, i.e. years of schooling and inequality in earnings. There is general agreement that there is a crude correlation between level of earnings and level of schooling. Using comparative data, Blaug showed that in the USA, UK, India and Mexico, the more schooling people received, the higher their earnings. Other studies, including some in the UK, have shown the same correlation.[31] There is a strong controversy, however, about the validity of this correlation when family background is taken into account. Becker, reviewing existing data in the USA, found that further education was significantly correlated to high earnings after making allowances for both ability and social-class background.[32] Bowles, on the other hand, claimed that social-class background was more important than years of schooling in determining a person's earnings.[33] Jencks, referring to income and not only to earnings from work, found that if family background and measured

2 Vic George

intelligence were taken into account, years of schooling had only a negligible effect on income. He estimated that 'an extra year of elementary or secondary schooling really boosts future income less than 4%; an extra year of college boosts it about 7% and a year of graduate school boosts it about 4%.'[34]

To conclude this section, it can be said that the available evidence suggests that innate intelligence has little effect on earnings. Years of schooling are a more important factor, though the extent of influence exerted on level of earnings is not agreed upon. How does this conclusion relate to the functional explanation of inequality? Though the functional thesis does not concentrate explicitly on intelligence, it does imply that intelligence is one of the main factors a society has to take into account in deciding who are the right people for the right jobs. Since economic reward is the main criterion of the importance of jobs in society, according to the same thesis, the implication is that intelligence and income as well as earnings from work are related. All the statistical evidence, however, shows that there is no such correlation. The functional thesis fares only slightly better statistically with regard to years of schooling, assuming that this is another of the factors that a society takes into account in the allocation of the right people to the right positions.

Cultural characteristics
Motivation is central to the functional theory. Incentives are necessary to attract the more able people to the more important positions in society and they are also necessary to motivate them to carry out their duties satisfactorily. Personal attitudes towards achievement and success are family- and sub-culturally based, and they can, according to some writers, influence economic success and failure.[35] The culture of poverty thesis by Oscar Lewis and the cycle of deprivation notion by Sir Keith Joseph are variations of the 'achievement motives' school but confined to the low-income groups and couched in sociological, anthropological or social policy language rather than in a psychological framework. Oscar Lewis's culture of poverty thesis is the most developed theoretically, and it is on this that this section will concentrate.

Lewis maintains that poor communities have a culture of their own which is significantly different from and at variance with the culture of the rest of society. For analytical purposes, it can be said that the culture of poverty consists of three inter-related groups of items. First, a certain pattern of objective living conditions: low income, unemployment, irregular work, inadequate housing, low educational achievement, ill-health, and so on. Second, a certain pattern of objective forms of behaviour: early sexual experiences, promiscuity, illegitimacy, family violence, family authoritarianism, short childhood period, nonparticipation in formal or informal social agencies, and general lack of community stability. There is no attempt in the literature to define and quantify these forms of behaviour in a way in which the reliability and validity of Lewis's research findings can be tested by others. Third, a certain pattern of subjective values, attitudes and beliefs that are congruent with the behavioural characteristics and the objective conditions. These values include fatalism, inability to defer gratification of pleasure, strong anti-authority feelings, marginality, helplessness, dependency, inability to plan, and so on. Again, Lewis does not define these values in an operational way so that his findings can easily be tested by others.

Under what conditions does the culture of poverty develop? It develops as a response to certain difficult socio-economic conditions. It develops as a means through which the poor can cope with the hopeless socio-economic conditions they face. Not all groups that live in conditions of poverty develop the culture of poverty. Lewis offers six characteristics of societies in which cultures of poverty can develop. Such societies are based on a cash economy, they have low wages and persistently high rates of unemployment; their dominant value system stresses profit-making and upward social mobility; and failure in such societies is seen as the result of personal inadequacies. Thus the culture of poverty does not develop in caste-type societies in spite of the existence of abject poverty, or in poor communities with a tradition of learning and a stable community organisation, or in socialist societies where private profit does not exist. The culture of poverty develops particularly 'when a stratified social and economic system is breaking down or is being replaced by another, as in the case of the transition from feudalism to capitalism or during periods of rapid technological change.'[36] The culture of poverty is thus a reaction and an adaptation on behalf of the poor 'to their marginal position in a class-stratified, highly individuated capitalist society.'[37]

Once the culture of poverty comes into existence, it acquires an entity of its own and becomes immune to the influence of improved socio-economic conditions in society. Once it acquires its own entity, it perpetuates itself through the socialisation of children. Lewis is very emphatic about the crucial importance of early socialisation.[38]

> By the time slum children are aged six or seven they have usually absorbed the basic values and attitudes of their sub-culture and are not psychologically geared to take full advantage of changing conditions or increased opportunities which may occur in their lifetime.

This is one of the strongest claims of social determinism for human behaviour – almost as strong as biological determinism. The influences of the school, the mass media, the labour market and so on are considered ineffective in countering the family and neighbourhood influences of early schoolhood.

Does the culture of poverty really exist? Bearing in mind Lewis's failure to define and measure adequately the various living conditions, forms of behaviour, and particularly the values that inspire and perpetuate the culture of poverty, attempts by other researchers to test his thesis have been hampered. The majority of such studies have been carried out in Latin American cities where conditions were considered by Lewis as most favourable for the development of the culture of poverty. These were studies of poor urban communities formed by recent rural immigration. On the whole, they have not substantiated Lewis's thesis. Rather they have shown that such communities struggle against all odds to improve their socio-economic condition through their own efforts and organisations in the absence of any sustained or substantial government plans to help them. They do not lack in aspirations and in efforts to improve themselves even though their achievements are not spectacularly high.

In a study of 620 slum dwellers in Caracas City, Schwartz concluded that the culture of poverty thesis was not substantiated. There were isolated families which one might consider as showing some of the traits of the culture of poverty, but there was no evidence to support the view that the culture of poverty had developed as a widespread adaptation by the whole slum community to its marginal position in the class-stratified society of Venezuela.[39]

In a study of a squatters' community of several hundred people in Lima, Peru, Turner discussed how they set up their makeshift houses against government opposition and how they enlarged and improved these houses over the years. The community set up its schools, shops, associations and other social institutions to provide a supporting social environment. Nothing in his account of the *bariada* shows that the families exhibited the culture of poverty traits reported by Lewis in his various studies.[40]

In a study of a similar community in Brazil, the *favelas* of Rio, Bonilla found no evidence to support the culture of poverty thesis. It is true that the *favelados* suffered from unemployment, illiteracy, ill-health, unsatisfactory housing conditions, etc. These, however, as he points out, 'remain prevailing conditions not only in the *favela* but elsewhere in the city and throughout the vast rural spaces of Brazil.'[41] In a survey of the opinions of 200 *favelados* he found that they shared with skilled workers the belief of an open, mobile society where children can reach top positions in society irrespective of their family background. He also found that the *favelados* took as much, if not more, active interest in political activities as the skilled workers. He concluded that 'a great many *favela* families are relatively stable, have fairly regular employment and are even rigidly conventional by middle-class standards.'[42]

Lewis's thesis has also been criticised by some of his fellow anthropologists on the grounds that he has mistaken the situation of poverty as being the culture of poverty.[43] According to the situation of poverty thesis, the poor acknowledge and aspire to the dominant value system of society; but since the fulfilment of this value system is beyond them, they may develop a complementary value system for everyday living. The fact that successive generations of poor people have similar subcultures is, according to the situation of poverty thesis, not the result of the irrevocable and faulty socialisation of children but because each generation is faced with the same socio-economic problems and has the same inadequate resources to solve these problems. R.T. Smith's work on the Caribbean family,[44] and Liebau's work in the USA are two examples of the situation of poverty thesis.

Liebau studied the lives of two dozen Negro men who spent their time on a street corner in Washington. They were men who were generally unemployed and who withdrew from their responsibilities as husbands and fathers by finding refuge on the street corner. Liebau's two main conclusions were, first, that these men saw themselves as failures both in employment and family life precisely because they had internalised the dominant values of the wider society which stress economic success and the role of the father as the family breadwinner. Second, because of their persistent failures, they had turned to the street in order to conceal their failure. This gave them some respite from their painful experiences in wider society. He summarises his thesis as follows:[45]

From this perspective, the street corner man does not appear as a carrier of an independent cultural situation. His behaviour appears not so much as a way of realising the distinctive goals and values of his own sub-culture, or of conforming to its models, but rather as his way of trying to achieve many of the goals and values of the larger society, of failing to do this and of concealing his failure from others and from himself as best he can.

The implications of the culture of poverty and of the situation of poverty thesis are fundamentally opposed to each other. The culture of poverty maintains that further government services in full employment, education, health, social security and so on will be under-utilised by the poor or, if fully utilised, largely wasted; the value system of the poor must first be changed before they can benefit from these services. From the situation of poverty thesis, the problem of poverty can be solved by improved government services, particularly if they are provided in ways in which they are freely and easily accessible to the poor. The culture of poverty sees the culture of the poor as the reason for the existence of poverty. The situation of poverty locates the cause of poverty in the structure of society. The former is part and parcel of the functional explanation of inequality; the latter belongs to the conflict explanation, as the next section will attempt to show.

Data on the utilisation of public services according to social class does not lend either a consistent or a strong support to the culture of poverty. The utilisation of the education and health services by the poor increased in this country as a result of the structural changes introduced in the provision of these services during and immediately after the Second World War. The number of the unemployed varies according to the state of the economy and the consequent demand for labour. In some aspects of the health service and of the education service the poor make less use of the services than others. In other aspects of these services they do the opposite. Personal and cultural explanations have been offered by some, and structural and institutional explanations by others. There is little scientific empirical evidence from this country; but most of the recent evidence from the USA, and particularly from some of the programmes initiated under the War on Poverty, have provided experimental evidence supporting the structural, institutional explanation. A number of neighbourhood health centres were established in deprived areas which provided free services in a non-stigmatising way to poor people. The take-up of health services increased and people's awareness of the need and value of medical services increased. Reviewing the evidence from several experimental projects under the Office of Economic Opportunity, Riessman concludes that 'the health behaviour of the poor can be radically altered and within a relatively short period of time, by introducing structural changes in the way the services are offered.'[46] Support for structural explanations comes also from the well-known Vicos Project. Vicos is a small village in the Andes of Peru which for centuries was in a state of abject poverty and illiteracy. A team of American social scientists descended on the village in the early 1950s, bringing with them generous financial resources. New methods of agriculture were introduced, a school was started, health services were provided, villagers were paid wages for their work, and a community organisation was set up. Within two years agricultural production increased, school attendance and health improved, and generally the life of the villagers changed. All this came about without any programmes designed to change the value system of the villagers.[47]

Structural factors
The structural explanation of the distribution of inequality and poverty

follows naturally from the conflict model of society and from the two/ three-dimensional view of power. In a society where power is unequally distributed, it is natural that the weak groups will lose out in the competitive pursuit of economic and other valued rewards.

In capitalist societies conflict (and the unequal distribution of power) is along both class lines and occupational group lines. In socialist societies it is between occupational groups only. Deutscher's view of the difference between the USSR's stratification system and that of western European societies is valid. 'I make a distinction,' he writes, 'between economic or social inequality and class antagonism. The difference between highly-paid skilled workers and unskilled workers/ labourers is an example of an inequality which does not amount to class antagonism; it is a difference within the same social class.'[48]

In a capitalist advanced industrial society where the means of production and distribution are in the hands of private individuals, it is logical that there will be inequality between the owners of wealth and the rest of the population. Whether one views the situation from the Marxist perspective of 'surplus value' and 'exploitation' or from the capitalist perspective of 'rightful reward' for the investment of one's capital, the end result is the same.

Private profit is the single most important feature of capitalism. There would be no logical reason for capitalists to invest their capital if this were not to result in profit. It is true that in some capitalist countries government intervention and trade union power set limits to the amount of profit – and for short periods these limits may be severe – but they cannot abolish it altogether without abolishing the capitalist system itself. In capitalist societies where inheritance of wealth is legal, class inequalities are perpetuated along family lines. Most owners of large amounts of capital have fathers who were also wealthy, as the next chapter shows.

Thus a capitalist form of production creates inequalities between the owners of large amounts of capital on one hand and the rest of the population on the other. But how can one explain income inequalities among the non-owners of wealth along structural lines? By the power which they possess as members of different occupational groups to extract favourable terms from their employers. As Westergaard and Reisler put it, 'The labour market in effect is a patchwork of markets where skilled and unskilled blue-collar and white-collar employees, men and women, workers in this industry and that, one region and another, sell their labour on different terms.'[49] But what exactly is it that gives one occupational group more power than another?

It is important to distinguish between the top professional, top managerial and top Civil Service positions on one hand and the rest of the non-owners of capital on the other. The former are also more likely to be owners of large or moderate amounts of capital, and they exhibit a close proximity to the capitalist class as a result of similar social origins and cultural affinity. The power they possess is partly the result of their marketable skills and partly the result of their explicit or implicit alliance with capital. The relationship between the two sides is of a symbiotic type: capital bestows power on them and they in turn subscribe to the survival of the general principles of the capitalist order. The power of the top professional groups is legitimised through the society's value system so that it is generally accepted as justifiable. Also, professional associations zealously guard their powerful positions through extended forms of training and restrictive practices. The fact that the general public may accept the privileged economic position of the top professionals is not because of the greater functionality to society of these occupations but because of the ability of the professions to convince the public of their greater importance. In the last analysis, the main function of a profession is to protect the interest of its members rather than its clients.

Inequality among different working-class occupations is the result of their different power, which in turn is due largely to what Parkin calls their marketable skills,[50] i.e., length of education and training; and, to a lesser extent, to such other factors as trade union organisation, demand for their products and other structural factors. Anderson, who explains inequality along orthodox Marxist lines, agrees with this view: 'The ability to market a scarce and inelastically demanded skill or service is unquestionably the most decisive factor in determining competitive occupational reward.'[51] Other things being equal, the greater the marketable skills of an occupational group, the greater its power and hence the stronger its bargaining position with employers. Unskilled and semi-skilled occupations have little power and they have thus generally been the lowest-paid groups in society. Working-class groups use their power not only against employers but also against other working-class groups in their jostling for positions on the socio-economic ladder.

Thus we find that the hierarchy of earnings from work approximates length of education and training, though it does not fit them perfectly. Professionals receive higher salaries than skilled workers, and these in turn earn higher wages than unskilled workers. In spite of variations of earnings within the same occupation, Atkinson's comments are true. He states that 'the earnings tree showed that a headmaster is likely to earn three times as much as a farm labourer, that a hospital consultant is likely to earn twice as much again, and top executives many times more.'[52] This general picture is distorted by a variety of other factors, the main four of which are family background, sex, ethnic origin and geographical variations. All these are institutional factors that are beyond the control of the individual. They, and other less significant factors, modify the power relationship of different classes and groups but they do not alter the central thesis of the conflict model of inequality. The importance of family background on occupation and income manifests itself in many ways, but in none more clearly than in the preponderance of ex-public school and ex-Oxbridge students, whose family background is predominantly middle and upper class, among company chairmen.[53] It is worth repeating that the influence of family background is most crucial to the structuralist thesis, for it affects not only occupations and income but also education and training. Thus, though both individualistic and structural explanations attribute a great deal of importance to education, the latter see family background as even more important than education. That sex is an important determinant of earnings is suggested by the fact that the average earnings of all full-time female employees have been consistently about half that of men for the whole of this century. This is confirmed by the evidence that, even taking the level of education and age into account, the earnings of women remain at about the same proportion of the earnings of men.[54] Discrimination against women in terms of the kinds of job open to them and in terms of promotion is the first main explanation of their inferior position in both the earnings and the occupational ladder. The second explanation is the cultural indoctrination of both men and women that certain jobs are not suitable for women. In these ways, women have formed the largest section of the low-paid over the years.

The literature documenting discrimination against immigrants in general and their weaker position in the labour market is massive. Immigrants tend to perform the least desirable jobs in terms of pay, hours of employment, conditions of work and status. Daniel concluded that 'it is fair to say that coloured immigrants are more often employed in one type of job . . . and where this was true it was the most menial and unattractive type of job, for which it had been impossible to attract white labour.'[55] The same picture applies to immigrants in France, Germany, Switzerland and other countries of the Common Market.[56] The USA has an even better-documented history of discrimination against immigrants. After centuries in the USA, Negroes are still inferior to whites in terms of income, even after taking into account level of education and ability.[57] There are, of course, many individual reasons for individual acts of discrimination, but the explanation of the immigrants' inferior position in the labour market must be a structural one.

For advanced industrial societies, Bohning hypothesised that, once an industrial country 'unable to change its social structure in the face of labour shortages in socially undesirable and low-wage jobs, resorts to importing foreign workers, the social job structure is thereby rigidi-fied.'[58] In this way, low-paid manual jobs that are essential to economic development and profit are filled by resort to mainly immigrant rather than native workers. The least powerful and least secure group occupies the bottom of the occupation and income league. Once this pattern gets established it becomes very difficult to change. Tradition lends support to power to perpetuate inequality.

Geographical variations are observable in all industrial countries, both as regards regions and particular parts of cities. In the UK, regional variations have persisted in spite of substantial government efforts to even them out. Thus employment opportunities, unemployment rates, occupational status, earnings and other such indicators are superior in South-East England and inferior in Scotland and Northern Ireland.[59] In cities, people living in certain parts are more deprived in terms of education, housing, income and so on than other city dwellers. Again, in spite of a number of government projects, such inner-city depriva-tions continue.[60]

Power influences the position of different groups in society not only in terms of earnings but also in terms of employment, housing, health, education and other socially desirable goods. There is substantial evi-dence that by and large one type of disadvantage is related to another to create an intricate web of disadvantages. There are exceptions to this general principle, such as some unskilled workers whose incomes are lower than those of other manual workers occupying council housing and thus being less disadvantaged in housing terms than some skilled workers. This, and perhaps a couple of other exceptions, do not alter the validity of the web of disadvantage argument; i.e., that low wages are the common denominator of social disadvantage. This has been adequately documented,[61] and some of this will be reviewed in the next chapter.

Berthoud's pinball analogy of the operation of the intricate web of disadvantage is helpful. It is in two parts: 'first, those of lower class have a high chance of suffering a first problem, which can then lead to others, and secondly, even after the first problem is experienced, the causal link has a higher chance of connecting with the second prob-lem.'[62] The reason why the balls played by the poor ring up mis-fortune at every bounce has already been referred to. It is the structural inability of the poor to compete effectively in the important markets of employment, education and housing which affect life chances in society. Structural explanations thus insist that, more often than not, the origin of many social and economic disadvantages can be traced back to the person's occupation and income. Moreover, the social, political and economic systems operate in ways in which at best modify only slightly and at worst exacerbate the disadvantages which low-income groups suffer.

Conclusion

If the conflict rather than the functional theory explains the existence of inequality and poverty, structural factors rather than individual characteristics account for most of the groups and individuals in poverty or in low pay. This is not to deny that there are individuals who, because of such adverse personal characteristics as severe physical or mental handicap, cannot compete effectively in the labour market. Rather it is to stress that these are a very small minority of the poor and the low-paid. The vast majority are accounted for by structural factors.

References

1 B.S. Rowntree, *Poverty: A Study of Town Life*, Macmillan, 1901, p. 117.
2 V. George, *Social Security and Society*, Routledge & Kegan Paul, 1973, p. 47.
3 OECD, *Public Expenditure on Income Maintenance Programmes*, 1976, p. 63.
4 Quoted in A. Atkinson, *Poverty in Britain and the Reform of Social Security*, Cambridge University Press, 1969, p. 17.
5 P. Townsend, 'Poverty as Relative Deprivation', in D. Wedderburn (ed.), *Poverty, Inequality and Class Structure*, Cambridge University Press, 1974. The need was met by Townsend's *Poverty in the U.K.*, Penguin, 1979, published too late for discussion here.
6 M. Douglas, 'Relative Poverty', in A.H. Halsey (ed.), *Traditions of Social Policy*, Blackwell, 1976.
7 T.H. Marshall, 'Value Problems of Welfare Capitalsim', *Journal of Social Policy*, vol. 1, no. 1, January 1972.
8 K. Davis and W.E. Moore, 'Some Principles of Stratification', *American Sociological Review*, vol. 10, no. 2, April, 1945.
9 M. Tumin, 'Some Principles of Stratification: A Critical Analysis', *American Sociological Review*, vol. 18, no. 4 August 1953.
10 W. Wesolowski, 'Some Notes on the Functional Theory of Stratification', *Polish Sociological Bulletin*, 3–4, 1962.
11 W. Buckley, 'Social Stratification and the Functional Theory of Social Differentiation', *American Sociological Review*, vol. 23, no. 4 August 1958.
12 R.H. Tawney, *Equality*, Allen & Unwin, 1931.
13 H.J. Gans, *More Equality*, Random House, 1973.
14 R.A. Dahl, 'The Concept of Power', *Behavioural Science*, vol. 2, July 1957.
15 R.A. Dahl, *Who Governs?* Yale University Press, 1961, p. 336.
16 P. Bachrach and M.S. Baratz, 'Two Faces of Power', *American Political Science Review*, vol. 56, 1962.

22   Vic George

17 P. Bachrach and M.S. Baratz, *Power and Poverty: Theory and Practice*, Oxford University Press, 1970, p. 49.
18 Ibid., p. 49.
19 M.S. Lukes, *Power: A Radical View*, Macmillan, 1974, p. 24.
20 Ibid., p. 25.
21 Ibid., p. 45.
22 P. Worsley, 'The Distribution of Power in Industrial Society', *Sociological Review Monograph*, 8, 1964, pp. 22–3.
23 R. Holman, 'Poverty: Consensus and Alternatives', *British Journal of Social Work*, vol. 3, no. 4, Winter 1973.
24 Gans, op. cit., ch. 4.
25 J. Ryan in *Race, Culture and Intelligence*, edited K. Richardson and D. Spears, Penguin, 1972, p. 53.
26 A.H. Halsey, 'Class Difference in Intelligence', *British Journal of Statistical Psychology*, vol. 12, Part I, May 1959.
27 H.J. Eysenck, *Race, Intelligence and Education*, Temple-Smith, 1971, p. 61.
28 See H. McGurk, *Growing and Changing*, Methuen, 1975; M. Rutter and N. Madge, *Cycles of Deprivation*, Heinemann, 1976.
29 Ch. Jencks *et al.*, *Inequality*, Penguin, 1975, p. 221.
30 S. Bowles and V. Nelson, 'The Inheritance of IQ and the Inter-generational Reproduction of Economic Inequality', *Review of Economics and Statistics*, vol. 56, 1974.
31 M. Blaug, *An Introduction to the Economics of Education*, Penguin 1972, Ch. 2.
32 G. Becker, *Human Capital*, Columbia University Press, 1964.
33 S. Bowles, 'Schooling and Inequality from Generation to Generation', *Journal of Political Economy*, vol. 80, 1972.
34 Jencks *et al.*, op. cit., p. 223.
35 D. McLelland *et al.*, *The Achievement Motive*, Appleton-Century-Crofts, 1953.
36 O. Lewis, *La Vida*, Random House, 1966, p. xlv.
37 Ibid., p. xliv.
38 Ibid., p. xlv.
39 A.J. Schwartz, 'A Further Look at Culture of Poverty: Ten Caracas Barrios', *Sociology and Social Research*, July 1975.
40 J.C. Turner, 'Barriers and Channels for Housing Development in Modernizing Countries', *Journal of the American Institute of Planners*, vol. 33, no. 3, 1967.
41 F. Bonilla, 'Rio's Favelas', in *Peasants and Cities*, ed. W. Mangin, Houghton Mifflin, 1970, p. 75.
42 Ibid., p. 75.
43 Ch. Valentine, *Culture and Poverty*, University of Chicago Press, 1968.
44 R.T. Smith, 'Culture and Social Structure of the Caribbean', *Comparative Studies in Society and History*, vol. 6, 1963.
45 E. Liebau, *Tally's Corner*, Little Brown, 1967, p. 222.

46 C.K. Riessman, 'The Use of Health Services by the Poor', *Social Policy*, vol. 5, no. 1, May–June 1974.
47 H. Dobyns, P. Doughty and H. Lasswell (eds.), *Peasants, Power and Applied Social Change: Vicos as a Model*, Sage Publications, 1964.
48 I. Deutscher, *The Unfinished Revolution, Russia 1917–1967*, Oxford University Press, 1967, p. 54.
49 J. Westergaard and H. Reisler, *Class in a Capitalist Society*, Heinemann, 1975, p. 347.
50 F. Parkin, *Class, Inequality and Political Order*, MacGibbon & Kee, 1971, p. 21.
51 Ch. H. Anderson, *The Political Economy of Social Class*, Prentice-Hall, 1974, p. 85.
52 A. Atkinson, *The Economics of Inequality*, Oxford University Press, 1975, p. 74.
53 P. Stanworth and A. Giddens, 'An Economic Elite: A Demographic Profile of Company Chairmen', in P. Stanworth and A. Giddens, *Elites and Power in British Society*, Cambridge University Press, 1974.
54 Office of Population and Census Statistics, *General Household Survey, 1973*, HMSO, 1976.
55 W. Daniel, *Racial Discrimination in England*, Penguin, 1968, p. 120.
56 S. Castles and G. Kosack, *Immigrant Workers and the Class Structure in Western Europe*, Oxford University Press, 1973.
57 Jencks et al., op. cit., also L. Broom and N. Glenn, *The Transformation of the Negro*, Harper, 1965, ch. 6.
58 W. Bohning, *The EEC and the Free Movement of Labour*, Oxford University Press, 1973, p. 53.
59 B. Coates and E. Rawstron, *Regional Variations in Britain*, Batsford 1971.
60 S. Holterman, 'Areas of Urban Deprivation in Great Britain', *Social Trends*, no. 6, HMSO, 1975.
61 Westergaard and Reisler, op.cit.; F. Field, *Unequal Britain*, Arrow Books, 1973; M. Rutter and N. Madge, *Cycles of Disadvantage*, Heinemann, 1976.
62 R. Berthoud, *The Disadvantage of Inequality*, PEP, Macdonald & Janes, 1976, p. 182.

2 Poverty and inequality in the UK

Vic George

This chapter will first review briefly the extent of inequality in income, wealth and earnings. It will then discuss more fully the extent of poverty, the groups in poverty, the reasons why the country's social security system has failed to achieve one of its main objectives, the abolition of poverty among people not at work, and the failure of the wages system in respect of those at work.

Distribution of income

A person's income includes all money payments and receipts in the form of earnings from work, social security benefits, investment interest and profits. The existing data on income distribution are unreliable, partly because the records of some of the sources of income are inaccurate and partly because some other sources of income are not included at all in the various estimates of income distribution. The net effect of these errors and omissions is to underestimate the extent of income inequality in British society.

People's sources of income vary in importance. For the lowest income group, though earnings from work is the most important source, social security benefits constitute a substantial source of income. Thereafter, earnings from employment begin to dominate until one reaches the top income groups, where income from profits and from investment interests becomes far more important. Indeed, the top 1 per cent income group receives more of its income from profit and investment than from employment. This, in a sense, is the first important aspect of inequality in income: a small minority of very rich people receive most of their income as a result of the work effort of the majority of the working population.

Data on income distribution in the UK use as their income unit the tax unit adopted by the government for taxation purposes. The tax unit is the income of a single person or the combined income of a married couple. Table 2.1 indicates a substantial reduction in the proportion of the national income accruing to the top 1 per cent and the top 10 per cent. This apparent redistribution has been in favour of the middle-income groups and not the low-income groups. Thus the proportion of income received by the bottom 50 per cent of income units remained constant throughout the whole period both before income tax - 23.7 per cent - and after income tax - 26.5 per cent. On the other hand, the proportion of income received by the middle-income groups - 11 to 50 per cent - increased to absorb the whole of the loss made by the top 10 per cent of the income units.

TABLE 2.1 *Distribution of income in the UK, 1949-72*

Quantile group	Before income tax					After income tax				
	1949	1959	1964	1967	1972	1949	1959	1964	1967	1972
%	%	%	%	%	%	%	%	%	%	%
Top 1	11.2	8.4	8.2	7.4	6.4	6.4	5.3	5.3	4.9	4.4
2-5	12.6	11.5	11.3	11.0	10.8	11.3	10.5	10.7	9.9	9.8
6-10	9.4	9.5	9.6	9.6	9.7	9.4	9.4	9.9	9.5	9.4
Top 10	33.2	29.4	29.1	28.0	26.9	27.1	25.2	25.9	24.3	23.6
11-20	14.1	15.1	15.5	15.2	15.8	14.5	15.7	16.1	15.2	15.8
21-30	11.2	12.6	12.6	12.6	13.1	11.9	12.9	12.9	13.0	13.2
31-40	9.6	10.7	10.9	11.1	11.0	10.5	11.2	11.1	11.0	11.2
41-50	8.2	9.1	9.2	9.1	9.2	9.5	9.9	8.8	9.7	9.5
51-60		7.5	7.4	7.7	7.5		7.2	8.0	7.7	8.0
61-70	23.7	5.9	5.8	6.0	5.9	26.5	6.6	5.6	7.1	6.5
71-80		4.4	4.3	4.8	4.8		5.2	5.1	4.9	5.5
81-100		5.3	5.2	5.6	5.8		6.0	6.5	7.1	6.8
Total population	100.0	100.0	100.0	100.0	100.0	100.0	100.0	100.0	100.0	100.0
Gini co-efficient	41.1	39.8	39.9	38.8	37.4	35.5	36.0	36.6	33.5	33.1

Source: Royal Commission on the Distribution of Income and Wealth, Report No. 1, HMSO, Cmnd, 6171, 1975, Table 15, p.45.

This general conclusion is subject to many criticisms and provisos. In the first place, income from occupational fringe benefits (company expense accounts, company cars, company housing, holidays at the company's expense, etc.); income from dividends and interest taxed at source which remains unreported; and income from life insurance and superannuation funds; all these are not included in the estimates of income distribution. Thus Westergaard and Resler have recently esti-mated that if these were taken into account, the proportion of income received after income tax by the top 1 per cent of income units has remained unaltered since the end of the Second World War.[1]

A number of demographic changes are likely to have affected the distribution of income, though it is difficult to be precise about the direction of this effect. The number of persons in receipt of social security benefits and the number of students in receipt of government grants has increased faster than the economically active population, with the result that the number of incomes at the bottom of the income distribution has also increased. The increased number of married women at work has pushed tax units upwards, since a husband's and a wife's income are aggregated. This has resulted in an increased proportion of income accruing to the upper middle-income groups, but not so much to the top income groups.

Finally, the effects of direct income taxes tend to give a somewhat unreal picture of the extent of redistribution because they do not take into account indirect taxes which bite more on the incomes of the low-income groups.

The recent changes in taxation policy introduced by the Conservative government in June 1979 are likely to increase income inequality. These changes not only reduce direct tax rates and increase indirect taxation but they also reduce substantially tax rates levied on high incomes.

Distribution of earnings from employment

We referred in the first chapter to the general relationships between earnings from employment on the one hand and occupation and sex on the other. These and other relationships will be discussed more fully in this section.

That there is a broad correlation between type of occupation and earnings is shown by the fact that the median earnings of both non-manual men and non-manual women are higher than the earnings of manual men and manual women respectively in full-time occupation. Nevertheless, a number of manual occupations command earnings that are higher than those of some of the non-manual occupations. Skilled manual workers' earnings today exceed the earnings of clerical workers, even though other conditions of their employment (holidays, pensions, etc.) may be inferior. Moreover, the differences in earnings between non-manual and manual workers have narrowed over the years, due mainly to the relative fall in the salaries of the professional groups and of clerical workers. During the period 1913-60, Routh has estimated that the relative position of unskilled and semi-skilled manual workers has remained the same; the position of professionals, clerks and, to a lesser extent, that of skilled manual workers, has deteriorated; while the position of managers and administrators and of foremen has improved. Later figures do not change this general picture.[2]

The life patterns of earnings of manual and non-manual workers differ substantially. Manual workers reach the ceiling of their earnings at an early age, usually before they are thirty years old. Thereafter, their wages decline slowly but steadily, so that by the time they retire their earnings are not much higher than they were when they first entered employment. Professionals' salaries, on the other hand, rise slowly but substantially by the time they reach the age of forty. After that their salaries tend to remain at the same high level until they approach retirement, when their salaries begin to decline slightly. This difference in life earning patterns between the two groups has shown little change over the years.

TABLE 2.2   *Gross earnings of full-time male manual workers, Great Britain, 1886–1974*

Year	Median earnings £ per week	Lowest decile %	Median %	Highest decile %
1886	1.2	68.6	100.0	143.1
1906	1.5	66.5	100.0	156.8
1938	3.8	67.7	100.0	139.9
1960	14.2	70.6	100.0	145.2
1974	41.8	68.6	100.0	144.1

Source: Department of Employment, New Earnings Survey, HMSO, 1974.

As one would expect, the earnings of non-manual workers are considerably more dispersed than those of manual workers, partly because of the wider diversity of non-manual occupations and partly because earnings of non-manual workers tend to vary more among different age-groups. A very striking feature of the distribution of earnings of male manual workers is that it has changed very little during the last one hundred years, as Table 2.2 shows. General market forces of supply and demand, trade union power, increasing economic national affluence and the like have not improved the position of low-paid workers *vis-à-vis* that of their better-paid colleagues. Recent government pay policies, though sometimes explicitly trying to protect the low-paid against inflation and even to improve their position, have not proved at all successful.

The earnings of women in full-time employment have remained consistently lower than those of men both in manual and non-manual occupations. The median weekly earnings of women in full-time manual occupations constituted 50.2 per cent of the corresponding wage for men in 1906, 53.5 per cent in 1960, 54.0 per cent in 1974 and 65 per cent in 1976. A similar picture emerges from a comparison of women and men in non-manual occupations. It is too early yet to be certain about the effects of recent legislation making discrimination against women illegal, but all the indications so far suggest that it is one of several factors that is associated with the improvement in the earnings of women compared with those of men.

Finally, there are regional variations in earnings, particularly among manual workers. For non-manual workers, differences in earnings are less marked and for some groups they are non-existent. The general picture for the earnings of all adult male workers in different regions is as follows: Assuming that the figure for the whole of the UK was 100 in 1973, then the figure for Northern Ireland was 87, for East Anglia 92, for the South-East 105, and for the West Midlands 105.[3] These ratios have shown a marked stability over the years and a close relationship to other forms of regional deprivation. There are, moreover, sharp differences within regions as between regions. Thus, Wilding has shown that not only were workers' earnings in Wales, on the whole, slightly lower than those in England, but that there were also 'considerable regional disparities within Wales and a basic division between the high-wage area of the industrial south and the low-wage areas of central, northern and west Wales.'[4] The same can be said of other regions in the country.

Distribution of wealth

It is generally agreed that the existing methods of estimating the distribution of wealth are unreliable. Whether they are so unreliable that they render worthless all estimates of wealth distribution is a matter of contention. The method which has been used by the government, and which is the most generally quoted, is the so-called multiplier method. In brief, this method estimates the wealth of the living on the estates of those who die during any one year. Its deficiencies are glaring and they are explicitly stated by the Inland Revenue which works out such estimates. The Royal Commission on the Distribution of Income and Wealth reluctantly accepted this method as the least inadequate of the various existing methods of wealth estimation. The Commission made various adjustments to the Inland Revenue data and reached different estimates of wealth distribution. Table 2.3 is taken from the Report of the Commission and it is a summary of its various estimates.

It is not only the estimation of wealth which is problematic but also its definition. Generally speaking, personal wealth is so defined as to

TABLE 2.3   *Distribution of personal wealth in Great Britain, 1972*

Quantile group (%)	Inland Revenue estimate (%)	Adjusted estimates	
		Probable range (%)	Preferred estimate (%)
Top 1	29.9	27–29	28.1
Top 5	56.3	51–55	53.9
Top 10	71.9	64–69	67.3
Top 20	89.2	79–84	82.4
Bottom 80	10.8	16–21	17.6

Source: Royal Commission on the Distribution of Income and Wealth, Report No. 1, HMSO, Cmnd 6171, 1974, Table 56, p.125.

include cash, life assurance policies, land, buildings and certain durable goods. Dwellings are one of the major wealth items, and for the small wealth owners they account for most of their wealth. Thus, for those whose total wealth assets are less than £5,000, their house accounts for 60 per cent of their total wealth. For the top wealth owners (those whose total wealth assets were £200,000) housing constitutes only 8 per cent of their wealth. For this latter group it was shares and securities that formed the largest single item of their wealth: 60 per cent of their total wealth. Clearly this indicates that this small minority of 0.2 per cent of wealth owners commands immense economic power in British society. This, of course, has always been the case. Lydall and Tipping estimated that 1 per cent of the population owned 81 per cent of company stocks and shares in 1954, and that 10 per cent of the population owned 98 per cent.[5]

Though the concentration of wealth in contemporary Britain is substantial, it is likely that it is less than what it was at the beginning of this century. Inland Revenue estimates of wealth distribution go back only to 1960. Before that, various estimates were made by individual researchers using the Inland Revenue method of estimation but with fewer refinements. The picture that emerges is that apparent wealth concentration declined substantially over the years. This general conclusion has been questioned by various writers, particularly Titmuss, on the grounds that this redistribution of wealth was to a very large extent redistribution within families. In an effort to avoid increasingly heavier rates of estate duty over the years, wealthy husbands transferred some of their wealth to their wives and children.[6] That this hypothesis is true is supported by the evidence that the redistribution of income was mainly from the top 1 per cent to the next 4 per cent of wealth owners, and that the proportion of total wealth owned by women increased substantially during this period.

TABLE 2.4   *Distribution of personal wealth 1911–60 in England and Wales*

Quantile group (%)	Percentage share of wealth (%)				
	1911–13	1924–30	1936–38	1954	1960
Top 1	69	62	56	43	42
Top 5	87	84	79	71	75
Top 10	92	91	88	79	83
Bottom 90	8	9	12	21	17

Source: Royal Commission on the Distribution of Income and Wealth, Report no. 1, HMSO, 1974, Table 41, p.97.

The Inland Revenue data published since 1960 show that the decline in the share owned by the top 1 per cent of wealth owners continued during this period and that the redistribution was not in favour of the next 4 per cent but in favour of the next 15 per cent. These trends, however, do not reflect changes in the concentration of stocks and shares or in land but in other forms of wealth, particularly house ownership. During this period the proportion of people buying their house increased substantially and, moreover, the price of houses increased faster than the general price index. In 1973 dwellings accounted for two-fifths of the total net wealth compared with one-fifth in 1960. Increased house ownership may thus account for most of the redistribution of wealth since 1960.

TABLE 2.5   *Distribution of personal wealth 1960–73 in Great Britain*

Quantile group (%)	Percentage share of wealth (%)		
	1960	1970	1973*
Top 1	38.2	29.0	27.6
Top 5	64.3	56.3	51.3
Top 10	76.7	70.1	67.2
Top 20	89.8	89.0	86.4
Bottom 80	10.2	11.0	13.6

Note: The estimate for 1973 differs from that in Table 2.3 because of the assumption in this table that persons not covered by the Inland Revenue estimates have no wealth. In Table 2.3 it was assumed that such persons owned a small amount of wealth.

Source: Royal Commission on the Distribution of Income and Wealth, Report no. 1, HMSO, 1974, Table 45, p.102.

For the top wealth owners, inheritance of wealth is the rule rather than the exception. Harbury and McMahon looked at the estates of deceased males in 1956 and 1965 which amounted to £100,000 or more. One half of those whose estates were £100,000 or more had fathers who had left over £100,000 and 70 per cent had fathers who had left more than £25,000. Moreover, when they compared their findings to a similar study by Wedgwood for the years 1924-6[7] they found that 'the role of inheritance in the creation of the personal fortunes of top wealth owners . . . has not changed very much since the mid-twenties.'[8] Though the evidence can be faulted on several minor counts, it does suggest strongly that self-made men account for only one-third of the top wealth owners; the remaining two-thirds owe their wealth inheritance to their parents.

Extent of Poverty

The early industrialisation and consequent rapid urbanisation of this country meant that though Britain was one of the first European countries to reap the economic benefits of the new order, it was also one of the first countries to experience the effects of such social problems as urban poverty, slums, crime, ill-health and the like. By the second half of the nineteenth century, a number of government reports and private publications documented the prevalence of these problems in a rather unsystematic way. It was not until the end of the century that poverty studies began to be carried out in a planned and scientific way. Charles Booth's massive study of poverty in London at the turn of the century[9] and Seebohm Rowntree's scientific study of poverty in York in 1899 were the first to set the pattern of future poverty studies.[10] The contribution of these two researchers to the understanding of poverty was not of a methodological kind only. They also contributed to the growing social awareness that poverty and its relief could not be left to private hands. Government intervention on a more generous basis was necessary. There were, of course, other and more important reasons – political and economic – why government action for the relief of poverty became imperative at this period.[11]

Rowntree's influence on social policy dealing with poverty continued right up to the second half of this century through his other two studies of poverty in York in 1936[12] and 1950.[13] It was, however, his first study which raised and tried to answer in a methodologically rigorous manner some of the basic questions of defining and measuring poverty. As mentioned briefly in the previous chapter, he defined poverty in purely subsistence terms. 'Families were in poverty if their total earnings were insufficient to obtain the minimum necessaries for the maintenance of merely physical efficiency.'[14] A person thus lives in subsistence poverty if the food he eats, the clothes he wears and the house he lives in are such that his health suffers. Rowntree acknowledged the austerity of his list of necessities but he felt that this was necessary partly in order to ensure that no one could criticise him of exaggerating the extent of poverty. This is how he described his poverty line:[15]

> A family living upon the scale allowed for in this estimate must
> never spend a penny on railway fare or omnibus. They must never
> go into the country unless they walk. They must never purchase
> a halfpenny newspaper or spend a penny to buy a ticket for a
> popular concert. They must write no letters to absent children,
> for they cannot afford to pay the postage. They must never con-
> tribute anything to their church or chapel, or give any help to a
> neighbour which costs them money. They cannot save nor can they
> join a sick club or trade union, because they cannot pay the neces-
> sary subscriptions. The children must have no pocket money for
> dolls, marbles or sweets. The father must smoke no tobacco and
> must drink no beer. The mother must never buy any pretty clothes
> for herself or her children, the character of the family wardrobe as
> for the family diet being governed by the regulation, 'nothing must
> be bought but that which is absolutely necessary for the main-
> tenance of physical health and what is bought must be of the
> plainest and most economical description'. Should a child fall ill
> it must be attended by the parish doctor; should it die, it must be
> buried by the parish. Finally, the wage earner must never be absent
> from his work for a single day.

Having decided which commodities were necessary for physical efficiency, Rowntree had to face the more difficult problem of the quantity and the quality required for each commodity. He solved this problem differently for the various commodities. As far as housing is concerned, he allowed for each family a sum of money equivalent to the amount of rent paid. He acknowledged that ideally he should have estimated the cost of having houses that were adequate to maintain families of different sizes. He decided against this because of the diffi- culties involved in reaching such estimates, and strangely enough be- cause there were not enough adequate houses for all his sample in York. The latter is clearly an irrelevant argument because what he was con- cerned with was the cost and not the availability of adequate housing. Thus his findings on the extent of poverty were an underestimate of the actual position. He acknowledged that at least 26 per cent of his sample lived in accommodation which was either unsatisfactory or slums. The rent paid for such housing was only about half of the rent paid by the other working-class families in his sample.

For clothing he adopted a different methodological approach. The estimate of the amount of money necessary to purchase clothing for physical efficiency was based largely on the replies of his working-class respondents to the following questions:[16]

> What in your opinion is the very lowest sum upon which a man can keep himself in clothing for a year? The clothing should be adequate to keep the man in health and should not be so shabby as to injure his chances of obtaining respectable employment. Apart from these two conditions, the clothing to be the most economical obtainable.

The estimate was also based on discussions between the interviewers and the respondents about the cheapest ways in which clothing items could be purchased and the average length of time such items would last. Clearly this is a different approach from the one which he used to estimate the cost of housing.

He concentrated his attention most on the question of diet because food is the basic necessity for physical efficiency. He arrived at the necessary amount of money for a diet adequate for subsistence by making three successive estimates: first, he estimated the number of calories that are necessary for physical efficiency. He relied on the studies of Professor Atwater in the USA and of Dr Dunlop in Scotland, who found that when prisoners doing moderately heavy work were fed upon certain diets that contained a certain number of calories, they neither gained nor lost in body weight. He distinguished between men, women and children, but found it difficult to differentiate between different occupations. Second, he had to find the type of diet that could provide this number of calories. He rejected the idea of using prison diets because they were 'so extremely stringent as to be punitive in character and would not serve as a basis for a standard diet for the independent poor.'[17] He chose instead the diets used in workhouses, but after excluding fresh meat from these diets. He accepted but did not attempt to justify that his diet standard 'is therefore less generous than that which would be required by the Local Government Board.'[18] Third, he found out the prices of the foodstuffs in his diet paid by working-class people in York. Thus he arrived at the amount of money necessary for food to maintain merely physical efficiency.

In spite of all his attempts to exclude cultural considerations in his estimates of food, Rowntree did not quite succeed. It is true that his diets were most unappetising but not culture-free. The fact that he chose a reduced workhouse diet rather than a prison diet was a decision based on cultural considerations. Subsequent studies have also shown that people can obtain the same number of calories from even drabber and hence far cheaper diets if only they could behave according to the wishes of researchers and ignore the social life of the community.[19] In his 1936 study, Rowntree came to half-recognise the argument that poverty means more than lack of basic necessities for human survival. It means that poor people should partake of the social life of their community. He thus made allowances for such cultural necessities as radio, books, newspapers, beer, tobacco, presents and holidays, though the amount of money he allowed for this was both arbitrary and inadequate. Rowntree's studies influenced the level of insurance and assistance benefits recommended by the Beveridge Report in 1942 and introduced by the post-war legislation in 1948. What is surprising is that the level of these benefits was less generous than the level of Rowntree's poverty line in 1899 in relation to the average wages.[20] [21]

Though the amount of national assistance benefits has been increased many times since 1948, the amount of benefit today as a proportion of average gross weekly earnings of male manual workers has not changed, as Table 2.6 shows. This stable relationship between national assistance benefits and average wages is not unexpected. Should the level of benefit *vis-à-vis* average gross wages be raised substantially, it would mean that many wage earners, particularly those with children, would be worse off financially in employment than on national assistance benefits. The lack of co-ordination, however, between social security and taxation policies has inadvertently resulted in an improvement of the supplementary benefit scales *vis-à-vis* average net earnings. Taxation of below-average wages has become increasingly heavy during the last decade, due to a number of reasons which cannot be discussed here. Not surprisingly, pressure from various quarters has been mounting to remedy the situation and to streamline taxation, social security and rent and rate rebate policies. Table 2.6 gives a slightly misleading picture of the standard of living of people on supplementary benefit because its comparisons with earnings are made at those dates annually when benefits were increased. While this is satisfactory for making comparisons over the years, it neglects the fact that in between the annual rises, the level of benefits *vis-à-vis* earnings is lower than the figures in Table 2.6.

Rowntree's studies have greatly influenced many contemporary studies of poverty, all of which have used the level of national assistance (now known as supplementary benefit) benefits as their poverty line. It is only recently that some new approaches have been put forward. Prominent among these is that of Townsend mentioned in the last chapter. He points out that the resources of any family consist of more than its cash income. He suggests five possible types of resource: cash income, capital assets, value of employment benefits, value of public social services in kind and private income in kind. He argues, in brief, for a broader definition of resources than has been used in

TABLE 2.6   *Supplementary benefit ordinary scale rates, excluding rent, as a percentage of average gross and net earnings* of male manual workers aged 21 and over*

Date	Single householder		Married couple	
	Gross	Net	Gross	Net
July 1948	17.6	22.9	29.4	36.1
July 1955	17.6	22.5	29.6	35.7
April 1961	17.8	24.9	29.9	39.3
Sept. 1971	18.9	29.8	30.8	47.2
Nov. 1975	17.3	29.8	28.2	47.5

*Net earnings for this purpose are taken as gross earnings less income tax, national insurance contributions, and average rent and rates.

Source: HMSO, Report of the Supplementary Benefits Commission for the Year Ended 31 December 1975.

poverty studies so far. Similarly, he argues for a broader definition of the necessities of life. Instead of the traditional consumption list used by Rowntree and others, he puts forward the idea of 'style of living', which takes into account such nationally accepted social practices as going on holidays, inviting friends for a meal, eating out, birthday parties, possessing such household amenities as a WC, hot and cold water, etc. He then attempts to relate the wider concept of resources to the wider concept of style of living to estimate the extent of poverty or deprivation in society. In his words:[22]

> It is hypothesised that with a diminishing level of resources people will engage less fully in the national 'style of living'. Below a certain level it is further hypothesised that participation will fall off more sharply. More exactly as resources diminish at the lower levels of the distributional range participation will diminish disproportionately.

In this way he constructs a deprivation index. Townsend's approach is a refreshing departure from the traditional straightjacket of poverty studies, even though it still leaves open the question of where the cut-off point lies between deprivation and non-deprivation. It questions in a very fundamental way the distribution of income and wealth in society, for it sees poverty and inequality as being part of the same problem. For this reason it is unlikely to have any effect on social policy in the foreseeable future.

Thus, the extent of poverty in Britain has traditionally been measured by the proportion of people whose incomes are below the supplementary benefit level, or on the same level or just above it. Our knowledge of the extent of poverty in Britain is limited in a number of ways. First, the available evidence refers to the condition prevailing in society at any one time. It is a snapshot view of poverty. It does not tell us very much of the extent of intra-generational and inter-generational poverty. In his first study, Rowntree recognised this when he referred to the cycle of poverty through which individuals go from childhood to old age. Certain stages in this cycle are more likely to immerse working-class people in poverty than others. During their lifetime people may move in and out of poverty, not only because of changing socio-economic conditions but also because of changes in their family structure. Rowntree acknowledged that the numbers of people he found to be in poverty 'represent merely that section who happened to be in one of these poverty periods at the time the inquiry was made.'[23] Second, the available evidence is based on small local studies or on calculations involving government data that are inadequate because they were collected not specifically to estimate poverty but to construct other types of social and economic indices. Third, many studies of poverty concentrate either exclusively or predominantly on income, with the result that the poor are divided into administrative categories corresponding to the provisions of the social security system. What is lost sight of is that those with low incomes suffer from other social disadvantages, and that the various administrative groups of poverty are or have been largely part of the same social class.

Fourth, the apparent precision of the supplementary benefit scales is misleading. In fact, there is no one poverty line but various poverty lines. Apart from the unemployed, other supplementary benefit recipients after two years move on from the temporary to the permanent benefit scales, which are higher. In addition, a large proportion of people receiving insurance and supplementary benefits are also granted discretionary weekly allowances for special needs (extra heating, extra clothing, special diets) and discretionary lump sums for unexpected emergencies. These additional allowances and grants are unevenly paid out, with the result that people who receive the same basic benefit are in fact receiving unequal amounts from the Department of Health and Social Security.

In spite of these reservations, there appears to be a strong measure of agreement that the extent of relative poverty is substantial, and that it has not decreased over the years. Rowntree's three studies established that the extent of poverty in York was 10 per cent in 1899, 18 per cent in 1936, and 1.5 per cent in 1950. The higher level of poverty in 1936 was due partly to the economic depression of the period and partly to the fact that the poverty line was relatively more generous than that used in 1899. The lower level for 1950 was due mainly to the social policy legislation, including food subsidies, introduced in the 1940s, and partly to some methodological issues relating to the survey itself. The low figure for 1950 helped to increase the general feeling in the country during the 1950s that full employment, regular wages and comprehensive social security benefits had eradicated poverty.

During the late 1950s and early 1960s several studies of specific groups showed that poverty was much higher than had been considered. Townsend's study of old people,[24] Marris's study of widows,[25] and the study by Cole and Utting of the economic circumstances of old people[26] were the most important studies which helped to create a new under-standing of the depth and breadth of poverty in British society. The study, however, which re-established poverty as a national issue was the examination of government data relating to the incomes and ex-penditures of families in the whole country in 1960 and 1953 by Abel-Smith and Townsend, in 1965.[27] The study showed that poverty was not only substantial, but that it had increased during the two years under consideration. These findings were substantiated by two govern-ment studies: one of the financial circumstances of retirement pen-sioners in 1965,[28] and the other of the circumstances of families with two or more children.[29]

From the mid-1960s onwards, the country has also witnessed the growth of several pressure groups campaigning vigorously for the im-provement of social security provisions for children in general, for the unemployed, the disabled and one-parent families. Governments have also spent larger sums than before both on supporting research into poverty and deprivation and in setting up experimental projects in very deprived areas. Poverty has been firmly established as a national issue, with all political parties committed to its abolition but not taking firm action when in government. By and large, implicitly rather than ex-plicitly, government anti-poverty programmes have been based on individualistic explanations of poverty discussed in the last chapter. A series of programmes tried to deal with different groups in poverty or with different aspects of poverty by providing some extra resources, by trying to streamline administrative structures, and by attempting to involve people in the implementation of some of the programmes. The basic assumption was that the socio-economic system was basic-ally sound and that what was needed was some minor surgery work to revitalise or infuse more blood into some of its parts. Not surprisingly, these programmes proved to be nothing more than cosmetic surgery, though they provided some help to some of the poor: a few nurseries, a couple of housing advice centres, some welfare rights centres, some financial help to schools in deprived areas, and so on. The failure of these programmes in both the USA and in Britain to abolish or reduce poverty is not unexpected by those who view it in structural terms.

The exact proportion of the British population in poverty is not known. The various national estimates are based on government data from the Inland Revenue and the Family Expenditure Survey. Estimates based on Inland Revenue data by Gough and Stark have shown higher proportions of people with incomes below the national assistance scales, 9.4 per cent in 1963,[30] than estimates based on data from Family Expenditure Surveys. Thus Abel-Smith and Townsend's study found that 3.8 per cent of the population in the United Kingdom had incomes below the national assistance scales, while Atkinson found a very similar figure: 3.4 per cent in 1969.[31] Government estimates, based again on Family Expenditure Survey data, which have given figures around 3.0 per cent slightly underestimate poverty because they wrongly assume that all people receiving supplementary benefit do not have incomes below the scales. This discrepancy between poverty figures, based on Inland Revenue or Family Expenditure Survey data, is due to the fact that the first refer to nuclear family units while the second refer to household units. Thus, single old people living with their children will be counted separately in the Inland Revenue data while they will be considered as part of the household in the Family Expenditure Survey figures.

The importance of this in estimating the extent of poverty is brought out by Fiegehen and his colleagues. They analysed the Family Expenditure Survey data for 1971 in the usual way according to household units and according to nuclear family units. They found that 4.3 per cent of households totalling 3.0 per cent of individuals had incomes below the supplementary benefit level, or 12.5 per cent of nuclear families totalling 8.8 per cent of individuals. On household data 1.7 million people in the country were in poverty; on nuclear family data, the figure was 4.7 million.[32] In summary, it can be said that a minimum of 3.5 per cent of the population of the UK (two million persons) or a maximum of about 9 per cent (almost five million people) live in poverty; i.e., have incomes below the supplementary benefit scales. The exact figures lie somewhere between these two extremes.

People in receipt of supplementary benefit receive not only an amount equivalent to the statutory scale rates plus an amount for their rent, but also various discretionary grants for extra clothing or heating, special diets or other exceptional needs. The award of these discretionary grants and allowances varies a great deal from one office to another but on a national basis they increase the value of the basic statutory allowances considerably. It is, therefore, generally agreed that the poverty line should not be the basic supplementary benefit scale rates plus rent, but that a proportion of the basic allowance should be added to it. Abel-Smith and Townsend found that while only 3.8 per cent of the population had incomes below 100 per cent of the national assistance scale rates, 9.0 per cent had incomes below 120 per cent of the scale rates and 14.2 per cent had incomes below 140 per cent of the basic scale rates. Similarly, other private researchers and government reports have since provided estimates of people living below the poverty line, on it, or just above it. Local surveys of poverty have confirmed that the various calculations of the extent of poverty in the whole country are not excessive and that poverty is not decreasing. Coates and Silburn in their study of a working-class district in Nottingham found that 37 per cent of their sample lived at or below the poverty line, and 40 per cent below 140 per cent of the national assistance scale rates.[33] A study of an estate in west Belfast found that 19 per cent of the population had incomes below the supplementary benefit scales, and 67 per cent had incomes below 140 per cent of the basic scale rates.[34] Young's studies of poverty in London in 1974 showed that 18 per cent of his sample in the district of Camden and 29 per cent of the sample in the district of Bethnal Green had incomes less than 120 per cent of the supplementary benefit scale rates.[35]

Tables 2.7 and 2.8 present a summary of the statistical evidence on the extent and composition of poverty in Britain. The main point of Table 2.7 is that the proportion of people living below, on, or just above the poverty line was not lower in 1974 than in 1960 when Abel-Smith and Townsend first analysed the Family Expenditure Survey data. If anything, it is slightly greater because, while they found 14.2 per cent of the population with incomes below 140 per cent of the national assistance scale rates, Table 2.7 shows that 15 per cent live below 120 per cent of the same scale rates. Fiegehen *et al.* arrive at a similar conclusion in their analysis of the Family Expenditure Survey data. The proportion of the population in relative poverty, i.e. those whose incomes fell below the current scales of national assistance, did not change between 1953 and 1973. The proportion of people in absolute poverty, i.e. those whose incomes fell below a constant 1971 absolute living standard, 'declined from about a fifth of the population in 1953/4 to about a fortieth in 1973.'[36] As they themselves point out, however, this was due to the fact that the whole nation became more affluent during this period rather than to social security policies favouring the poor. These different figures illustrate the problems involved in making comparisons about the extent of poverty over time.

Groups in Poverty

We start the discussion of the groups in poverty with the working poor; i.e., that group of families in poverty where the father is in full-time employment. One of the most disturbing findings of the Abel-Smith–

TABLE 2.7   *Families and persons normally with low net resources in Great Britain, December 1975*[1]

	Family resources					
	Below supplementary benefit level and normally not receiving it		Normally on supplementary benefit[2]		Above supplementary benefit level but within 20% of it	
	Families	*Persons*	*Families*	*Persons*	*Families*	*Persons*
	(thousands)[3]					
Families under pension age:						
Married couples with children	130	570	120	550	200	920
Single persons with children	50[4]	150	260	760	20[4]	80
Married couples, no children	60	120	70	130	60	130
Single persons, no children	260	260	340	340	130	130
Families over pension age:						
Married couples	140	280	280	560	400	800
Single persons	450	470	1,370	1,370	690	690
All families	1,090	1,840	2,430	3,710	1,500	2,750
	(percentage)[5]					
Families under pension age:						
Married couples with children	2	2	2	2	3	4
Single persons with children	7	8	40	41	4	4
Married couples, no children	1	1	1	1	1	1
Single persons, no children	4	4	5	5	2	2
Families over pension age:						
Married couples	7	7	13	13	19	19
Single persons	11	11	34	33	17	17
All families	4	3	10	7	6	5

Notes:
[1] Families are included in this table if the head is either normally receiving supplementary benefit or if the family's net income less net housing costs less work expenses is less than 120% of their supplementary benefit level scale rate. Figures in the table take account of a further analysis of the FES data where the head of a household was self-employed, and include revised estimates of a few figures published in earlier Parliamentary answers.
[2] This analysis of the FES treats respondents according to their normal income and employment situation within the three months preceding the interview; these figures exclude persons who have received supplementary benefit for less than three months in order that the information should be consistent with that obtained from the FES.
[3] Rounded to the nearest 10,000.
[4] Subject to considerable sampling error.
[5] Rounded to the nearest whole percentage.

Source: Central Statistical Office, *Social Trends*, no. 8, HMSO, 1977, Table 6.33, p.116.

Townsend study was that inadequate wages were the single most important reason for poverty, accounting for over one third of the poor. The importance of this factor was corroborated by the publication of the government study 'Circumstances of Families', two years later. Until then, the social security system did not play any direct part in alleviating low pay. Three main plans were then being considered by governments to remedy this situation. First was the substantial improvement of the existing scheme of taxable family allowances, which would benefit all families with children in and out of work but which would help particularly the low-paid, since they do not pay much income tax. This was rejected on the grounds that the gross expenditure would have been substantial and even the net expenditure would have been too high. Second was the introduction of a minimum wage. Again, this was rejected on the grounds of cost, possible effects on levels of unemployment and prices, and because it would not abolish poverty since a minimum wage is not related to the size of the family.[37]

The third possibility, the one that was adopted, was a system whereby low wages were supplemented according to family responsibilities. This is the family income supplement scheme, which provides a weekly allowance to families with children where the main breadwinner is in full-time employment and where the gross combined earnings of husband and wife fall below a certain level that varies according to the number of dependent children in the family. The amount of the supplement covers only half the entitlement and does not exceed a certain amount per week. It is paid only after an application is made by the main family breadwinner.

The family income supplement scheme had in-built conditions from the start that would prevent it from achieving its purpose – to abolish poverty among families where the father was at work. The fact that the supplement itself is not paid in an automatic way but only after an application by the low-paid has meant that the take-up rate has not been 100 per cent but it has ranged from 50 per cent to 75 per cent in spite of substantial government publicity. Statistics concerning take-up rates are extremely unreliable because there is no way at present of knowing who is eligible.[38] The fact also that the scheme does not take into account family expenditures on housing has meant that families with low pay and high rent end up in poverty in spite of any additions they may receive from the family income supplement scheme, unless they apply for such other means-tested benefits as rent and rate rebates. Finally, the restrictions placed on the proportion of the entitled amount that can be paid meant that the government was prepared to allow some families to live in poverty rather than risk affecting work incentives. It was feared that, if the whole amount of entitlement was paid, men might not try to improve their wages through harder work or change of job. A subsequent government study of the scheme concluded that it had no effect on work incentives. Low-paid workers who refuse to change jobs that would provide them with slightly higher wages do so not because of fear of losing their family income supplement, but because they get used to their job. There was no evidence from the study either that offers for overtime work were turned down because of potential loss of the family income supplement.

In spite of these criticisms, the scheme has helped to reduce the extent of poverty among families where the father is in full-time employment. The same government study found that without the family income supplement 'the proportion of respondents who were living below the "supplementary benefit line" rose from 13 per cent to 29 per cent.[39] Family income supplement is of particular help to those fatherless families where the mother is at work, because of the low wages of women and the fact that the scheme provides an allowance for the absent father.

TABLE 2.8   *Immediate reasons for poverty*

Reason	Percentage of people in poverty			
	1936 Rowntree	1960 Abel- Smith and Townsend	1972[a] Government estimate	1971[b] Fiegehen et al.
Old age	15	33	67	48
Inadequate wages	42	40	6[c]	20
Unemployment	29	7	7	10
Sickness and disability	4	10	8	
One-parent family	10	10	11[d]	10
Other	–	–	–	12[e]
Total	100	100	100	100

Notes:
a Hansard, Written Answers, 20 May 1974, cols 45–8, and December 1974, cols 514–15; b G.C. Fiegehen *et al.*, op. cit., Table 5.8, p.66; c includes people off work for illness or unemployment for less than three months; d includes some unclassified persons; e this group includes 'Being female – not retired' and 'other reasons -- unoccupied', which includes sickness and disability.

The second reason for the decline in the size of this poverty group is the increased proportion of married women at work. Between 1951 and 1971 the proportion of married women who worked nearly doubled from 22 per cent to 42 per cent. It is true that wives with no dependent children are more likely to work than wives with dependent children.

Similarly, wives with dependent children of school age were more likely to be at work than wives with children of pre-school age. Nevertheless, the activity rate of all groups of wives increased between 1951 and 1971. Wives' earnings are crucial to family budgets for all income groups. For the low-paid they make all the difference whether the family lives below or above the poverty line. A government analysis of family expenditure survey data for two-parent families showed that the number of families with the father in full-time employment but living below the level of supplementary benefit doubled if the wife's earnings were excluded.[40] Finally, the reduction in the size of this poverty group owes something to the relative increase of family allowances in the late 1960s. Though the amount of the family allowance is still small by the standards of some European countries, it is, nevertheless, bigger than it was in 1960, even in relation to the gross national average wage. Britain is thus still in search of a policy that can ensure that poverty among the working population is abolished. Government expenditure on the family income supplement is far too small to be able to deal adequately with such an important problem, and it is more than likely that new initiatives will be needed in this field in the next few years. The replacement of the family allowance by child benefits in 1977 was a slight improvement in the sense that they are payable in respect of all the children in the family, whereas the family allowance scheme excluded the first child.

Among the non-working population, government policy since the Second World War has been that poverty was to be abolished through a comprehensive system of national insurance benefits paid as of right to all those who satisfied the insurance contribution conditions, and through the safety net of the means-tested national assistance scheme for the small and declining minority that somehow slipped through the insurance benefit network. This was the central idea of the Beveridge Report which fired the imagination of the British people during the War, and on which the whole complex structure of the reorganised social security system was based. That poverty among the non-working section of the population has not been abolished has been established by the various studies mentioned above. The role of national assistance has not turned out to be as originally envisaged either. The number of national assistance claimants and their dependants as a proportion of the total population in Britain has increased over the years, with the result that in 1975 one person in eleven in the whole country relied on supplementary benefit to a greater or lesser extent. The main reason for the dominant role of the national assistance/supplementary benefit scheme has been that from the start the amount was higher than any insurance benefit because it included, for the vast majority of the recipients, an addition for rent. Demographic factors, the welfare rights movement, rising aspirations, as well as the more liberal administration of the scheme since the late 1960s have helped to boost the numbers relying partially or completely on supplementary benefit.

Table 2.9 shows that two thirds of all supplementary benefit recipients today are retirement pensioners. One in five of all retirement pensioners rely, in varying degrees, on supplementary benefit – a figure which is not higher than the figure for the unemployed or the sick and certainly lower than that for single-parent families. The dominance by the elderly of the supplementary benefit scheme and of the distribution of poverty in society reflects largely their demographic dominance and not their inferior treatment by the social security system.

TABLE 2.9   *Persons receiving supplementary benefit, UK, December 1975*

Category of beneficiaries	Per cent
Retirement pensioners	60.2
Unemployed with national insurance benefit	4.8
Unemployed without national insurance benefit	14.5
Sick and disabled with national insurance benefit	2.8
Sick and disabled without national insurance benefit	6.0
Single-parent families with dependent children	10.8
Others	0.9
Total	100.0

Source: Central Statistical Office, *Social Trends,* no. 7, HMSO, 1976, Table 5.23, p. 120.

Why are there so many old people with incomes below the supplementary benefit level, let alone on it or just above it? The vast majority of retirement pensioners receive their retirement pension as of right, but since this does not include an allowance for rent or allowances for such exceptional needs as extra heating or special diets, one fifth of them have to apply to the local supplementary benefits offices for extra benefits which are paid after a personal means test. Evidence from various studies shows that the elderly are treated more sympathetically than other groups when applying for means-tested additions to their pensions. Yet many of them do not apply for such benefits. The government enquiry in 1965 showed that there were three inter-related reasons why retirement pensioners did not apply for supplementary benefit: dislike of means-tested benefits because they considered them as stigmatising; a feeling of pride that they could manage with what they had; an ignorance of whether they were entitled to means-tested benefits and how to apply for them.[41] Research into means-tested benefits has since shown that, in spite of greater publicity, these problems still remain; and they are not confined to either old people or to the supplementary benefit scheme. They cover all age-groups and all means-tested benefits where the onus is on the individual to apply, and which involve a personal means test.[42]

Which groups among the elderly are likely to be in poverty? Social-class background, age and sex are the three main determinants of poverty in old age. Retirement pensioners who had been in manual and particularly unskilled occupations are more likely to be in poverty than others, because they are less likely to have any savings or an adequate occupational or private pension with which they can supplement their retirement pension. The government survey of 1965 showed that income from savings was not an important source of income in old age, generally speaking; but, as one would expect, it was less important and even non-existent for those from manual occupations. The comparative study of old people in the USA, Britain and Denmark substantiated this and many other findings of the government survey.[43]

The same government study showed that whether a retirement pensioner had an adequate occupational pension or not made all the difference between living in poverty or not. Three out of ten of retirement pensioners with manual occupation backgrounds received an occupational pension; the corresponding proportion for those with non-manual occupation backgrounds was six in ten. Moreover, the average occupational pension received by those with a non-manual occupation background was three times greater than that received by retirement pensioners with a manual occupation background. That this picture has not altered much is shown by the subsequent reports of the Government Actuary. Thus, in 1971, 62 per cent of all male employees and 28 per cent of all female employees were covered by an occupational pension scheme; the corresponding proportions for manual workers were 56 per cent and 18 per cent; for non-manual workers, the proportions were 87 per cent and 56 per cent. Among the manual occupations, it was the lowest paid and the least secure in employment that were likely to be excluded.[44] Moreover, occupational pension schemes for non-manual workers provided larger sums and on more favourable conditions than schemes for manual workers.

That poverty is more likely with advancing age among the elderly is self-evident. The very old are less likely to be in part-time employment, they are less likely to have occupational pensions, they are more likely to have used up their savings, and they are more likely to have increased needs due to failing health. For these reasons, it was no surprise that the government study of 1965 found that, while only one in five of all retirement pensioners relied exclusively on their retirement pension and their supplementary benefit, the proportion among those aged eighty-five and over was almost one in two.[45]

TABLE 2.10   *Coverage of occupational pension schemes in firms and organisations with such schemes in December 1971*

Category	Private firms (%)	Public sector (%)	Total (%)
Non-manual:			
Men	75	94	81
Women	36	60	45
Manual:			
Men	45	68	51
Women	19	25	19
Total	47	71	53

Source: Government Actuary, 'Occupational Pension Schemes, 1971'. HMSO, 1972.

Equally self-evident is the greater risk which retired women on their own run of being in poverty in comparison with men. Women live longer than men, they are less likely to be covered by adequate occupational pensions, they are less likely to work beyond the retirement age, they are less likely to have worked regularly during their working life, and when they did their earnings were lower than those of men. These demographic, occupational and social security factors inexorably lead to greater poverty among women on their own than men during old age. Thus the government survey of 1965 showed that of all old people in poverty during old age, 32.3 per cent were married couples, 8.1 per cent were single men and 59.6 per cent were single women.[46]

The recent reorganisation of retirement pensions will allocate more resources to the elderly, but it is unlikely that it will do away with the maldistribution of resources according to class, age and sex. The new emphasis on earnings-related pensions will benefit least the low-paid and, unless women's wages improve substantially in the future, women will continue to feature prominently among the elderly poor. Occupational pension schemes, envisaged to work in partnership with the state pension scheme, will continue to provide benefits in the same unequal way that they have done up to now, though the position of manual workers will improve slightly. As for the special problems of the very elderly, the new pension scheme makes no special provisions at all.

Social security provision for the sick and the disabled is so fragmented that it makes any discussion of the financial condition of the disabled very difficult. Governments have tended to deal with the financial problems of the disabled not according to the degree of disability but according to the source of disability. Thus the war-disabled receive the most generous benefits, followed closely by those who were disabled as a result of an occupational accident or occupational illness. Those who were disabled as a result of an ordinary illness or accident receive insurance benefits that are lower in amount and granted on conditions less favourable than those for the war-disabled and industrially disabled. Finally, those who were born disabled receive the least generous benefits or no benefit at all, and it is among this group that poverty is most likely to be found.

The government study of the disabled in 1968 showed that 30 per cent of the disabled were receiving supplementary benefit and another 7 per cent – representing 250,000 people – appeared to be entitled to supplementary benefit but were not receiving it.[47] These appeared high figures, and two further government studies were carried out to explore the situation further. Unfortunately, these studies helped to confuse rather than clarify the situation. By the time the two follow-up studies were conducted, some of the disabled had moved away, others had died, and others did not want to take part in the survey. Bearing these and other methodological points in mind, the two studies found that poverty was not as widespread as was first considered. They found that at least 70,000 people were eligible to receive supplementary benefit and were willing to apply for it. A further 100,000 were not willing to claim supplementary benefit, though an unspecified proportion were entitled to it.[48]

Other private studies have confirmed the view that poverty among the disabled is more prevalent than among the general population. Sainsbury concluded her findings as follows:[49]

As many as 48% of the households represented in the sample reported resources of below 140% of the basic national assistance scale, compared with 18% of the United Kingdom generally. Whereas about 5% of households nationally had incomes below the basic national assistance scale – this was true of 14% of the households in the sample. Of course, there was a disproportionate number of elderly persons in the sample and this might be expected to inflate the proportion of low income households. But an above average number of younger persons in the sample belonged to low income households. 10% of persons below pensionable age belonged to households where the total income was below the basic national assistance scale, compared with 5% of households nationally.

The main reasons for poverty among the disabled are that some receive no benefit from the state at all, others receive inadequate benefits, and others are in low-paid occupations and suffering from rates of unemployment three to five times higher than the national average rate of unemployment. Pressure groups for the disabled have campaigned vigorously in recent years for a disability benefit paid as of right to all the disabled according to the degree of disability and irrespective of insurance contribution conditions, or the cause and place of disability. The major political parties have from time to time expressed support for this plan, but neither political party, when in government, has shown much enthusiasm in implementing its pledges.[50] Thus poverty among the disabled will continue in the foreseeable future until the disjointed form of incremental social security planning gives way to the comprehensive plan that groups for the disabled and others have long advocated.

As far as poverty during sickness is concerned, it is clearly manual workers who are most likely to experience it. In the first place, they are more likely to be absent from work on account of sickness than non-manual workers. This is particularly true for unskilled workers, whose rates of sickness absence from work are three times higher than those of professional men of the same age-group.[51] In the second place, they are less likely to receive any benefits from occupational sick pay schemes which would supplement any government insurance benefit they may receive. Wedderburn and Craig found that while only 46 per cent of manual workers in the industries they studied were covered by an occupational sick pay scheme, the corresponding proportion for non-manual workers was about 63 per cent. They also fared much less well with regard to the length of time benefit was paid and to the amount of the benefit.[52] Similarly, a government study showed that 'people in less skilled jobs and people with the lowest incomes before their illness started were less likely to receive sick pay' from their employers.[53] The lowest-paid and the unskilled predominated among the long-term sick, who were less likely to receive sick pay. Moreover, the same groups 'who are best off financially while they are sick because they receive sick pay are also likely to find it easiest to return to work because they have a job to go to.'[54] In general, then, the unskilled are most exposed to the health hazards of work and least protected by government or occupational schemes.

The same observation is even more true in the case of the unemployed. The rate of unemployment is closely related to social class: the lower the social class of the occupation the higher the incidence of unemployment. Unskilled manual workers have been experiencing unemployment rates two to three times higher than those of skilled manual workers and six times higher than those of the professional and managerial groups. The Census for 1971 showed the following rates: In class I, the unemployment rate was 1.4 per cent; class II,

2.2 per cent; class III (non-manual), 3.0 per cent; class III (manual), 4.2 per cent; class IV, 5.2 per cent; and class V, 11.8 per cent. The duration of unemployment, too, is similarly related to social class, as Table 2.11 shows.

TABLE 2.11 *Occupational group and long-term unemployment, men, January 1978*

Occupational group	Men unemployed for over 1 year	All unemployed men
	%	%
Managerial and professional	4.0	8.0
Clerical and related	10.0	8.0
Other non-manual	2.0	3.0
Craft and similar occupations, incl. foremen	9.0	16.0
General labourers	56.0	40.0
Other manual occupations	19.0	25.0
All occupations	100.0	100.0

Source: 'Statistics on Long-Term Unemployment', *Department of Employment Gazette*, June 1978.

Various writers have referred to this relationship between social class and unemployment. Reid concludes from official data that 'unemployment among manual workers is both more common and less likely to be alleviated.'[55] Daniel, commenting on his survey of the unemployed, concluded that 'our findings combine to show that the problem of unemployment remains very much a problem of the male manual working class.'[56] Age, sex, ethnic group and regional variations are other important dimensions of unemployment, but they do not negate the role of social class.

How does the social security system deal with the financial problems of unemployment? A flat-rate insurance benefit is provided for a maximum period of twelve months, and an earnings-related insurance benefit for the first six months of unemployment. Those with inadequate employment records will not be entitled to these insurance benefits, or will be entitled to reduced amounts. These are most likely to be the unskilled workers. Moreover, the combined amount of flat-rate and earnings-related unemployment benefit should not exceed 85 per cent of the unemployed person's previous gross wage – a rule which affects adversely the low-paid. Supplementary benefit can be paid when the unemployment benefit runs out, or when there is no qualification to unemployment benefit, or when the unemployment benefit is inadequate. The amount of supplementary benefit paid to the unemployed, however, is lower than the amount paid to other population groups in the sense that the unemployed do not qualify for the long-term rates, irrespective of how long they may have been unemployed. Unemployment benefit can be refused for periods of up to six weeks for those who are considered to be avoiding taking up employment, who left their job voluntarily or because of industrial misconduct, and so on. Also, until mid-1976, the wages stop rule ensured that no unemployed person received more in supplementary benefit than he was earning while in employment – a rule which obviously affected the low-paid with families. Again, all these rulings affect the unskilled unemployed more than other groups of unemployed people.[57]

The various unfavourable rulings contained in the unemployment benefit scheme and in the supplementary benefit scheme relating to the unemployed are designed to enforce industrial discipline as far as possible and not to undermine work incentives. Even with these conditions, the fear still persists that many of the unemployed are 'voluntarily' unemployed because of the existence of social security benefits, particularly the earnings-related benefits and redundancy benefits introduced in the mid-1960s. An official article, however, summarising the evidence, concluded that 'several investigations have been made, and several econometric studies, but they have not produced any conclusive evidence to support this hypothesis.'[58]

Table 2.12 indicates the failure of the insurance system for the unemployed. No other insured population group – the elderly, the sick, the widowed, or the disabled – is covered so inadequately by its insurance benefit. It is not surprising, therefore, that poverty among the unemployed is substantial. Sinfield's study of a small group of long-term unemployed men found that more than one third of the total sample had incomes below the supplementary benefit level. Over one half of the unemployed with children as against one fifth of those without children had incomes below their supplementary benefit entitlement.[59] A study of a larger sample of unemployed by Hill found that 17 to 18 per cent of the married householders who were unemployed for over four weeks had incomes below the supplementary benefit level. In general, too, Hill found that 'there was little question that the majority of the unemployed were living . . . on what can be described as no more than subsistence incomes.'[60]

These studies were conducted before the abolition of the wages stop, and it can be argued that the proportion of the unemployed with incomes below the supplementary benefit level is not as high today. On the other hand, unemployment rates have risen very considerably in the last five years, standing at about 6.0 per cent of the labour force in 1977 compared with less than 2.0 per cent in the 1950s. The fact that

the unskilled, the disabled, the immigrants and other weak groups
suffer from higher unemployment rates and particularly from long-
term unemployment does mean that poverty among the unemployed
may have increased recently, for these are the very groups which are
not protected well by the insurance scheme and have to rely on supplementary benefit. A study by the Department of Health and Social
Security in 1978 showed how limited the incomes of unemployed men
were: 67 per cent of the men in the sample had incomes equivalent to
their supplementary benefit entitlement, 21 per cent had incomes
above it; and 12 per cent had incomes below it.[61]

TABLE 2.12   *Unemployed men aged 18 and over:
benefit and credit position*

Receiving unemployment and/or supplementary benefit		
Unemployment benefit only	4397	30.9%
Unemployment benefit and supplementary benefit	1351	9.5%
Supplementary benefit only; unemployment benefit exhausted	4039	28.4%
Supplementary benefit only: other cases	1606	11.3%
Receiving no benefit		
Unemployment benefit exhausted	869	6.1%
Claim disallowed	220	1.5%
Claimant disqualified	124	0.9%
Claim not decided	726	5.1%
Non-claimants	878	6.2%
Total sample	14210	100.0%

Source: 'Characteristics of the Unemployed: Analysis by
Occupation', *Department of Employment Gazette,* HMSO,
vol. 82, no. 5, May 1974, Table 7, p.389.

The loss to the community from high unemployment rates is as
manifold as it is substantial. Not only have social security benefits to
be paid but, as Forester points out, society also loses in many other
ways.[62]

Society *loses* the income tax revenue it would have gained had the
unemployed been in employment. It *loses* the indirect taxes on the
consumption of extra goods and services that would have been
bought. And it *loses* the national insurance contribution which

52   Vic George

would have been paid by both employers and employees. Most important of all, in economic terms, society loses the value of the goods and services which the unemployed would have produced. (And this is not to speak of any personal and psychological costs of unemployment).

The position of one-parent families has received a great deal of attention in the last ten years by both government and private reports and research studies. One family in ten is a one-parent family, and one child in ten lives in a one-parent family. Of all one-parent families, five-sixths are fatherless families (i.e. headed by a mother) and the remaining one-sixth are motherless families (i.e. headed by a father). Of the fatherless families, the separated are the largest group (190,000), followed by the widowed and the divorced (120,000 each), with the unmarried being the smallest sub-group (90,000). As Table 2.13 indicates, their main sources of income are earnings from work, maintenance payments, supplementary benefit and insurance benefits for widows. For social security purposes, however, one-parent families fall into two groups: widows, who are entitled to insurance benefits which are payable irrespective of any other income from work or from

TABLE 2.13   *Main sources of income of one-parent families, 1971

Main source of income	Number of families
Fatherless families other than widows' families:	
Earnings	140,000
Maintenance	50,000
Supplementary benefits	200,000
Other	10,000
Widows' families:	
Earnings	50,000
Widows' benefits	60,000
Other	10,000
Motherless families:	
Earnings	90,000
Supplementary benefits	10,000
Total number of one-parent families:	620,000

*Main source is the largest source of income

Source: 'Report of the Committee on One-Parent Families' (Finer Report), Cmnd 5629, HMSO, 1974, Table 5.1, p. 244.

elsewhere which they may have; and all the other one-parent families, which can apply for means-tested supplementary benefit. For this reason and also because many widows receive an occupational widows' pension, widows are better off financially than other fatherless families. Very much on par with widows' families are the motherless families due to the fact that in the vast majority of these families the father goes out to work.[63] The separated and the unmarried are the worst off financially, with the divorced occupying the middle position.

The average income and the average adjusted income of fatherless families is less than half that of two-parent families, according to a government study.[64] One-parent families are also worse off than two-parent families in terms of housing, health and school achievement of their children. Reviewing all the evidence, the Finer Committee concluded that[65]

> in terms of families with children . . . there can be no other group of this size who are as poor as fatherless families of whom so many lack any state benefits other than supplementary benefit or family allowance, whose financial position is so uncertain and whose hope of improvement in their situation is relatively so remote.

As Table 2.7 showed, one half of all persons in a family of a single person with dependent children had incomes just below the supplementary benefit level, equivalent to it, or just above it at the end of December 1975. This proportion is very similar to that arrived at by the Finer Report, even though its figures refer to families rather than persons in the families. Of the total 620,000 one-parent families, an estimated 45 per cent had incomes just below, equivalent or just above the supplementary benefit level. It is also possible that the single parent definition of Table 2.7 is wider than that used by the Finer Report. With all these qualifications, however, the proportion of one-parent families who have to manage on very restricted incomes is by any standard excessively high.

The tragedy of fatherless families, other than widowed, is that they can hardly escape from the poverty they are in: whether they rely on supplementary benefit or whether they decide to go out to work makes little difference to their financial position. Women's wages are low and child-minding is expensive, with the result that, generally speaking, it does not pay to go out to work. It is even worse for mothers who try to manage on part-time earnings supplemented by maintenance payments from the husband. The Finer Report showed that it was this group of fatherless families that had incomes below the supplementary benefit level – a total of 43,000 families or 8 per cent of all fatherless families.[66] Maintenance payments by the husband are usually small in amount, they are paid irregularly, and they involve the mother in a great deal of trouble in her efforts to enforce regular payment.[67] Relying on supplementary benefit over long periods of time is a crippling experience materially, socially and morally. The various studies of fatherless and motherless families provide abundant evidence for this.[68] The social security system, through its cohabitation rule, makes any semi-stable relationships with men difficult if not impossible. Women who are thought to be living as common-law wives have their allowances stopped or reduced. Every year an average of 8,000 such cases are investigated and in about 3,500 the allowance is withdrawn or reduced.[69]

The Finer Committee was very critical of the large-scale dependence of fatherless families, excluding widows, on means-tested supplementary benefit. It is therefore difficult to understand why they recommended a new benefit which was itself to be means tested. They rejected proposals for an end-of-marriage allowance which would provide a benefit as of right to all one-parent families on similar lines to the benefits now provided to widows.[70] In the meantime, the government has rejected the Finer recommendation for a new means-tested benefit. Thus the fastest growing group in poverty – the one-parent families – is still without adequate social security provision, and its numbers are likely to continue to grow as fast in the future as they have been doing during the last few years.

It was Rowntree in his first study of York who coined the phrase 'life cycle poverty' to describe the stages that the family's financial status goes through. In all families, poverty is most likely during retirement and during the child-bearing stage. Relative affluence is most likely during the in-between period. Child poverty is thus a real risk in society, and for many this type of poverty is more disturbing than other types because children are not to blame for their condition. They are the future citizens on whom the economic strength of the country depends, and they are also the future parents on whom the welfare of the next generation of children depends. Child poverty thus evokes more public sympathy than any other form of poverty.

The revelation by Abel-Smith and Townsend that a large proportion of children was living in poverty was particularly disturbing. They showed that in 1960 29 per cent of all persons living in poverty (i.e. with an income below 140 per cent of the national assistance scale rates plus rent) were below the age of fifteen. Expressed differently, 17 per cent of all children (two and a quarter million children) were living in poverty. The Ministry of Social Security study of families with two or more children confirmed these findings for 1966; and Table 2.14, which is extrapolated from government statistics for 1975, also lends support to the view that child poverty is a major problem in British society. As would be expected, children of large families are more vulnerable than children of small families,[71] but it is a mistake to believe that the biggest proportion of children in poverty come from large families. Thus the Ministry of Social Security study showed that families with the father in full-time work, with two children, made up over a third of all families in poverty; and for families with two children or three children, the corresponding proportion was one half. Expressed differently, of all children in poverty, 38 per cent lived in families with two or three children. Thus child poverty is due as much to the parents' low wages as to the largeness of the size of the family.[72]

TABLE 2.14   *Number of children living in families with low incomes, December 1975*

Type of family	Below supplementary benefit level, normally not receiving supplementary benefit	On supplementary benefit	Above supplementary benefit level but within 20% of it	All children in poverty
Married couples	310,000	310,000	520,000	1,140,000
Single persons	100,000	500,000	60,000	660,000
Total	410,000	810,000	580,000	1,800,000

Source: Extrapolated from Table 2.7.

Children in poverty, like adults in poverty, are very likely to suffer from other forms of deprivation. Thus Wedge and Prosser's study of a national sample of 10,504 children born in the week of 3–9 March 1958 showed that a significant proportion of these children at age eleven in 1969 were multiply deprived. One in four had grown up either in a one-parent family or in a large family with five or more children where individual care and attention would have been more difficult than in other families. A similar proportion of one in four were living in poor housing conditions; i.e., grossly overcrowded or in housing with no hot water supply. At least one in seven of the children was living in families with low income, i.e. at the level or below the level of supplementary benefit. These individual deprivations overlapped, and one child in every sixteen was experiencing all three forms of deprivation. The authors refer to this group of children as the socially disadvantaged compared with the disadvantaged, i.e. suffering from one disadvantage only.[73] Disadvantaged children were shorter than ordinary children, more likely to have suffered from illness and accidents, more likely to suffer from a hearing or speech impairment, more likely to attend schools for the educationally sub-normal, and had lower reading scores in the ordinary school. As one would expect, social class was an important variable in the distribution of disadvantage among children. 'Fewer disadvantaged children were thus from middle-class homes, fewer of them had middle-class grandparents, fewer had parents who had stayed on at school beyond the minimum age and fewer of their parents read newspapers or books.[74] Thus the disadvantages as well as the advantages were social-class based not only within the same generation but also across generations.

Though the various groups of people in poverty have been discussed separately, there is a common thread joining most of them together: they belong to the manual, particularly the unskilled, occupational groups. The unskilled workers earn wages that are lower than those of other occupational groups; they are more likely to have larger families and to suffer from unemployment, sickness and disability; vice versa, they are less likely to be covered by occupational schemes for sickness, widowhood and retirement; they are less likely to satisfy to the full the insurance contributions entitling them to the various insurance benefits; and they are, of course, less likely to have any savings or strong financial support from their extended family network. Bearing in mind that these misfortunes are inter-connected, the unskilled are not only more likely to find themselves in poverty but more likely to remain in it. As a 1978 government report on lower incomes put it:[75]

> The effects of disadvantage can be cumulative. There are links between the incidence of low skills, low earnings, sickness disablement and spells of unemployment, and those who have less earnings from work are also likely to have lower incomes when out of work. Poor housing conditions are less clearly associated with lower incomes but those with lower incomes are more likely than others to occupy poor housing.

Conclusion

Income and wealth inequalities are almost as great today as they were at the beginning of this century, though the concentration of both has been dispersed from the top 1 per cent to the top 10 per cent of the population. Some of this dispersal is illusory, for it is dispersal from husbands to wives or other members of the family. In spite of the various forms of personal and company taxation, these inequalities have survived and, on present evidence, they will continue in the future. Poverty, too, has survived in spite of the fact that the standard of supplementary benefit level today in relation to average earnings is similar to the standard of absolute poverty adopted by Rowntree in 1899. The social security system provides financial help to millions of people in need but it fails to ensure that no one has an income below even the basic supplementary benefit level for two main reasons. First, many of those who are entitled to supplementary benefit fail to apply for a variety of reasons. Second, many of those in receipt of supplementary benefit receive reduced amounts, again for a variety of reasons. Theoretically, it is quite possible to abolish this form of poverty among the non-employed section of the population through administrative changes. In practice, however, it may not be possible, partly because of cost and partly because some of the existing rulings that are responsible for some of the poverty reflect core social values relating to work and the family. Poverty among the working population is much more difficult to abolish. The family income supplement is a pale shadow of the supplementary benefit scheme. Any attempt to extend the supplementary benefit scheme to the working population will be resisted, not only because of the cost involved, but also because it will be seen to undermine work incentives. For these reasons, poverty, even narrowly confined to income only, will continue to exist in Britain.

The inability of the government to solve the problem of poverty among the working poor means that any real improvement in the supplementary benefit scales is impossible. These scales were calculated at least thirty years ago and, though they have been increased several times since, they have not been basically re-thought. To solve the problem of low pay and poverty, as at present defined, means some reduction of inequality. To improve the scales of supplementary benefit (i.e. to raise the poverty line) means a further reduction of inequality. The prospects are, therefore, that Britain will go on trying to help its poor; but until the question of inequality comes into the political arena, poverty will continue to exist.

References

1 J. Westergaard and H. Reisler, *Class in a Capitalist Society*, Heineman, 1975, Table 2, p. 42.
2 G. Routh, *Occupation and Pay in Great Britain, 1906–1960*, Cambridge University Press, 1965, Table 48.
3 HMSO, 'Abstract of Regional Statistics', 1974, p. 147.
4 P. Wilding, *Poverty: The Facts in Wales*, Child Poverty Action Group, 1977, p. 13.
5 H. Lydall and D. Tipping, 'The Distribution of Personal Wealth in Britain', *Bulletin of Oxford University Institute of Economics and Statistics*, February 1961.
6 R. Titmuss, *Income Distribution and Social Change*, Allen & Unwin, 1962.
7 J. Wedgwood, *The Economics of Inheritance*, Routledge & Kegan Paul, 1929.

8 C. Harbury and P. McMahon, 'Inheritance and the Characteristics of Top Wealth Leavers in Britain', *Economic Journal*, vol. 83, 1973.

9 C. Booth, *Life and Labour of the People of London*, Macmillan, 1902.

10 S. Rowntree, *Poverty: A Study of Town Life*, Macmillan, 1901.

11 B. Gilbert, *The Evolution of National Insurance in Great Britain*, Batsford, 1966.

12 S. Rowntree, *Poverty and Progress: A Second Social Survey of York*, Longmans, 1941.

13 S. Rowntree and G. Lavers, *Poverty in the Welfare State*, Longmans, 1951.

14 Rowntree, op. cit., 1901, p. 117.

15 Ibid., pp. 167-8.

16 Ibid., p. 140.

17 Ibid., p. 138.

18 Ibid., p. 131.

19 G. Stigler, 'The Cost of Subsistence', *Journal of Farm Economics*, vol. 27, 1945.

20 V. George, *Social Security and Society*, Routledge & Kegan Paul, 1973, p. 47-8.

21 R. Berthoud, *The Disadvantages of Inequality*, PEP, Macdonald & Janes, 1976, p. 26.

22 P. Townsend, in D. Wedderburn (ed.), *Poverty, Inequality and Class Structure*, Cambridge University Press, 1974, p. 35.

23 Rowntree, op. cit., 1901, p. 137.

24 P. Townsend, *The Family Life of Old People*, Routledge & Kegan Paul, 1957.

25 P. Marris, *Widows and their Families*, Routledge & Kegan Paul, 1958.

26 D. Cole and J. Utting, *The Economic Circumstances of Old People*, Codicote, 1962.

27 B. Abel-Smith and P. Townsend, *The Poor and the Poorest*, Bell, 1965.

28 Ministry of Pensions and National Insurance, 'Financial and Other Circumstances of Retirement Pensioners', HMSO, 1965.

29 Ministry of Social Security, 'Circumstances and Families', HMSO, 1967.

30 I. Gough and T. Stark, 'Low Incomes in the United Kingdom', *Manchester School*, vol. 36, 1968.

31 A. Atkinson, *Poverty in Britain and the Reform of Social Security*, Cambridge University Press, 1969.

32 G.C. Fiegehen, P.S. Lansley and A.D. Smith, *Poverty and Progress in Britain, 1953-1973*, Cambridge University Press, 1977, Tables 3.6, p. 29 and 4.5, p. 47.

33 K. Coates and R. Silburn, *Poverty: The Forgotten Englishmen*, Penguin, 1970, p. 67.

34 E. Evason, 'Measuring Family Poverty', *Social Work Today*, vol. 4, no. 3, 1974.

35 M. Young, (ed.), *Poverty Report, 1975*, Temple Smith, 1975, Table 6.2, p. 99.
36 Fiegehen *et al.*, op. cit., p. 111.
37 Department of Employment and Productivity, 'A National Minimum Wage', HMSO, 1969.
38 D. Stanton, 'The Take-up Debate on the UK Family Income Supplement', *Policy and Politics*, vol. 5, no. 4, June 1977.
39 Department of Health and Social Security, 'Two-Parent Families in Receipt of Family Income Supplement', 1972, HMSO, 1975, p. 87.
40 Department of Health and Social Security, 'Two-Parent Families: A Study of their Resources and needs in 1968, 1969 and 1970', HMSO, 1976.
41 Ministry of Pensions and National Insurance, op. cit., Table III, 21, p. 42.
42 R. Lister, 'Take-up: The Same Old Story', *Poverty*, no. 34, Summer, 1976.
43 E. Shandas *et al.*, *The Old in Three Industrial Societies*, Routledge & Kegan Paul, 1968.
44 Government Actuary, 'Occupational Pension Schemes', HMSO, 1972.
45 Ministry of Pensions and National Insurance, op. cit., Table II 2, p. 12.
46 Ibid., Tables III.2 and III.4, pp. 20–1.
47 A. Harris *et al.*, 'Income and Entitlement to Supplementary Benefit of Impaired People in Great Britain', HMSO, 1972.
48 C. Smith, 'Entitlement to Supplementary Benefit of Impaired People in Great Britain', HMSO, 1972.
49 S. Sainsbury, *Registered Disabled*, Bell, 1970, pp. 70–1.
50 The Disability Alliance, 'Poverty and Disability', London, 1976, pp. 1–2.
51 Office of Population and Census Statistics, 'General Household Survey', HMSO, 1973, table 8.10.
52 D. Wedderburn and Ch. Craig, 'Relative Deprivation at Work', in *Poverty, Inequality and Class Structure*, op. cit., table 7.1, p. 144.
53 Office of Population Censuses and Surveys, 'Prolonged Sickness and the Return to Work', HMSO, 1975, p. 90.
54 Ibid., p. 91.
55 I. Reid, *Social Class Differences in Britain*, Open Books, 1977, p. 88.
56 W. Daniel, 'The Reality of Unemployment', *New Society*, 9 September 1974.
57 A. Sinfield, 'Poor and Out of Work in Shields', in P. Townsend (ed.), *The Concept of Poverty*, Heinemann, 1970.
58 'The Unemployment Statistics and their Interpretation', *Department of Employment Gazette*, vol. 82, no. 3, March 1975, p. 181.
59 Sinfield, op. cit., p. 228.
60 M. Hill, *Men Out of Work*, Cambridge University Press, 1973, p. 139.

61 M. Clark, 'The Unemployed on Supplementary Benefit', *Journal of Social Policy*, vol. 7, part 4, October 1978.
62 T. Forester, 'Who, Exactly, are the Unemployed?' *New Society*, 13 January 1977.
63 V. George and P. Wilding, *Motherless Families*, Routledge & Kegan Paul, 1972.
64 A. Hunt *et al.*, 'Families and their Needs', HMSO, 1973.
65 The Finer Report, 'Report of the Committee on One-Parent Families', HMSO, 1974, p. 269.
66 Ibid., p. 254.
67 O.R. McGregor, *et al.*, *Separated Spouses*, Duckworth, 1970.
68 D. Marsden, *Mothers Alone*, Allen Lane, 1969.
69 F. Field, *The Facts*, Child Poverty Action Group, 1975, p. 21.
70 R. Lister, *Social Security: The Case for Reform*, Child Poverty Action Group, 1975, pp. 56–7.
71 H. Land, *Large Families in London*, Bell, 1969.
72 Ministry of Social Security, op. cit., tables III.4, A.3, A.4.
73 P. Wedge and H. Prosser, *Born to Fail?* Arrow Books, 1973, pp. 11–17.
74 Ibid., p. 32.
75 Royal Commission on the Distribution of Income and Wealth, *Lower Incomes: Report No. 6*, Command 7175, HMSO, 1978, p. 152.

3 Poverty and inequality in Belgium

Jos Berghman*

Attitudes and policies towards poverty

Since the end of the Second World War there have been several distinct phases in the development of Belgian attitudes and policies towards poverty. The first phase, beginning immediately after the liberation in 1944, was characterised by a great deal of activity in the field of social policy. This was to some extent influenced by events in other countries, as for example the publication of the Beveridge Report. However, Belgium's post-war reforms were also inspired by some quite different considerations from those underlying the Beveridge strategy.[1] As had happened before the War, the main initiatives leading to the reforms stemmed from trade unions and employers' organisations and particularly from a *Projet d'accord de solidarité sociale*, a plan for social and economic reconstruction formulated by the so-called social partners. While this called for considerable improvements in social protection, it still reflected the traditional continental view that social policy was mainly concerned with 'normalising' the relationships between the two sides of industry rather than with the wider (Beveridge) issues of citizenship.[2]

This helps to explain why the main results of the reforming activity of this first phase were changes in the social provisions made for employed persons, especially social insurance provisions. Decrees issued in 1944 and 1945 created a new system of social insurance for persons under contract of employment, including for the first time compulsory health, disability and unemployment insurance. The decrees also raised the existing old-age and survivors' pensions and, much more substantially, the children's allowances and family benefits which Belgium had pioneered in the early 1930s. Public servants were not fully incorporated into this social insurance system, but continued to be covered by special and more generous statutory provisions. Special

* I would like to thank Mr R.J. Lawson, University of Southampton and co-editor, and Professor Dr H. Deleeck and my colleagues at the Centrum voor Sociaal Beleid (Centre for Social Policy), University of Antwerp, for their advice and criticism.

arrangements were also made for miners and seamen. By contrast, in
the early post-war period the only compulsory insurance measures
for the self-employed were children's allowances and related benefits.
A separate scheme for the self-employed had been introduced in 1937
and its benefits were improved and extended after the war. However,
its main allowances continued to be set (as they still are today) at lower
levels than the children's allowances for employees.

Thus the post-war reforms created a system of social insurance
which, to quote Professor Deleeck, 'aimed at fighting poverty as it
specifically presented itself amongst employees, and not at fighting
poverty in general'.[3] Moreover, in its benefits and administration the
system tended to focus on what Deleeck has called 'the ordinary
employee with an ordinary career and an ordinary family life'. This
was partly because the right to adequate protection remained dependent on work records and contribution periods, while the levels of
most benefits varied with the individual's wage level.[4] But another
reason was to be found in the important role played by employers'
organisations and the labour movement in the policy-making and administrative processes of social insurance.[5] The new system was divided
into various financially and administratively independent sectors
managed by councils of employer and employee representatives under
the chairmanship of an administrator representing the Minister of
Social Security. Trade unions and friendly societies[6] were also en-
trusted with much of the daily administration of unemployment
insurance and medical care, sickness and disability benefits, and they
acquired a quasi monopoly over many of the social services run by
social insurance schemes as well as over legal aid in social matters.
Hence the system was not only technically complicated, but also one
which was not likely to respond much to the needs of groups who for
some reason were not affiliated to organisations of the labour movement, or were not well organised, or were marginal to the production
process.[7]

As to the task of fighting poverty in general, this continued to be
the responsibility of local social assistance committees, whose activities were quite separate from social insurance and were on the whole
little affected by the post-war reforms. Under an Act of 1925 a social
assistance committee was set up in each commune, mainly to provide
financial assistance, to take any measures to prevent destitution and to
secure any help for medical care.[8] This was an entirely decentralised
system managed at the local level by a committee which, after having
set up a 'social investigation', had complete discretionary power to
decide whether a person or family was in need and the kind and
amount of assistance that should be awarded. It followed that assistance benefits varied from one commune to another, depending on,

for example, the financial resources of the local committee or the size and skill of its professional staff.

The individual character of each decision, which in theory was meant to lead to a fair assessment of personal and family needs, made it impossible to develop any set of national assistance levels.[9] Hence there was no official poverty line in Belgium, nor indeed any national policy on minimum social incomes. Some reference to national minimum benefits was to be found in the social insurance legislation, where it was accepted that certain groups should be provided with higher pensions and allowances than a mere application of insurance principles would have yielded.[10] However, a bewildering disparity was apparent not only among the different social insurance sectors but also within the same sector.[11] These minima were also based on certain contribution and work conditions: only 'full career' pensioners, for example, could qualify for minimum pensions.

After the burst of reforming activity in the early post-war period Belgian social policy entered a new phase that was to last until the end of the 1960s. This phase saw some important developments in certain sectors of social security, especially in the pension arrangements for employees.[12] Legislation in the 1950s related pension rights more closely to revalued lifetime earnings, and there were a number of *ad hoc* adjustments to existing pensions to bring them more in line with changes in national prosperity. There was also a gradual extension of the field of application of social insurance, as some new schemes were created for previously excluded groups. For the self-employed an old-age and survivors' pension scheme was introduced on a compulsory basis in 1956, and this was followed by compulsory medical care insurance in 1964. In 1967 these provisions were co-ordinated in the so-called 'social statute of the self-employed', to which sickness pay and disability benefits were added in 1970.

Despite these developments, the basic character of Belgian social insurance and assistance policies was not really changed during this phase. The new pensions for the self-employed provided only very modest benefits, in most cases well below any acceptable subsistence standards, while the initiatives for changes within the general social insurance system still came from the 'social partners' and tended to emphasise the needs of the ordinary employee. Since successive governments preferred to follow the 'social partners' rather than elaborate different policies, there was little opportunity for a critical or fundamental reappraisal of social insurance, nor indeed of social policy as a whole. Another consequence of this state of affairs and of the continued reluctance of central government to interfere with the activities of social assistance committees was that hardly any information was available at the national level about the existence of poverty or its incidence amongst different social groups.

This, at least, was the situation until the second half of the 1960s, when the problem of poverty began to re-emerge as a public issue of some political significance. As Deleeck has put it:[13]

After twenty-five years of social security and in the midst of welfare, the existence of modern forms of poverty was discovered. The point at issue was quite an extensive group of people who had been unable to participate in the general prosperity.

One of the earliest estimates of the size of this group was made by the *Nationale Aktie voor Bestaanszekerheid* (National Action for Security of Subsistence), a master organisation of several poverty action groups created in this period to enhance public awareness of the problems of the 'forgotten' or 'disinherited' groups. In its 'Manifesto of the Disinherited' (1967) it claimed that more than 900,000 people, about 10 per cent of the Belgian population were living in poverty.[14]

Inevitably this was only a very rough estimate based on an arbitrarily chosen poverty line. As one would expect, the absence of any official poverty standards and the difficulties in interpreting the available data on earnings and social benefits led to some quite significant differences in the findings of some of the reports produced in this period. As regards the elderly, for example, an investigation by the *Centre de recherche et d'information socio-politiques* (CRISP), also published in 1967, claimed that 300,000 old people, representing 19 per cent of the elderly, were in poverty.[15] This was followed by another and well-documented study at the Department of Social Security by J. Mertens, who concluded that in 1969 around 25,000 retired couples and 100,000 single pensioners – 9.5 per cent of the elderly – had incomes below his poverty lines.[16]

There was also some interesting research in this period into the treatment of the poor by social assistance committees; this provided evidence of people's reluctance to apply for assistance, at least until virtually all other possibilities were exhausted.[17] This was the main conclusion of P. Schoetter's study of five social assistance committees which together gave assistance to 702 families.[18] Similar findings, and the general inadequacy of social assistance benefits, were reported in a survey of families helped by the Brussels social assistance committee.[19]

In spite of the limited and loose character of some of these studies, they all proved their usefulness in focusing public attention on hitherto neglected problems. Indeed, the campaign on behalf of the 'disinherited', which was supported by a number of private members' bills in parliament, quickly succeeded in convincing government and parliament that some important changes were needed in the basic framework of Belgian social policy. Between 1969 and 1976 a number of acts were voted through parliament which together gave evidence of new priorities, especially in the treatment of the poorest sections of the community. In these developments it was no longer the social partners, but parliament and government that took the initiative.

In December 1969 a private member's bill was introduced to 'universalise' children's allowances, which up to that time were provided only within the framework of the different schemes for employees, miners, seamen, civil servants and the self-employed. Although the field of application of these schemes had been extended since the War, it was pointed out that children in some of the very poorest families (e.g., in certain one-parent families) had no legal entitlement to the allowances, the amounts of which were considerably higher in Belgium than in most other countries. Instead of introducing a universal right to children's allowances, the government amended the bill and changed its title to the Guaranteed Children's Allowances Act.[20] As a result children with no right to allowances in one of the social security schemes would be paid family allowances by the administration of the general social insurance system for employees. Since the new benefits were to be financed out of general taxation and not by social security contributions, it was argued that their levels should be set at the same levels as the children's allowances for the self-employed.[21] Furthermore the guaranteed allowances were to be awarded only after what by any comparative standards was a fairly stringent means test.

Under an act passed on 27 June 1969 some provision was also made for the remaining 3 per cent of the population not covered by the social insurance provisions for medical care.[22] In contrast to the guaranteed children's allowance regulation, this established a voluntary insurance system for 'persons not yet covered'; anyone in this category could become a member of the general social insurance scheme by paying voluntary contributions.

As for replacement incomes, the first significant development was an Act of 1 April 1969 introducing a guaranteed income for the elderly. This was a means-tested benefit administered by the general pension scheme for employees, and aimed essentially at old people who were not compulsorily insured or who had only limited pension rights. The basic payments were set initially at 30,000 BF per annum for couples and 20,000 BF for single persons. These were very low levels: for couples they represented little more than 20 per cent of the average gross wages of male industrial workers, and for single people only 13.5 per cent. However, for couples and single persons respectively, pensions of up to 6,000 BF and 4,000 BF per annum and other incomes up to 9,000 BF and 6,000 BF per annum were exempted from the means test.

When in parliament the bill was criticised, first because of the small amounts awarded, which were clearly less than was provided by most social assistance committees, and second because the guaranteed income was to be confined to the elderly. The Minister of Social Security, however, argued that financial constraints prohibited the extension of the benefit to the whole population and that the government did not consider the amounts as representing a subsistence minimum but a basic guaranteed payment which might be supplemented by social assistance committees.[23] In fact, he already knew at the time of the debate that a committee on social assistance of the *Vereniging van Belgische Steden en Gemeenten* (Association of Belgian Towns and Communes) had met to elaborate some kind of general assistance standard to act as a guideline for individual social assistance committees and that its proposed levels, which were to be followed by most of the larger communes, were set well above the new guaranteed minimum.[24]

Despite its limitations, the 1969 Act marked a turning point in Belgian social policy, since for the first time some sort of nationally guaranteed income was adopted. Moreover, once the initiative on this matter had been taken by parliament, there was to be persistent parliamentary pressure for improvements in the benefits and for the extension of the principle to other groups. As regards the level of the benefit, there have been some quite significant increases in the 1970s. As Table 3.1 in the next section shows, by 1976 the basic amount for a single person represented 22.4 per cent of average male industrial wages and for a couple 30.9 per cent. Since 1973 there has also been a special supplementary payment for severely disabled old people.[25]

Although there were several private members' bills[26] which attempted to introduce a guaranteed minimum for all citizens, it was not until 1974 that the government finally accepted the principle. The Act of 7 August 1974, which came into effect on 1 January 1975, established a 'right to a subsistence minimum' for every Belgian citizen: this was extended the following year to citizens of other European Community countries, displaced persons and political refugees.[27] This benefit was again made subject to a means test and its basic allowances were set at the same levels as the guaranteed income for the elderly. In spite of its title it was still assumed that some supplementation by social assistance would be needed to bring the benefits up to an acceptable minimum standard. Moreover, unlike the arrangements for the elderly which still continue to be run by the social insurance authorities, the local social assistance committees were made responsible for administering the new scheme under the general supervision of the Minister of Public Health, the Minister competent for social assistance. The scheme is also financed equally by central government and the local social assistance committees. In the parliamentary debates some amendments were moved to have the provisions financed entirely by central government, out of a surtax on the higher income brackets, but they were all rejected.

As far as other means-tested benefits are concerned, the Act of 27 June 1969 introduced new provisions for the disabled, in an attempt both to co-ordinate the fragmented and inadequate legislation covering those who were not receiving insurance benefits and to secure them at least a minimum income. A Royal Decree of 24 December 1974 brought these provisions into line with the other minimum benefits by providing the disabled with basic allowances set at the same levels as the 'right to a subsistence minimum', to which an important supplement was added that varied with the degree of disability. Finally, the Act of 8 July 1976 should be mentioned, which replaced the social assistance committees by 'public centres for social welfare' and established for the first time a legal right to social aid. Although this Act has created new possibilities for the co-ordination of social work[28] and for more co-operation between various local welfare services, it has not changed drastically the organisation of financial assistance. It is highly doubtful that this has yet been freed from the stigma of the old social assistance committees.

Thus a new set of social provisions has been established since 1969, involving for the first time the development of national policies towards the poor in general. Significantly, the 1970s have also seen some much more systematic research than previously into economic aspects of poverty; it has used poverty standards set above the relatively meagre official minimum levels and has hence focused attention on the needs of many households, including many families of low wage earners and the poorer self-employed, largely unaffected by the new policies on minimum benefits.

This was a feature of an important investigation of poverty in the early 1970s by a group of young social scientists calling themselves *Werkgroep alternatieve ekonomie* (Working Group on Alternative Economics).[29] The Group made estimates of the minimum budget requirements of different types of household and arrived at levels which were considerably higher than the national minimum standards. As Table 3.5 in the next section shows, they were also between 15 per cent and 20 per cent higher than the social assistance levels in Antwerp, one of the more generous local assistance authorities; though for single persons the Working Group's minimum was roughly 10 per cent less than the Antwerp minimum. On the basis of an analysis of social security statistics the Group calculated that just over 1,400,000 people, about 14.5 per cent of the Belgian population, were living in poverty.[30] Of these, 960,988 persons (68.6 per cent of the total) were living in families where the head of the household was at work. The next section will discuss more fully the poverty lines and findings of this study, and also those of a more recent investigation undertaken at the Centre for Social Policy of the University of Antwerp.

After preliminary research in Greater Antwerp,[31] it organised a national sample survey, in order, among other things, to construct inductively a set of social subsistence levels for different types of household.[32] The results of the survey suggested that in 1976 24 per cent of households had incomes below these social subsistence levels.

Other recent developments have contributed to a broadening of the debate about poverty. As we shall see in the third section, when examining the relationship between poverty and inequality, the past decade has seen a growing awareness of the interdependence of various forms of deprivation and their links with the wider issues of class and inequality. Although there are still many gaps in our knowledge of these issues, it has become increasingly clear that the post-war welfare state has done much less to reduce social inequalities than was earlier assumed to be the case. Hence poverty is no longer being seen as a problem relating to certain groups who were somehow forgotten in the burst of legislative activity after the War, but as a much more fundamental and formidable issue.

The measurement and extent of poverty

Poverty lines
Before looking more closely at the evidence of poverty in Belgium today, some further analysis is needed of the social assistance standards associated with central and local government policies, as well as the poverty lines used in the surveys by the Working Group on Alternative Economics and the Centre for Social Policy. With the introduction of the 'guaranteed income for the elderly' (GIE) and the 'right to a subsistence minimum' (RSM), central government has established what is, at least in principle, a guaranteed national minimum level of living. One might describe it as Belgium's official poverty line, though (as was pointed out earlier) it has been an assumption underlying central government policies that the poorest sections of the community would not rely solely on this national assistance but continue to receive some supplementary aid from local authorities. Clearly many people do receive this extra aid, but unfortunately no information is available on the extent of take-up; nor indeed on people who for one reason or another may not apply in the first place for the means-tested national benefits.

That the official national poverty line is still set at a very low level is apparent when comparisons are made with average wages. As Table 3.1 shows, in spite of considerable increases in the national assistance rates in recent years, in October 1976 the allowances for couples and single persons represented little more than 30 per cent and 22 per cent respectively of the average wages of male manual workers in industry. It should be added here that, unlike local social assistance, no provision is made under the national legislation for rent or heating allowances. Moreover, the figures in Table 3.1 refer to the payments made to people living in their own homes: under the RSM legislation those living together with persons other than dependent children receive half the payments made to couples.

TABLE 3.1 *Poverty lines in BF and as a proportion of average gross wages of male manual workers in industry (monthly)*

As for October	National guaranteed income GIE-RSM*				Antwerp standard, including rent and heating**				Average wage
	couples		single persons		couples		single persons		
	BF	%	BF	%	BF	%	BF	%	BF
1969	2,602	20.25	1,735	13.50	5,200	40.47	3,680	28.64	12,848
1970	2,974	20.87	1,983	13.92	5,200	36.49	3,680	25.82	14,248
1971	3,468	21.89	2,312	14.59	5,400	34.09	4,550	28.73	15,838
1972	3,789	22.12	2,526	14.74	6,030	35.19	5,300	30.93	17,132
1973	4,511	22.27	3,007	14.84	7,660	37.82	6,170	30.46	20,254
1974	5,368	21.93	4,155	16.97	8,440	34.48	6,800	27.78	24,477
1975	6,806	25.65	4,960	18.69	11,120	41.91	8,620	32.49	26,527
1976	9,075	30.90	6,569	22.37	12,380	42.16	9,620	32.76	29,363

* 'Guaranteed income for the elderly' (GIE) and 'right to a subsistence minimum' (RSM — from 1975 onwards).
** Social Assistance Committee, now Public Centre for Social Welfare, of Antwerp.

Source: Calculations based on 'Overzicht van het economisch en sociaal leven', *Statistisch Tijdschrift*, NIS, Brussels, monthly; *Statistisch Jaarboek van de Sociale Zekerheid*, Ministerie van Sociale Voorzorg, Brussels, annually; and information provided by the Public Centre for Social Welfare of Antwerp.

Table 3.1 also illustrates the development since 1969 of the social assistance standard that has been elaborated by the social assistance committee of the city of Antwerp, and which in consultation with the surrounding communes has been used in the entire conurbation. This standard is probably one of the more generous in Belgium: when rent and heating allowances are included the levels are approximately 10 per cent higher than those recommended by the Association of Belgian Towns and Communes, and it can be assumed that many authorities, though mainly the larger communes, stick more closely to these recommendations. Quite a lot of smaller committees, on the other hand, still continue to grant assistance without reference to any general yardstick and without making any regular adjustments to their rates in line with changes in prices or wages.

The Antwerp rates shown in Table 3.1 are made up of three elements which together represent 90 per cent of the minimum unemployment benefits. These are a basic allowance, which in October 1976 was 7,320 BF for single persons and 9,780 BF for couples, a housing allowance of 1,100 BF and 1,400 BF respectively, and a heating allowance, granted from September until April, of 1,200 BF for both single persons and couples. No account is taken in the table of extra housing allowances, dietary payments and study grants for schoolchildren which the Antwerp authorities may also provide. The decrease in the relative value of the Antwerp standard between 1970 and 1974 can be explained by the fact that there were no changes in housing and heating allowances in this period; though for single persons this was compensated by increases in the relative value of the basic allowances.

The comparisons in Table 3.1 clearly show that the poverty line set by the central government is considerably lower than that in Antwerp: in October 1976 the former represented for couples and single persons respectively only 73.3 per cent and 68.3 per cent of the latter. One implication of this is, of course, that central government was at that time contributing much less than 50 per cent to the financing of the 'right to a subsistence minimum' in Antwerp. It should be emphasised, however, that the figures in the table refer only to minimum payments.

TABLE 3.2 *Monthly disposable income in BF of recipients of national minimum benefits with income from other resources, October 1976*

	Guaranteed income for the elderly		Right to a subsistence minimum	
	couple	single person	couple	single person
Full amount of benefit	9,075	6,569	9,075	6,569
Maximum disregarded income:				
pensions	1,458	1,167		
other resources	1,042	833	1,042	833
Maximum disposable income:				
in BF	11,575	8,569	10,117	7,402
as a proportion of average wages (%)	39.42	29.18	34.45	25.21
as a proportion of Antwerp standard (%)	93.50	89.07	81.72	76.94

Exemption rules in the means tests and any adjustments of social assistance benefits to individual needs may result in higher disposable incomes. Moreover, as Table 3.2 shows, the effects of the exemption rules (i.e. disregarded income) are to bring the national assistance rates closer to the local rates, especially for pensioners.

Turning to the 'unofficial' poverty lines mentioned earlier, Table 3.3 shows the minimum budget for a standard family with two children

TABLE 3.3   *Minimum budget for a standard family with two children (10-14 years), Working Group on Alternative Economics, 1972*

	BF/month
Food	4,749
Beverages	750
Housing	2,940
Clothes	1,500
Other expenses	1,700
Total	11,639

Source: Werkgroep Alternatieve Ekonomie, *Armoede in België*, De Nederlandse Boekhandel, Antwerp, 1972, p. 14.

aged between 10 and 14 years that was calculated by the Working Group on Alternative Economics. This was used by the Group as a basis for estimating the minimum income requirements of other types of household: thus a single person's requirements were set at 5,000 BF a month, those of a couple without children at 8,200 BF, and those of a couple with one child at 10,000 BF. From the third child onwards the Working Group assumed that children's allowances would be sufficient to cover additional expenses. Table 3.4 shows the 'social subsistence levels' arrived at by the Centre for Social Policy for some types

TABLE 3.4   *Social subsistence levels, Centre for Social Policy, October 1976*

Type of household	BF/month
Retired single person	9,700
Active single person*	12,300
Retired couple	13,000
Couple (1 retired, 1 active)	16,500
Active couple without children	19,600
Active couple with 1 child	24,300
Active couple with 2 children	27,000

*'Active' refers to persons under normal pensionable age, which in Belgium is 60 years for women and 65 for men.

Source: Centrum voor Sociaal Beleid, *Bestaanszekerheid en Sociale Zekerheid*, CSB, Antwerp, mimeographed, 1977, p. 15.

of household. These are essentially subjective estimates, based on the incomes of households who in the Centre's survey declared that they could 'just scrape along' on their actual incomes.

Finally, in Table 3.5 an attempt is made to compare the official and unofficial poverty lines discussed here for six different types of household. To make the levels comparable with those of the Working Group on Alternative Economics it is assumed that children are aged between 10 and 14 years: hence study allowances have been added to the Antwerp rates, and the guaranteed children's allowances with age supplements to the national RSM benefits. The Working Group's calculations have also been adjusted for changes in average wages. As the table shows, there are some quite considerable differences between all

TABLE 3.5   *Poverty lines for some types of household as a proportion of the national guaranteed income standard, October 1976*

	Centre Soc. Pol.	Altern. Econ.	Antwerp standard	National standard
	%	%	%	BF
1 Retired single person	147	130	146	6,569
2 Active single person	187			
3 Retired couple	143	154	135	9,075
4 Active couple without children	215			
5 Active couple with 1 child	257	181	150	9,454
6 Active couple with 2 children	226	167	140	11,946

four poverty lines, but especially between the Centre for Social Policy's measures for active persons, those under normal retirement age, and the other poverty standards. In the Centre's research the subjective assessment of a 'social subsistence level' by an active couple without children amounted to exactly two-thirds of the average wages of male manual workers in industry or well over double the official national poverty level for a couple.

The poor
We can now attempt to find out what proportion of the population falls below these poverty lines, and the incidence of poverty amongst different social groups. Obviously, all estimates have to be treated with some caution, because of biases and deficiencies in the various sources of data. This is particularly true of the estimates of the working poor, since there are many difficulties in interpreting the information available on earnings and other sources of income. The social security schemes for employed persons and the self-employed persons collect data on the incomes of individual contributors, but they provide no

information on the composition of a contributor's family or the existence of other sources of income. Tax statistics, on the other hand, do provide such data, but give an inaccurate picture of the situation of those with low incomes. The position as regards social security beneficiaries, especially pensioners, also presents problems. Although quite detailed information is available on individual pension rights, relatively little is known about possible combinations of social insurance pension rights with civil service pensions or the number of pension recipients in the same household. The position of very poor pensioners is also difficult to assess because of inadequate data on the combination of GIE payments with local social assistance or on the disregarded income of those with means-tested benefits.

What are probably the most reliable estimates of the numbers of the working poor and their families are to be found in the studies of the Working Group on Alternative Economics and the Centre for Social Policy. The Working Group's calculations are given in Table 3.6, where it will be seen that almost a million persons were estimated to be living in families where the head of the family was working and the family income fell below the Group's poverty line. This represented approximately 11 per cent of employed and self-employed persons and their dependants: it also accounted for just over two-thirds of the poor in the Working Group's study. The survey by the Centre for Social Policy

TABLE 3.6 *Estimated number of persons living in families where the head of the family is at work and with incomes below the Working Group's poverty line, 1969*

		Number of persons
Single wage earners		40,587
Married wage earners	without children	66,972
	with 1 child	250,959
	with 2 children or more	378,944
Self-employed		223,526
Total		960,988

Source: Werkgroep Alternatieve Ekonomie, op. cit., pp. 15 ff.

suggests an even higher proportion, though this would seem to be due mainly to the different definitions of poverty. According to the Centre's calculations, 14 per cent of families where the head of the family was working had incomes below the Centre's 'social subsistence levels'. These poverty ratios would, of course, be much lower if one used an official poverty line like the Antwerp standard, but unfortunately no estimates are available based on this kind of yardstick. However, if the Working Group's calculations are correct, it would seem that in the early 1970s about 10 per cent of the labour force and their families had incomes below approximately 120 per cent of the Antwerp standard. This is a surprisingly high figure, especially when one remembers the assumptions made by the researchers about the effects of children's allowances: from the third child onwards the allowances were assumed to cover the children's subsistence requirements.

Who, then, are the working poor? The studies of the Working Group and the Centre for Social Policy found a somewhat higher incidence of poverty amongst the self-employed than amongst employed persons, though in both studies low wage earners made up the largest single group in poverty. In the Working Group's survey, for example, low wage earners, mainly unskilled manual workers, and their families accounted for 52.7 per cent of all persons in poverty, the self-employed and their families 16.0 per cent, the retired 25.4 per cent, and other non-active persons and their families 6.0 per cent. As for the self-employed, the Centre for Social Policy found that the risk of poverty was greatest amongst farmers and their families, 46 per cent of whom had earned incomes below the Centre's social subsistence levels.[33] But the self-employed poor also included many small retail traders and artisans, who in Belgium as elsewhere have suffered from the growth of supermarkets and increasing concentration in industry and commerce.

As with other European Community countries, the future trends in relation to the working poor are somewhat difficult to assess. It seems clear that economic pressures will lead to a further decline in the numbers of self-employed persons, particularly the poorer groups. There is likely to be growing pressure to raise the minimum wage, which was finally introduced after several years' discussion in 1975. In October 1976 the minimum gross wage, from which social security contributions and other taxes have to be paid, was 18,524 BF or 63 per cent of the average gross wages of male manual workers in industry. At the same time, however, the recent rise in unemployment has clearly increased the risks of poverty amongst many of these families, especially by reducing the possibilities for women or young people to work and hence add to the family income.

What, then, is the situation of families where the head of the household is unemployed? In the Working Group's study persons in these families accounted for only 2.9 per cent of the total number of persons in poverty, though this of course was before the economic recession. Moreover, the Working Group based its calculations on the estimated numbers of 'structurally unemployed', the overlapping categories of unemployed persons with a partial or total incapacity to work, of persons in protracted unemployment and of the older unemployed (aged 45 and over). Whereas the Group supposed that in general a short period of unemployment would not lead to a situation of poverty, it was assumed that the majority of the around 40,000 structurally unemployed were living in poverty.[34]

Since the Working Group's study unemployment rates have increased substantially, though so too have unemployment benefits. These were previously flat-rate benefits, but since 1 November 1971 they have been calculated as a percentage of previous wages. During the first year all unemployed persons get 60 per cent; afterwards persons who are not the head of a family get only 40 per cent of previous wages.[35] Furthermore, benefits may not fall below the minimum rates indicated in Table 3.7.

TABLE 3.7   *Minimum rates of unemployment benefit, October 1976*

Category	Monthly minimum rate (BF)
1 Heads of a family	12,800
2 Other employees of full age	9,850
3 Employees aged 18-20	6,900
4 Employees under the age of 18	4,350

Source: Calculated from Ministerie van Sociale Voorzorg, *Statistisch Jaarboek van de Sociale Zekerheid 1975*, Brussels, 1977.

Although their level is higher than the GIE-RSM standards, the minimum unemployment rates remain low when compared with other poverty lines.

It seems clear that a considerable proportion of the structurally unemployed would be receiving benefits at the minimum rates. Precisely how many families are involved is difficult to assess, because the statistics cover a number of overlapping categories. The annual statistics show,[36] for example, that at the end of June 1976 persons with a partial or total incapacity to work receiving unemployment benefit numbered 34,950 and 21,802 respectively. At the same time 46,743 recipients had been unemployed for more than two years and 65,556 unemployed persons were aged 45 and over. There were also 20,625 males, aged 45 and over, and with a partial or total incapacity to work, who were in a situation of protracted unemployment. From all this it looks as if about 45,000 families of unemployed persons have been receiving the minimum rates of benefit for a fairly long period.

Despite the problems of interpretation mentioned above, official statistics provide some interesting insights into recent trends relating to the elderly poor, especially the very poorest old people, who receive the 'guaranteed income for the elderly'. As Table 3.8 shows, the numbers receiving this benefit have declined during the 1970s, from 86,172 in 1971 to 68,784 in 1976. This decrease, which has of course occurred when the value of the guaranteed income has increased quite significantly in relation to average wages, seems to be due mainly to changes in the social security pension formulae and to recent legislation which has greatly liberalised the conditions of eligibility in the social

TABLE 3.8   Recipients of the guaranteed income for the elderly, 31 December

Category − rate	1971	1972	1973	1974	1975	1976
Married men − couple	10,163	8,832	7,567	6,568	5,883	5,473
Married men − single person	1,285	1,191	1,025	936	819	812
Unmarried men − single person	12,305	11,176	10,304	9,544	9,136	8,980
Married women − single person	2,732	2,669	2,470	2,275	2,118	2,154
Unmarried women − single person	47,440	46,132	44,587	42,821	42,382	42,286
Widows, entitled to old-age or survivors' pension, receiving GIE supplement	12,247	11,177	10,318	9,731	9,247	9,079
All recipients	86,172	81,177	76,271	71,875	69,585	68,784

Source: RROP, Jaarlijkse statistiek van de pensioengerechtigden 1977, Brussels, p. 13.

insurance schemes. Table 3.8 also indicates that the national minimum benefit is received predominantly by women, and especially unmarried women, who in 1976 accounted for 61 per cent of all the beneficiaries. This category would include, for example, single women who have taken care of sick relatives and for that reason have never been compulsorily covered by one of the social insurance schemes or have developed only partial pension rights. As one would expect, a significant number of GIE recipients are ex-self-employed persons or persons with 'mixed pensions', those who moved at some stage in their careers from one pension scheme to another.[37]

Perhaps the most revealing recent figures on poverty amongst the elderly are those provided in the Centre for Social Policy survey. As Table 3.5 has shown, the Centre's social subsistence levels for a retired single person were virtually the same as the Antwerp standard and for a retired couple were just over 5 per cent higher than this official local poverty line. The Centre's calculations suggested that in 1976 no less than 38 per cent of single pensioners and 36 per cent of retired couples had incomes below these levels.[38] This would clearly include many old people with pension rights under the social insurance schemes for employed persons as well as the schemes for the self-employed.

As far as the disabled are concerned, one is confronted with a highly fragmented system of social insurance and means-tested schemes, and hence much overlapping statistical information. However, a rough estimate of the numbers in poverty can be made using a Ministry of Labour survey of disabled persons and the calculations of the Centre for Social Policy. The Ministry survey, carried out in 1968, estimated the number of disabled persons under pensionable age at 668,200, or 513,000 when children were excluded.[39] The Centre for Social Policy found that 11.6 per cent of persons with some form of disability benefit were living in families whose income was lower than 75 per cent of the Centre's social subsistence levels: taking all family types together this 75 per cent level would be broadly comparable with the Antwerp standard (or perhaps, slightly lower). When applied to the Ministry's estimate, some 55,000 families would be in such a situation.

The absence of any specific policy towards single parents illustrates the fact that social security policies in Belgium have tended to emphasise and reinforce values relating to the 'normal' family. Whereas widows under the age of 45 and looking after children can claim a right to a survivors' pension, no special measures exist for other single parents with dependent children. The latter have to establish a right to social security children's allowances by either being employed or registered as unemployed or disabled persons.[40] If this is not possible they can have recourse to the means-tested guaranteed children's allowance scheme. No overall picture of the situation of single parents is available, since if they are social security beneficiaries they tend to be classified under the categories of 'employed', 'unemployed', 'disabled', 'pensioners', etc. In addition the social assistance authorities provide no special information on them, though this is part of a more general problem. As we have already implied, very little information of any sort is available on the activities of the local assistance authorities. Even the data on the 'right to a subsistence minimum' is of very limited value, at least as regards an assessment of poverty.[41]

Because of the many qualifications that have had to be made, it becomes extremely hazardous to give an overall estimate of the number of families living in poverty. Obviously, too, estimates depend on which poverty line is chosen. In summary, though, it seems likely that the number of households in poverty in Belgium today ranges from about 160,000 (about 5 per cent of households) to 780,000 (24 per cent), the former being the numbers that may be assumed to live at or below the official national poverty line, the latter representing those households with monthly incomes below the Centre for Social Policy's social subsistence levels.

Poverty, income inequality and other aspects of deprivation

In this final section we attempt to widen the discussion somewhat by looking at certain aspects of the distribution of income and wealth in Belgium, and at other forms of deprivation. These broader perspectives are, of course, crucial to an understanding of modern forms of poverty. However, once again there are problems in obtaining reliable and meaningful information on a number of important issues, partly due to the gaps and deficiencies in the official sources of data, but also because research into the inter-relationship between various forms of deprivation and disadvantage is still very much in its infancy.

Distribution and redistribution

The difficulties presented by the official statistics are clearly evident when one attempts to relate the findings of the 'poverty line' studies to the information available on the distribution of income and wealth, which is based on tax returns. The tax statistics pose a number of problems. First, the statistical unit is what is called the 'fiscal family': this may be a single person, including a non-dependent child living with his parents, or a married couple with or without dependent children. Hence several fiscal families may live together in one 'household', but information on such situations cannot be traced. Second, only families

TABLE 3.9   *Evolution of the share of wages in national income, 1948-75 (1953 = 100)*

year	Share of wages in national income* manual + non-manual workers together	manual workers	non-manual workers
1948	99.5	102.7	94.4
1953	100.0	100.0	100.0
1963	99.7	99.0	93.8
1970	100.0	100.5	79.6
1971	102.6	104.2	80.1
1972	103.1	103.8	80.7
1973	103.7	103.9	81.3
1974	107.0	107.4	83.6
1975	115.7	113.7	91.0

* After correction for changes in the active population.

Sources: Deleeck, H., 'Het aandeel van lonen en wedden in het nationaal inkomen, een aanvulling tot 1975', *De Gids op Maatschappelijk Gebied*, 1977, 2, pp. 168–72.

who fill in tax returns figure in the tax statistics; which means that no
account is taken of most of the families with incomes below the tax
thresholds. Third, as a result of tax evasion, tax avoidance and
exemption rules, taxable incomes can clearly differ quite significantly
from real incomes.

Another problem with this data is that the most detailed analyses
of it relate to the situation in the 1950s and 1960s, whereas it seems
likely that the 1970s have seen some important changes in distributional
patterns. As well as the social legislation of the 1970s there has also
recently been an unprecedented rise in the share of wages and salaries
in national income. As Table 3.9 shows, this wages and salaries quota
remained more or less constant between 1948 and 1970;[42] by contrast,
there was a 15.7 per cent rise in the combined share of wages and
salaries between 1970 and 1975, which seems to compensate for increases in inflation and unemployment figures.

TABLE 3.10   *The distribution of taxable income*

Income groups	Share in gross taxable income 1970*	Share in net taxable income 1968** Before taxes	After taxes
Bottom 10%	2.8	1.8	2.2
Bottom 10-20%	4.4	3.9	4.4
Bottom 20-50%	19.1	18.5	20.2
Top 20-50%	29.7	29.0	30.4
Top 10-20%	14.6	14.2	14.3
Top 10%	29.4	32.6	28.6

Sources: * 'De personele inkomensverdeling in België'. *Statistisch Tijdschrift,*
NIS, 1977, 5-6, p. 331.
** Boelaert, R., 'Herverdelende werking der inkomstenbelasting', *De overheid
in de gemengde economie — Referaten 11e VWEC,* Univ. pers Leuven, Louvain,
1973, p. 322-43.

As to the situation before 1970, it is perhaps appropriate here just
to summarise some of the main conclusions to be drawn from the
available data.[43] The general impression one gains from figures such as
those in Table 3.10 is of a markedly unequal distribution of income,
with direct taxation having surprisingly little redistributive effect. When
measures like the Gini coefficient are applied, there seems to have been
a slight increase in overall income inequality during the 1960s,[44]
mainly because of an improvement in the already excellent position of
managers and certain of the so-called 'liberal professions', especially
lawyers and doctors. In 1970 the average gross taxable income of
physicians and dentists was 582,852 BF, of lawyers 461,788 BF and of
managers or partners 417,255 BF; the corresponding figure for all

employees was 188,105 BF and that for non-active persons 132,714 BF.[45] As one would expect, differences like this partly resulted from inequalities in the distribution of wealth.[46] As one indication of this, Table 3.11 shows the distribution in 1970 of net taxable income from bank deposits, shares, dividends, etc. Only 7.1 per cent of 'fiscal families' had some taxable income from these sources, and 0.9 per cent had no less than 54.2 per cent of the total taxable income.

TABLE 3.11   *Distribution of income from bank deposits, shares, etc., 1970*

Income group (in 1,000 BF)	Proportion of fiscal families %	Fiscal families with taxable net income from bank deposits. . . as a proportion of		Proportion of taxable net income from bank deposits
		total fiscal families %	fiscal families from same income group	
0–<100	41.3	2.0	5.2	11.0
100–<500	56.3	4.1	7.3	34.8
500–<1000	1.8	0.6	34.2	15.1
⩾1000	0.6	0.3	55.0	39.1
	100.0	7.1		100.0

Source: Calculated from 'De belastingsaangiften van de natuurlijke personen voor het aanslagjaar 1970', *Statistisch Tijdschrift*, NIS, 1974, 2, pp. 135ff.

The relatively small redistributive effect of direct taxation seems to have been due both to the nature of the tax system and the incidence of tax evasion, the amount of which has been estimated at about 25 per cent and of which the higher income groups are proportionately more guilty.[47] As for the combined effect of indirect taxes and subsidies, a study by Verhé concludes that, with some qualifications, it may be assumed that their aggregate burden increases in line with rises in consumption.[48] However, whereas for manual workers this burden varies in proportion to the income level, for non-active persons it is regressive, and for non-manual workers only lightly progressive. Finally, some research has been done on the redistributive effects of the social security system. As far as redistribution in relation to wage earners is concerned it seems highly doubtful whether any significant vertical income redistribution has taken place, because of the emphasis on contributions, the existence of contribution ceilings, and the relatively more intensive use made of social security provisions by the higher-paid wage earners and their families. Hence only a horizontal redistributive effect remains, and this is related more to the insurance character of the social security system than to any purposes of national income redistribution.[49]

Other forms of deprivation
Here we may take first of all the question of housing. A number of studies have confirmed the close relationship between poverty of income and overcrowding and insanitary housing conditions.[50] Perhaps the most significant finding of the studies concerns Belgium's social housing policies, in which subsidies have been given to private builders and to housing associations which in principle, at least, build houses that low-income families might buy or rent at low cost. In practice, it seems that middle-income families have profited much more from these subsidies and that they are, for example, proportionately over-represented among families renting from the National Institute for Social Housing.[51] This state of affairs seems to be due mainly to the decreasing real value of the subsidies, to rent levels, and more generally to the fact that social housing policies seem to have been more influenced by economic than social objectives, let alone poverty policies.

No comprehensive information is available on the distribution of health or the use of health services. However, Table 3.12 illustrates the fact that medical consumption and the cost that it involves varies

TABLE 3.12   *Average cost of medical care for manual and non-manual workers – Belgian General Social Security Scheme, 1971 (in BF)*

	Manual	Non-manual
Consultation of:		
general practitioner	356.1	289.1
specialist doctor	175.5	255.0
dentist	127.6	217.1
Medicaments:	670.7	795.3

with income level: low-income categories are more inclined to call on 'cheap' medical care with a general practitioner, whereas higher-income categories are more open to preventive care and prefer to be treated by a specialist doctor.[52] Yet, as regards the need for medical care, it is generally accepted that the findings of the French CREDOC studies apply to Belgium.[53] Overall the distribution of medical care seems to be influenced by a double inequality: on the one hand low-income categories are in greater need of medical treatment, but on the other hand they find more difficulty in ensuring for themselves adequate medical care.[54]

The predominant importance for social inequality and deprivation of education and educational opportunities has been stressed in many studies. In Belgium growing attention has been given to this aspect from the 1960s onwards, as a result of the movement towards democratisation of university education. From research at the University of Louvain[55] it became clear that the proportion of students from lower-status groups being matriculated in the university was very limited. Table 3.13 illustrates that, despite the emphasis that has been put on the democratisation of university education, children of manual workers remain heavily under-represented. Furthermore, it was found that students from higher-status families prefer studies that lead to the high-status liberal professions, whereas students from low-status groups rather study sciences or applied sciences leading to careers in paid employment.[56]

TABLE 3.13   *Indexes of participation of male and female students in university education by professional category of their father (University of Louvain, KUL, academic year 1975–76)*

	Male	Female
Liberal and academic professions	383	465
Entrepreneurs	138	145
School teachers	663	682
Managers	94	112
White-collar workers	171	184
Blue-collar workers	35	23
Artisans, craftsmen	183	138
Small self-employed in trade and commerce	83	85
Farmers	86	80
All occupations	100	100

Source: De Lando, I., 'De sociale herkomst van de Leuvense studenten', *Politica*, 1977, 3, p. 220.

Subsequent research showed that unequal access to university education depends very much on the kind of secondary education, which in turn correlates with social status as indicated in terms of professional category of the father (Table 3.14). Thus the evidence for Belgium demonstrates the applicability of theories on the influence of social stratification on the unequal distribution of educational opportunities and success.[57] Though the average educational level has increased in the long run,[58] neither policies towards democratisation of university education nor a reorganisation of secondary education have been sufficiently adequate in effectively counteracting existing inequalities.[59]

As far as employment conditions are concerned there are several points of relevance to this discussion. A first point concerns the

TABLE 3.14 *Distribution of first-year pupils by kind of secondary education and by professional category of their father (City of Mechlin, 1973-74 in %)*

| Professional category of father | Kind of secondary education | | Technical Schools | |
| | Grammar Schools | | | |
	classic humanities	modern humanities		
I low	4.0	29.5	66.5	100
II	8.9	35.9	55.2	100
III	23.2	42.4	34.4	100
IV	42.0	43.0	15.0	100
V high	56.0	32.0	11.0	100
	18.7	37.4	43.9	100 (n = 1,811)

Source: Billiet, J., *Secularisering en verzuiling in het Belgisch onderwijs*, KUL, Louvain, 1975.

distinction between manual and non-manual workers. The importance of this distinction in Belgian social legislation, that is in both social security and labour legislation, is illustrated by the fact that in the latter two different labour contracts exist,[60] of which the contract for non-manual workers ensures a better security of employment by means of longer terms of notice. Though it gradually is being abolished, this distinction was and to some extent still is reflected in social security legislation by some differences in contribution rates and wage ceilings.

A second point relates to the division of the economy and to the organisation of labour relations by sectors of industry. In addition to economic factors the intensity of trade union membership helps to explain differences in security of employment and in wage levels.[61] Though the general membership level averages some 70 per cent on the national level, important differences exist among industries. In general it may be said that the most stable industries, where trade unionism is firmly rooted, not only provide a greater security of employment and higher wages, but have also managed to elaborate some additional private social security schemes. And though the importance of the latter remains relatively small in Belgium, they nevertheless tend to increase existing inequalities among industries.[62]

Finally, as far as differences between men and women are concerned, E. Lambrechts has shown how women have been treated as a secondary labour force. This can be illustrated by the evolution of the relative position of wage levels for women, which on the whole seems to have worsened in periods of economic recession whereas it improved in periods of recovery,[63] and by unemployment figures which have been proportionately high for women.[64]

Inter-relationships

By way of conclusion it may be interesting to return to the research of the Centre for Social Policy and to quote some of its findings on the factors determining security of subsistence in Belgium.[65] This will allow us to link the elements of the broader poverty definition with the narrower poverty line approach and to discuss the adequacy of the existing social policy measures.

It should be remembered that in the Centre's study security – and insecurity – of subsistence was originally defined as the degree by which a household's income is respectively larger and smaller than the social subsistence line. Subsequently, on this and on other variables that were thought to be indicative for security of subsistence, a factor analysis was worked out. The factor score of the first factor which the factor analysis provided was eventually used as the dependent variable.[66] For the variables by which the latter is determined a multi-variate analysis was worked out, the findings of which are summarised in Figure 1.

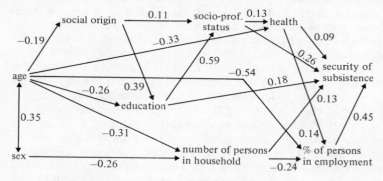

Figure 1. Determinants of security of subsistence

Note: Based on Path analysis with recursive modelling. The figures are β coefficients. For further explanation see text.

The influences of the variables age and sex of the head of the household on security of subsistence are indirect ones. In other words, age and sex exert an influence only through other variables such as health, the proportion of members of the household that are in employment, and the number of persons that constitute the household. The latter's direct positive influence is counterbalanced by its indirect negative influence through the degree of employment variable. Social origin, which is an index variable, has no direct influence, but it conditions the educational level of the head of the household, and this in turn exerts an important influence on his socio-professional status and on security of subsistence and thus highlights what has been said on the importance of education. The socio-professional status of the household exercises a direct influence which affirms the inequalities in income distribution and in the access to the welfare state that have been indicated previously. It also has an indirect influence through health which, in addition to a direct impact on the dependent variable, affects the proportion of household members in employment. The latter finally exerts the strongest direct influence on security of subsistence.

The most important general conclusions to which these findings have led when coupled with other analyses on the adequacy of the actual welfare system can be summarised as follows. The occurrence of either a social 'accident' or a low rating on a determining variable is only relevant to the extent that it conditions the ability to earn. In this the head of the household's employment, being the prime source of primary income, is the central point. If he is affected in this ability the situation can be adjusted in basically two ways: either by replacement incomes or by the existence of other income earners as may be the case in families with employed children. If the latter happens to be impossible the probability of insecurity is sharply increased, as is seen with families that are heavily dependent on replacement income sources.

As the social subsistence level is relatively high, it might have been assumed that the majority of households with replacement incomes would have been found with incomes below this level. Yet, because of the level of their replacement income, 48 per cent of such households managed to increase their income to above the social subsistence level. Only 11 per cent of them rate at least 25 per cent below this level. Hence it may be concluded that in general replacement incomes are adequate. However, to this statement many exceptions have to be made. They mainly have been found with pensioners, with recipients of disability benefits and with broken families, 80 per cent of the latter being young widows and divorcees with dependent children. Since the probability of social 'accidents' is spread unequally over social categories and the probability of insecurity is considerably increased when social 'accidents' coincide, intensifying one another, it appears that the welfare system, still conditioned as it is by insurance principles and providing for the 'normal', 'good' and isolated risks, fails in caring for more complicated situations. Instead of fundamentally correcting, it rather confirms social stratification.

References

1 J.-J. Dupeyroux, *Evolution et tendances des systèmes de sécurité sociale des pays membres des communantes européennes et de la Grand-Bretagne*, Luxembourg, ECSC, 1966, pp. 90–4.

2 J.-J. Dupeyroux, *Sécurité Sociale*, Paris, Dalloz, 1971, pp. 112ff.

3 Deleeck, H., 'Insécurité d'existence et le système de sécurité sociale en Belgique – 1974 – une enquête exploratoire', *Revue belge de Sécurité Sociale*, 1977, 1, p. 18.

4 C. de Clercq and W. Beirnaert, 'Een Belgisch stelsel van recht op bijstand', *Het Recht op Bijstand*, Cepess-documenten, 1968, 6, p. 144. E.g. for single men full-rate (old age) pensions are awarded only after 45 years of contribution and constitute 60 per cent of lifetime earnings; sickness benefits amount to 60 per cent of previous earnings.

5 H. Deleeck, 'Het Sociale Zekerheidsbeleid in België van 1945 tot 1975', *Ongelijkheden in de welvaartsstaat*, De Nederlandse Boekhandel, Antwerp, 1977; and G. Spitaels, *Réflexions sur la politique de sécurité sociale*, Bruxelles, Editions de l'université de Bruxelles, 1973.

6 The so-called 'mutualiteiten' (mutual aid societies).

7 H. Deleeck, 'Het mattheuseffect: over scheeftrekkingen in de verdeling van de collectieve voorzieningen', *De Gids op Maatschappelijk Gebied*, 1975, 11, pp. 717 and 730ff.

8 J. van Houtte, and J. Breda, *Behoeftige bejaarden en onderhoudsplichtige kinderen*, Van Loghum Slaterus, Deventer, 1976, pp. 53–55.

9 G. Muls, 'De betekenis van de openbare onderstand in België, *Het Recht op Bijstand*, Cepess-documenten, 1968, 6, p. 84.

10 M. Durieux, 'La notion d'état de besoin en droit belge', *Revue belge de Sécurité Sociale*, 1969, 2, pp. 209–23.

11 V. Teerlynck, 'De staat van behoefte in de Belgische sociale wetgeving', *Het Recht op Bijstand*, Cepess-documenten, 1968, 6, pp. 77–8.

12 T. Wilson (ed.), *Pensions, Inflation and Growth*, Heinemann, London, 1974, ch. 7.

13 H. Deleeck, 'Où va la sécurité sociale'. *Revue belge de Sécurité Sociale*, 1971, 1, p. 15.

14 'Nationale Aktie voor Bestaanszekerheid', *Manifest der meest onterfden*, Brussels, 1967.

15 CRISP, 'Le problème des déshérités en Belgique', *Courrier hebdomadaire*, Brussels, 1967, no. 379.

16 J. Mertens, 'Les ressources des personnes agées en Belgique', *Revue belge de Sécurité Sociale*, 1971, 8, pp. 749–99.

17 For a review see P. van Heddegem, 'Les besoins en matière de sécurité sociale: un inventaire provisoire', *Revue belge de Sécurité Sociale*, 1974, 9.

18 P. Schoetter, 'Sécurité sociale et assistance publique', *Revue belge de sécurité sociale*, 1966, 5, pp. 481–540.
19 M. Graffar, et al., 'Etude de la consommation de soixante familles assistées par le bureau de secours de la CAP de Bruxelles', *Revue de l'institut de Sociologie*, 1967, 1, pp. 115–72.
20 Act of 20 July 1971.
21 In contrast with the children's allowances for wage earners it meant that in October 1976 the basic guaranteed children's allowance for the first child was set at 379 BF, and that the first child was not entitled to age supplements. Other allowances, age supplements and maternity benefits were the same as in the wage earners' system (see Table).

TABLE *Family allowances in the social security system for wage earners (October 1976) in BF, and as a proportion of average gross wages of male manual workers in industry*

Children allowances (monthly)	in BF	%
Basic amount		
1st child	1,300	4.43
2nd child	2,063	7.03
3rd child	2,825	9.62
4th child	2,881	9.81
5th & following	2,902	9.88
Age supplement		
age 6–10 years	243	0.83
10–14 years	429	1.46
+14 years	694	2.36
Maternity benefits		
1st child	16,602	56.54
2nd child	11,451	39.00
3rd & following	6,160	20.98

Source: Ministerie van Sociale Voorzorg, *Statistisch Jaarboek van de Sociale Zekerheid 1975*, Brussels, 1977; and 'Overzicht van het economisch en sociaal leven', *Statistisch Tijdschrift*, NIS, Brussels, monthly.

22 W. Beirnaert, 'Werkingssfeer van de sociale zekerheid – evolutie en tendensen', *Het Recht op Bijstand*, Cepess-documenten, 1968, 6, p. 17.
23 P. Senaeve, *De bestrijding van de armoede in België*, Acco, Louvain, 1977, pp. 218–25.
24 Verslag van de Commissie 'Bijstand aan behoeftigen', *De Gemeente*, Vereniging van Belgische Steden en Gemeenten, Brussels, 1969, 2, pp. 82ff.; and 'Het verlenen van steun door de Commissies van Openbare Onderstand', *De Gemeente*, Vereniging van Belgische Steden en Gemeenten, Brussel, 1974, 11, pp. 619–20.

88   Jos Berghman

25 Royal Decree of 10 July 1973.
26 In 1968, 1969, 1971 and 1974.
27 J. de Busscher, 'L'institution du droit à un minimum de moyens d'existence', *Revue belge de Sécurité Sociale*, 1974, 10, pp. 1058ff.
28 Under the Royal Decree of 13 June 1974 social work agencies can be approved and subsidised by central government.
29 Werkgroep Alternatieve Ekonomie, *Armoede in België*, De Nederlandse Boekhandel, Antwerp, 1972.
30 Ibid., pp. 13–15.
31 H. Deleeck, 'Insécurité d'existence et le système de sécurité sociale en Belgique...', op. cit., pp. 1–22.
32 Centrum voor Sociaal Beleid, *Bestaanszekerheid en Sociale Zekerheid*, CSB, Antwerp, mimeographed, 1977. I would like to thank Mr J. Bouckaert, Director at the Ministry of Scientific Policy, for allowing me to quote from our recent research on 'Bestaanszekerheid en Sociale Zekerheid' (security of subsistence and social security), that being a part of the 'National Research Project for the Social Sciences', which has been financed by a grant from his ministry and is to be published in 1978.
33 Ibid., p. 25.
34 Werkgroep Alternatieve Ekonomie, op. cit., pp. 22–5.
35 Only wages under the corresponding social security contribution ceiling are taken into account. In October 1976 this ceiling figured at 27,950 BF. Hence the amount of the maximum unemployment benefit at the 60 and 40 per cent rates figured at 16,770 BF and 11,180 BF respectively.
36 Rijksdienst voor Arbeidsvoorziening, *Jaarlijkse telling van de op 30-6-1976 ingeschreven uitkeringsgerechtigde volledig werklozen*, Brussels, September 1976. In June 1976 active population was 4,031,480.
37 RROP., *Jaarlijkse statistiek van de pensioengerechtigden*, 1977, Brussels. Among wage earners' pension-, self-employed persons' pension- and mixed pension recipients respectively 2.32 per cent, 4.12 per cent and 6.45 per cent of pensioners were receiving a GIE supplement in 1976.
38 Centrum voor Sociaal Beleid, op. cit., p. 15.
39 Ministerie van Tewerkstelling en Arbeid, *Raming van het aantal mindervaliden in België*, Rijksfonds voor sociale reclassering van de mindervaliden, Brussels, 1968.
40 There has always been a possibility that they might obtain benefits by living in the household of an 'insured' relative.
41 The table has been based on the scarce information that is kept at the Ministry of Public Health. It shows that about 70 per cent of recipients receive full-rate benefits. The remaining 30 per cent proved to have other resources which resulted in partial benefit rates. It appears that only 10 per cent of recipients are couples, a majoirty of which can claim the full rate. 90 per cent of recipients are single persons, one fourth of which are living together with other persons than dependent children.

Number of RSM recipients by rate of benefit and by category
as a proportion of total number of RSM recipients

Rate	Category	Jan. 76	Dec. 76	July 77
		%	%	%
Full rate	I married couples	8.60	8.19	7.38
	II single persons	43.08	43.60	41.96
	III living together	15.35	19.05	19.52
Partial rate	I married couples	2.43	2.26	2.67
	II single persons	22.41	20.78	23.04
	III living together	8.07	5.96	5.35
	No information	0.06	0.16	0.08
	All RSM recipients	100	100	100
	n	8,520	11,501	14,722

Source: Ministry of Public Health

42 That is of gross wages: H. Deleeck, *Inkomensverdeling, sociale zekerheid en sociaal beleid,* De Nederlandse Boekhandel, Antwerp, 1972, pp. 91–116.
43 For a review of the Belgian literature on income distribution see H. Deleeck, *Ongelijkheden in de Welvaartsstaat,* De Nederlandse Boekhandel, Antwerp, 1977.
44 Distribution of taxable income before and after taxation: Gini-coefficients:

year	before	after
1964	0.3752	0.3312
1966	0.4000	0.3548
1968	0.3897	0.3427
1970	0.3997	0.3503

Source: K. Lotry, *De invloed van de belastinghervorming op de meting van de inkomensverdeling,* UFSIA, Antwerp, 1976.

45 'De personele inkomensverdeling in België, *Statistisch Tijdschrift,* NIS, 1977, 5–6, p. 326.
46 P. Duvivier, 'La répartition de la fortune mobilière en Belgique', *Courrier Hebdomadaire,* CRISP, 1972, no. 561.
47 M. Frank, 'La sous-estimation et la fraude fiscales en Belgique: ampleur et remèdes', *Cahiers économiques de Bruxelles,* 1972, no. 53, pp. 5–26; M. Frank, 'Belastingontduiking en fiscale onderschatting', *De Gids op Maatschappelijk Gebied,* 1956, 2, pp. 115–32; and M. Frank and D. Dekeyser-Meulders, 'La fraude fiscale réduit l'efficacité de l'impôt en tant qu'un instrument de redistribution des revenus', *Cahiers économiques de Bruxelles,* 1976, no. 71, p. 305–15.

48 W. Verhé, 'Herverdelende werking van de indirecte belastingen en de subsidies', *De Overheid in de gemengde economie – Referaten 11e VWEC*, Univ. pers Leuven, Louvain, 1973, pp. 344–59.
49 H. Deleeck, *Maatschappelijke zekerheid en Inkomensverdeling in België*, SWU, Antwerp, 1966; and Deleeck, *Ongelijkheden in de Welvaartsstaat, op. cit.*
50 *Werkgroep Alternatieve Ekonomie, Ongezond Verbeterbaar*, Kritak, Louvain, 1977, pp. 63ff.; NIS, *Volkstelling 1970*, deel 2A, 1975, pp. 64 and 141.
51 L. Goossens, 'Eigendomsverwerving van sociale woningen in België', *Bevolking en Gezin*, 1975, 1, pp. 18ff., B. de Cock, 'Woningbouw blijft in vraag voor "gewone" loontrekkenden en gezinnen', *De Gids op Maatschappelijk Gebied*, 1973, 10, pp. 837ff.; H. D'Hollander, 'Ongelijke verdeling van huisvesting', *De Gids op Maatschappelijk Gebied*, 1975, 2, pp. 95–110.
52 Werkgroep Alternatieve Ekonomie, *Dure Geneeskunde*, Louvain, 1975, p. 23ff.
53 C. Michel, 'La consommation médicale des Français', *Notes et Etudes documentaires*, 3584, La Documentation francaise, Paris, 1969.
54 Deleeck, 'Het mattheuseffect', op. cit., p. 720.
55 I. de Lanoo, *Stratificatieproblemen en democratisering van het universitair onderwijs*, De Nederlandse Boekhandel, Antwerp, 1969.
56 V. Claeys, *Universitair onderwijs als mobiliteitskanaal*, Universitaire pers Leuven, Louvain, 1974; and L. Vandekerckhove and L. Huyse, *In de buitenbaan – Arbeiderskinderen, Universitair onderwijs en sociale ongelijkheid*, Standaard, Antwerp, 1976.
57 The applicability of such theories has also been proved on educational success in primary education. Cf. B. Verbrugghe and L. Dulaing, 'De democratisering van het onderwijs, het ontnuchterend ontwaken uit een al te mooie wensdroom', *De Gids op Maatschappelijk Gebied*, 1977, 6–7, pp. 508ff.
58 Centrum voor Sociaal Beleid, op. cit., p. 41.
59 J. Billiet and J. Nizet, 'L'inégalité des chances ou la grande illusion', *La revue nouvelle*, 1974, 9, pp. 145–54.
60 Exception is made of particular labour contract legislation for, e.g., seamen, domestic staff, and apprentices.
61 As is illustrated by the fact that a national collective labour agreement on a minimum wage level was not signed before 1975.
62 H. Deleeck, *Inkomensverdeling, sociale zekerheid en sociaal beleid*, op. cit., pp. 157–74.
63 E. Lambrechts, 'Le travail féminin en Belgique – une approche sociologique', *Revue du Travail*, 1975, 9, pp. 605ff. Leroy estimated that at least 50 per cent of arrears in the average wage level for manual women workers in manufacturing industry has to be put down to either open or disguised discrimination: R. Leroy, *Les salaires féminins*, Editions Vie Ouvrière, Brussels, 1977, pp. 93–103.

64 In 1974 their level of unemployment amounted to 243 per cent as compared with the corresponding figure for men. Cf. *G.E.R.V.* 'De werkende vrouw – een statistische analyse', *F.E.R.V. -berichten,* 1976, 8, p. 73 and tables 61ff.

65 Centrum voor Sociaal Beleid, op. cit. The term 'security of subsistence' has been chosen in order to avoid any confusion with 'social security' which too easily refers to the existing social security system.

66 Based on a two-factor model with oblique rotation. The loading of the security of subsistence variable in this first factor was very high (.77).

4 Poverty and inequality in France

Adrian Sinfield

In 1976 the Organisation for Economic Co-operation and Development published two reports on its member countries, one on income distribution and the other on poverty.[1] These led *Le Monde* to tell its readers that their country had been awarded 'a gold medal' for its great and persistent inequality. Not only that, France also had one of the worst rates of poverty among the western industrial countries studied, despite its very high social expenditure.

In the same year the paper gave further emphasis to a number of national studies which broke 'the long and remarkable silence' and 'the groping in the dark' on the distribution of wealth, and provided detailed data on changes in the earnings spread over time. It headlined one article: 'Fortunes – much greater differences than had been thought', and another 'Wages: the same distribution as twenty years ago'.[2]

The picture of a country concerned with poverty and inequality was reinforced by another international study, published for the European Commission in Brussels with considerable publicity in March 1977. The French population as a whole was shown to be very much more aware of poverty, inequality and social injustice in their own country than were the people of Britain. The French believed that poverty persisted on a very much wider scale than did the British; and they were also much less likely to attribute it to personal failing or inadequacy and tended to place the blame for the much higher level of poverty on the injustice of their society. Indeed, almost half those interviewed in France believed there was poverty in their country compared with just over one-third in Britain; twice as many of these thought it due to injustice, and barely a third as many as in Britain considered it due to 'laziness and lack of will power'.[3]

Yet, despite the image that may be starting to emerge of a society that was aware and concerned to help its poor, poverty, deprivation and inequality seem to have received fairly little explicit attention in France in the last twenty years, compared, for example, with the USA, Britain or Sweden. Apart from individual, and recently growing, activity on a number of disparate issues, evidence of concern has been well below that in those other countries if one measures it by government activity in terms of committees, reports or legislation, by independent research initiatives, or by the extent of sustained and informed official or public debate, however confined this public may be.

The major exception to this picture that may account for some public awareness has been trade union concern with inequality linked to low pay. Their claims of pauperisation of the working class, seen as absolute in the 1950s and then more often as relative in subsequent years, may well have helped to shape popular perceptions. Even so, Jane Marceau reports evidence from the early 1970s of 'sheer ignorance on the part of the mass of the people of some of the important inequalities which remained in spite of "social protection"'.[4]

Nevertheless there have not been the many detailed analyses and discussions of poverty and measures to reduce it that have occurred in the USA and Britain. In these terms there is no poverty debate in France, no major poverty lobby, let alone any official anti-poverty programme. But any account of poverty simply based on the review of published materials and on discussion and correspondence with a small number of people, and undertaken from another country, must be at best regarded with a certain wariness. At worst it may reinforce stereotypes and pre-judgments, if not prejudices; confirm limited conventional wisdom of a foreign land; and mislead those who seek to gain lessons both for policy and the analysis of industrial capitalist societies from the growing number of comparative studies.

The French discussion of poverty

After 1945 the major problems of reconstruction, and an inflation which affected France earlier than most western countries, had the effect both of diverting attention from the specific problems of particular groups traditionally vulnerable to poverty and of exacerbating, or at best maintaining, regional and occupational differences in economic and social well-being. In addition the French social security legislation of 1945 and 1946 was seen as a 'working-class victory equal to the social reforms of 1936', and spoken of in terms of its social democratic spirit, solidarity and social justice.[5] Combined with the high rate of economic growth after the War, which brought about many evident changes in the society, it helped to create the belief of a poverty-free society even though the new social security scheme provided nothing for the unemployed – a reflection perhaps of the fact that France was less affected than many countries by the inter-war depression.

In early 1964, UNCAF (the Union Nationale des Caisses d'Allocations Familiales), one of the major national organisations in France allocating funds which could be said to combat poverty through its family allowances, let it be known that poverty had been eliminated in France and that consequently all funds spent on poverty research or on special action were wasted. In 1965 Alvin Schorr found little interest in poverty except for a gradually growing though limited awareness of the problem of the large families and the old.[6]

In 1965 Paul-Marie de la Gorce produced a summary of research relevant to poverty in *Poor France*, a book comparable in many ways to Michael Harrington's *The Other America*.[7] Despite a similar lack of clear references and often inadequately presented data, it did attempt the more comprehensive picture that others had failed to provide and gave some impetus to a national discussion of poverty. What limited debate there was had probably received its initial stimulus in February 1964 from a conference on poverty, or more precisely 'inadaptation', in the so-called economically advanced western societies organised by Alwine de Vos van Steenwijk of the Bureau de Recherches Sociales of Aide à Toute Détresse (A. à T.D.), was originally started by Abbé Pierre to aid the homeless sleeping in the Paris streets, and became increasingly involved with those existing, surviving without many benefits, in the 'bidonvilles' or shanty-towns on the outskirts of the larger cities.[8]

Concern over poverty in the USA provided another stimulus to the French debate in 1965 when, largely as a result of American encouragement, OECD held a trade union seminar on 'Low income groups and methods of dealing with their problems' to which Maurice Parodi presented a long and carefully documented paper on low income and poverty in France.[9]

But the French debate on poverty, let alone any attack on the problem, seemed to lose this initial momentum with perhaps the single exception of Aide à Toute Détresse, which extended its work not only outside the French shanty-towns to transit camps, hostels and temporary lodgings but to what it took as its new title, Le Quart Monde.[10] The Fourth World consists of those who remain in poverty within the modern, economically-advanced First World of market economies; and over the last decade the Fourth World movement has set up groups in New York, England, Holland and Belgium.

Apart from a wide variety of Fourth World publications reflecting a range of research and local community activity, there appears to have been little research or debate until the end of the 1960s, when Victor Scardigli and his colleagues at CREDOC began their steadily growing body of research into poverty and inequality.[11]

After his appointment as Prime Minister under President Pompidou in 1969, the 'energetic' Chaban-Delmas began work towards his 'new society' programme, 'a title conflated from Kennedy's "new frontier" and Johnson's "great society"', and very largely a response to the events of 1968. Although historically this may be seen as more of a discussion than a policy, the preparation of the Sixth Quinquennial National Plan of 1971–5 led to the initiation of a great deal of research and analysis on the distribution of household income, particularly by the National Statistical and Economic Studies Institute (INSEE).[12] From 1974 there has been a relatively steady flow of material from INSEE, often in its monthly journal *Economie et Statistique*, and from a number of other research institutes. Although few of these studies adopted a specific poverty or even low-income line, they did allow and encourage more firmly based debates on poverty and deprivation.[13]

Yet the absence of any single agreed measure of poverty or low income (such as the supplementary benefits scale rate plus rent compared with net income in Britain) seems to have inhibited the growth of any systematic debate even now. This is reinforced by the marked intellectual insulation that exists in France between different research institutes, different schools of thought and analysis, and different agencies and lobbies, so that it is much more unusual for one body to refer to work carried out in another than it is Britain.[14]

In consequence it is much more likely to be the journalist or committed layman who attempts to pull together the range of work that has been produced. And in this literature terms such as poverty, 'inadaptation', 'maladaptation', the outsiders, the sub-proletarians and the inhabitants of the underdeveloped France often appear to be seen as interchangeable means of identifying a very wide population covering an ill-defined and overlapping motley of, on one occasion, retired, drug addicts, children in care *or* in need of care and protection, unemployed, sick, maladjusted children in schools, low income recipients, the poorly housed, alcoholics, the mentally ill, the would-be suicides and suicides(!), criminals, *and* finally groups of 'marginals and asocials' or 'misfits'. Although these were formally listed in a table on 'general statistics on social inadaptation, excluding the physically and mentally handicapped', that writer and others appear to include them with those two other groups in discussions of poverty and exclusion.[15]

A major problem facing any analyst of the distribution of resources in France is the very limited material on recent incomes, let alone any changes in net economic power over time. The latest detailed data available at the beginning of 1978 are from the INSEE household and personal income and resources surveys of 1970.[16]

A particular difficulty with any other data available since 1970 is that it is largely dependent on tax returns; and reported income is generally believed to be a particularly low proportion of total personal income in France: 24 per cent in one comparative study published in 1969, against 75 per cent in the UK, 79 per cent in the USA, and 92 per cent in West Germany. Reliance on indirect taxation as the major source of fiscal revenue reduces the government's need to obtain fuller reports. The lost income belongs mainly to the lower-income groups, the self-employed (a large group with a wide dispersion of earnings), and the well-off.[17]

The extent of poverty in France

In the early 1970s, according to the OECD study, France ranked top with West Germany among the countries studied in the proportion of 'trend' gross domestic product devoted to income maintenance expenditure: 12.4 per cent compared with between 7 and 8 per cent for the UK, USA and Canada.

But France was also top of the eight countries in the proportion of population below the 'standardised' relative poverty line. By this measure 16 per cent of the French were poor compared with only 3 per cent in its equally high social spending neighbour, Germany, and 13 per cent in the USA, 11 per cent in Canada, and 7.5 per cent in the UK.[18]

The weight that should be put on this finding is particularly debatable for France, as the 'standardised' poverty line was based on a rounded and unweighted average of the various official or quasi-official poverty lines in six countries *excluding* France. The average of the other six gave a cut-off point of about two-thirds of the national private disposable income *per capita* for a one-person household and nearly two and one-fifth times that amount for a family of four. In France in 1972 the 'quasi-official' measure based on the minimum wage and pension was below one third of *per capita* private disposable income for a single person and three times that amount for four people, a level still below private disposable income *per capita*.[19]

The OECD estimate of 16 per cent is not out of line with the range of suggested percentages from within France. The report itself mentions René Lenoir's 15 per cent in 'The Outsiders' (despite the subtitle of the book "one Frenchman in ten") and Lionel Stoleru's 20 per cent in 'The fight against poverty in the rich countries'. In the mid-1960s Jules Klanfer had used data from De la Gorce's 'Poor France' to estimate that some seven million households lived in poverty – about 20 per cent of the total population, much the same level as in the USA, and in 1970 Jean-Pierre Launay subtitled his 'Underdeveloped France' 'fifteen million poor', a rate of some 28 per cent. In offering the most detailed account I have found, Stoleru stresses that it is only a very rough estimate and indeed gives no basic sources.[20]

The definition of poverty

There appears to be no clearly agreed measure of poverty in France or even an established group of alternative definitions, despite the OECD reference to a 'quasi-official' measure based on the minimum wage and pension. In a number of studies the level of minimum guaranteed earnings has been used – since January 1970 SMIC (Salaire minimum interprofessionel de croissance, a minimum growth wage) replacing SMIG (Salaire minimum interprofessionel garanti, the guaranteed minimum wage) which was first introduced in 1950.[21]

TABLE 4.1   *The poor in France, estimate of Lionel Stoleru, 1973-74*

1	The majority of farmworkers	600,000 estimated
2	The majority of labourers	1,100,000
3	Two-thirds of service workers	800,000
4	Half of the semi-skilled	1,300,000
5	A quarter of self-employed craftsmen and shopkeepers	800,000
6	Half of the elderly over 65	2,600,000
7	Two-thirds of widows with dependent children	1,000,000
8	Physically handicapped under 65	2,000,000
9	Socially maladjusted ('inadaptés') youth	1,000,000
	Estimated number of poor people	11,200,000
	Estimated number of poor families	3,000,000

The earlier measure was based on the concept of a minimum budget which met the most basic needs. The difficulty of fixing such an absolute poverty level objectively was recognised in large part because trade unions and employers' associations could not agree on where the minimum should be set. As Jean-Pierre Launay has argued, such a measure is a 'definition patronale' (bosses' definition), indicating the least they are prepared to pay rather than the least workers are prepared to accept.[22]

This is perhaps confirmed by the fact that before the major boost in SMIG in the politically-volatile atmosphere of Summer 1968, the 'smigards' had received frequent increases but had fallen well behind the rising average hourly rate for manual workers, which had gone up about 50 per cent faster. As a result, the number of workers directly benefiting from improvements in SMIG had fallen from 16 per cent to below 2 per cent between 1954 and the start of 1968.

Despite the 35 per cent increase in June 1968 (38 per cent outside Paris), which directly helped 12 per cent of workers, average wages after that continued to draw away from the minimum level. The introduction of SMIC in 1970 was an attempt to prevent the lowest wages falling behind. The act stated that 'SMIC guarantees the lowest-paid workers that their buying power will be maintained and they will have a share in economic growth'.[23] From the end of 1972, until the middle of 1974 at least, SMIC grew faster than the average hourly wage, and by 1975 it had caught up to the proportion of the average wage it had been in 1954.[24]

Although the use of SMIC to indicate the extent of poverty in work has a certain logic, its value for measuring low incomes for all groups is clearly more debatable. How much should it be adjusted to arrive at the net amount for equitable comparison of the income levels of those in and out of work, and for those outside the labour force altogether? Even for those in work it does not take account of family allowances and other benefits or taxes, social security and other contributions.

There is an additional problem in using SMIC as an indicator of poverty over time similar to the application of supplementary benefit levels in Britain. A more generous increase by a government that raises SMIC by more than prices or average earnings may show an increase of those in poverty outside the areas of employment covered by SMIC.

Poverty in work

SMIC is a useful indicator of poverty among workers, provided two factors are taken into account. One is the problems of relating a minimum hourly rate to weekly earnings data, which is partly dealt with by excluding part-time workers; the difficulty that remains here is that some will have worked more than the basic week of 40 hours and only the overtime will have taken them over the poverty line. The other major difficulty is the construction of a net monthly measure based on a gross weekly wage of 40 hours at SMIC rates minus contributions to Social Security, the complementary schemes for retirement and unemployment insurance. On this basis Nicole Borel suggests a cut-off point for July 1974 at 1500 F net per month for those in full-time work.[25] But this calculation takes no account of any payment of family allowances or other benefits nor of deductions of tax: and there are no comparable data for the analysis of poverty in work by family size at that date.

Borel's first finding was the large scale of the problem indicated by the measure suggested, and even by less generous ones. One-third of wage earners were receiving less than 1500 F net, one-fifth less than

1300 F, in July 1974. At both levels the clear majority of workers came from the private and semi-public sectors (69 per cent at 1500 F and 76 per cent at 1300 F). The second main finding was 'the very great inequality in the distribution of low pay'.[26] The risk of being in working poverty varied very much among different groups. Nearly nine out of ten domestic workers received less than 1500 F net a month, and over seven out of ten in local government and farming, compared with three out of ten in the main private and semi-public sectors, and less than two out of ten in central government. The difference between local and central government very largely reflects the much greater preponderance of established as opposed to temporary or non-established civil servants in the latter.

Women in full-time work are much more likely to be low-paid than men (44 per cent and 24.5 per cent respectively below 1500 F net). And, of course, women are also more likely to be in low-paying part-time jobs, especially those having to look after young children by themselves. In part women's greater risk of poverty in work reflects their greater concentration in low-paying sectors such as local government, where the proportion low-paid in each sex does not vary greatly. In public employment as a whole women are less likely to experience discrimination, and it is outside this area that the chance of low-pay for women is almost twice as great as for men.

The risk of low pay is much greater in four main industries, in addition to agriculture and domestic work: clothing, personal services such as hairdressing 74 per cent, hotel and catering 60 per cent, and textiles 51 per cent. Although tips may augment pay in some service industries, low earnings are still very prevalent. These are also industries likely to have an above average proportion of foreign workers who are particularly likely to be low-paid.

The risk of low pay is also of course considerably greater for those workers who do not receive the full protection of SMIC: apprentices, workers under 18 years of age, certain disabled workers, and those working within prisons. In addition many part-time workers are found in the low-paying industries, especially women with young children, but they are not included in the calculations above.

Finally, the self-employed are a very much larger proportion of the working population in France than in Britain. In general the data for this group are much more limited, but the available evidence indicates a much greater heterogeneity among them, and a wider dispersion of income. On 1966 data Scardigli considered that 'a large number of individuals in this group most certainly have very low incomes: small farmers, craftsmen, small shopkeepers'.[27] At the same date Klanfer reported that estimates suggested that there were as many on low incomes among the self-employed as in employment.[28]

How much of the picture would change if all benefits and taxes were taken into account is debatable. On 1966 analyses and estimates Scardigli concluded that 'the poorest families are not the principal gainers of the welfare programs for working families', and believed that the group immediately above these did better, even in obtaining more family allowances.[29] More recent analyses (which will be discussed in the section on families below) indicate that changes from 1972 onward have tended to benefit lower-income families.

Immigration and foreign workers – 'the pariahs of the nation'[30]

Paul-Marie de la Gorce's vivid phrase conveys the significance given in most of the non-statistical literature to the problems of immigrants and foreign workers, who are frequently mentioned in discussions of the 'asocials' or 'the poor'. The refugees from North Africa and to a lesser extent South-East Asia, the product of decolonisation and the move to independence in the French territories, were vulnerable to poverty because of their lack of those skills which were in short supply, the difficulty of obtaining accommodation, and the problems of adaptation to the host society.

Similar difficulties, and probably worse ones in recent years, have been experienced by foreign workers, especially those from Spain, Portugal and Africa, who seem particularly likely to finish up in the hardest and worst-paid jobs living in 'sub-human' conditions. The Algerians, Portuguese, Spanish and Italians each totalled between three-quarters and half a million in January 1972 according to the official data, with the Portuguese steadily diminishing in numbers. Moroccans and Tunisians then formed the next largest group.[31]

In 1972 one study found that foreign workers earned 17 per cent less than French workers. But a national average conceals the extent of inequality because foreign workers are more likely to be men in their prime working years in the industrial areas, which generally have higher rates of pay than elsewhere. Their very heavy concentration in manual jobs, especially the less qualified ones, is a major cause of the difference and this is likely to continue, given the small number in apprenticeships.[32]

These problems of the foreign workers are compounded by the fact that most – 'perhaps up to 80 per cent' in 1973 – have entered illegally and are the more willing to accept jobs at any wages and less prepared to fight for better working, housing and other conditions. The majority remain unskilled and limited to poor housing, and many are ineligible for most benefits. In 1973 the unions accused big employers of deliberately recruiting Moroccans and workers from Yugoslavia and Turkey to keep wage demands down and speed up the work routines. Recently increasing unemployment has intensified the potential conflict, with many arguing that the migrants should 'give up their jobs to French men and women if permanent joblessness is to be avoided.' Such views seem, implicitly at least, to be encouraged by government action, including such campaigns as 'Priority to Manual Workers' in 1976.[33]

The actual extent of poverty, rather than low earnings, among these groups, and the variation within them does not seem to have been analysed in any published material. The general consensus of the literature was well caught by Launay when he introduced a chapter on 'the foreigners' by saying this group, if any, experience poverty 'in the absolute sense of the term'.[34]

Families

The formal emphasis of French family support has traditionally been a horizontal rather than vertical redistribution of the costs of child-rearing, 'partly as a way of stimulating the birth rate but more generally to strengthen the family as an economic unit and social institution . . . as *la cellule sociale*, the primary source of a nation's stability and integrity', and one particularly supported by the Catholic church.[35] This policy has been evident in both taxation and social security. The tax *quotient familial* results in income being divided by the number in the family, dependent children counting as a half each, a system of particular benefit to those with high incomes, who are further helped by the large non-taxable family allowances. The range and variety of family allowances make any calculation of their total effectiveness even more difficult to assess.[36]

Major changes in the schemes from 1972 onward are believed to have provided a much greater transfer to poorer families, especially the larger ones. But certainly over the twenty years up to 1970 large families fell further behind the childless in their standard of living. This was particularly noticeable for the unskilled, domestic and farm workers.

In recent years there has been increasing 'harmonisation' and 'generalisation' of the range of family allowances, merging the different occupational schemes and extending coverage to family units without a wage earner. Since the beginning of 1978 residence, not active employment, has been the sole requirement for most programmes. And in 1977 a plan was announced to introduce a supplementary means-tested allowance to merge six existing schemes. It is estimated that 70 per cent of families will be eligible because 'the income ceiling is to be set at a fairly high level'.[37] Other developments have included an annual school re-entry allowance for families below a certain income with school-age children: for 1977 the size of that grant was tripled.[38]

In 1975 the basic tax-free cash allowance starting at £665 for children under ten provided a significant support for low-income families, and its combination with direct taxation meant greater support to poor families than in any other EEC country. A two-parent family with four dependent children on two-thirds of average earnings gained an amount after allowances and tax equal to 49.4 per cent of its income compared with 8.2 per cent in the United Kingdom. At average earnings the proportions were 33 per cent and −5.5 per cent respectively, and at five times average earnings −1.4 per cent and −40.9 per cent.[39] Even so, the most detailed calculations published by INSEE for 1975 show that at any wage level disposable income per head is still very much lower in large families than those with no or very few children, and the cost of bringing up a family clearly weighs particularly heavily on households headed by a low-paid worker.[40]

The 1975 analysis underlined the importance of high family allowances and a high tax threshold in helping poor families. The average unskilled worker with two children and a wife out of the labour force received between 28 and 37 per cent of the net household income in family allowances; the amount varies according to the age of children. A manager or higher professional would only have 2 per cent of disposable income in this way, but would benefit from the tax system.

The 1972 reforms play a large part in bringing about a greater redistribution to lower-income groups, although there are marked variations in the gains for families of different size and age at the same income level. One particularly ingenious analysis of the benefits that would be received over 17 years by a family during the birth and growth of four children, assuming 1975 legislation over that period, shows total benefits of 18,717 F to a labourer's family and 16,564 F to the professional or executive's family. This brings out very clearly both the inconsistencies that may arise from year to year as the family changes and the degree to which tax benefits reduce the extent of redistribution.[41]

There seems little discussion, let alone evidence, on any failure to take up means-tested benefits, and the calculations quoted above assume that all these have been received. Scardigli, however, mentioned 'the complications of official procedures' that applicants must go through to qualify for benefits as one of the factors that caused the poorest to lose out in the early 1970s, and may result in what might be regarded as concealed discrimination against some groups. Formal exclusion has been reduced by the extension of some benefits to foreign workers and their families.[42]

TABLE 4.2 Increase of financial help per child, for a family (with non-working mother) growing from none to four children over 17 years, holding 1975 laws constant throughout.

Years from first birth	Dates of successive births	Changing size & age of children[1]	Family head manual worker			Family head senior executive		
			Total net increase of family benefits[2][3] francs (%)	Change from row above[4]	Net increase per child of family	Total net increase of family benefits[2][3] francs (%)	Change from row above[4]	Net increase per child of family
0	Birth 1	1 A...	4 799 (7.9)	+ 4 799	4 799	2 559 (100.0)	+ 2,559	2 559
2		2 B... →↓	2 204 (17.2)	− 2 595	2 204	2 559 (100.0)	0	2 559
3	Birth 2	3 AB... →↓	7 620 (7.2)	+ 5 416	3 810	6 021 (71.8)	+ 3 462	3 011
6		4 BC... ↓↓	5 618 (9.7)	− 2 002	2 809	6 021 (71.8)	0	3 011
7	Birth 3	5 ABC... →↓↓	11 313 (4.8)	+ 5 695	3 771	10 168 (55.4)	+ 4 147	3 389
9		6 BCC... ↓↓↓	9 544 (5.7)	− 1 796	3 181	10 168 (55.4)	0	3 389
11	Birth 4	7 ABCD... →↓↓↓	16 205 (3.4)	+ 6 661	4 051	14 768 (45.7)	+ 4 600	3 692
15		8 BCDE... ↓↓↓↓	17 945 (3.0)	+ 1 740	4 486	15 918 (42.4)	+ 1 150	3 979
17		9 CDDE... ↓↓↓	18 717 (2.9)	+ 772	4 679	16 564 (40.7)	+ 646	4 141

Notes:
[1] The letters indicate the number and age of children at each stage: A under 2 years; B 3–5 years; C 6–9 years; D 10–15 years; E over 15 years old.
[2] The total net increase of family benefits is defined as the sum of the grants and the reduction in tax as a result of the 'family quotient' calculation.
[3] The figures in brackets indicate the portion of family benefits coming from the tax reduction.
[4] The age as well as the number of children effects the exent of the change from the situation in the row above.

One-parent families

One-parent families formed 6 per cent of all household units with more
than one person in 1968. Four out of five were headed by women and,
while the majority had only one child, one out of five had more than
two. In one-third of these units there was no worker, and among the
remainder the jobs held tended to be fairly low-skilled and poorly paid.
In consequence fatherless families had the lowest incomes in the 1970
survey, and those living with relatives tended to be the poorest of
these.[43]

Although single mothers are eligible for the general family allowances, access to other benefits and allowances has been generally determined by whether or not the mother is working, and so insured in her
own right and able to obtain the full health and income benefits available to workers and their dependants. For example 'the single wage
allowance' introduced in 1946 and means-tested since 1972, has been
available to divorced and unmarried mothers only if they are working,
while in two-parent families this benefit encourages the woman to stay
at home as part of the general pro-natalist policy. Only the separated
woman whose husband is in insured employment can receive this without working. However, the 'single parent allowance' of 1976 is not
dependent on employment, although it only provides support for
those with at least one child under the age of three.[44]

Overall the extent of support grows more with each child than in
Britain. In 1974 non-means-tested family allowances (including the
1971 special orphans' allowance) were equivalent to 4.2 per cent of
average gross earnings of male industrial workers for a one-child family;
14.5 per cent for two children, and 29.1 per cent for three children.
The figures for Britain were 2.2, 4.4 and 6.6 per cent respectively. The
various special allowances dependent on a test of income provided
additional support, although once again evidence of the rate of take-
up appears to be very limited. These benefits do not seem to be regarded in the same way as 'social aid' or assistance: although this may
be helpful for some, it does not offer an adequate safety-net because
many fail to apply, often because they are deterred by the conditions
and procedures. This residual programme, however, provides some
support for one- and two-parent families, 222,000 children at the end
of 1975. The monthly amount and its duration are fixed after an
enquiry by the local prefect's office.[45]

Poverty among those not in work

The risk of poverty is generally agreed to be much higher among those
out of work and their dependants. However, between 1962 and 1970

those outside the labour force gained more from the total effect of changes in taxation and social transfers than workers in the lower-paid groups. The gains made by workers in the first three years had largely been lost again by 1970. It is not yet clear what has happened since then, although the government's reactions to the 'Union de la Gauche' in 1972, especially after Giscard d'Estaing's election as president in 1974, included the proposal or introduction of many social reforms in social security and housing which would help the poorest, including those not in work. Many schemes ran into strong resistance from employers, but it is generally too early to see the overall effects of those that have been introduced.[46]

It should be emphasised that even a continued redistribution towards those outside the labour force may not necessarily prevent or reduce poverty among this group. Pensions and other benefits have generally been closely related to previous earnings and contributions, and the schemes have varied considerably among the different occupations. This has resulted in a relatively high level of income maintenance for many of the better-paid when they are not in work, and accounts for the high proportion of GDP going to income maintenance. But these schemes often have very low minimum rates well below any relative poverty line, and the public aid schemes are equally weak. In consequence, the inequality institutionalised in the social security system in France has become a major factor accounting for poverty among many of those in households not supported by a wage-earner.

The old

In most industrial societies the retired form the largest group of those not at work, and France has for long been among the countries with a high proportion of the population over 65.[47] Low labour force participation rates among this group, a high proportion living alone and often inadequate pensions have left the retired particularly vulnerable to poverty.

The Laroque report of some twenty years ago, comparable in some ways to a Beveridge report on the elderly, revealed their economic problems very clearly; but it is difficult to judge how major social security changes since then have helped the poorest of the elderly, in particular the very gradual replacement of the eleven basic retirement schemes by one pension system from the beginning of 1975.

In 1965 Parodi estimated that the position of the elderly had not changed significantly from the picture presented by a 1961 housing survey. Even allowing for some understating of income, he considered that at least half of the households headed by an old person were poor despite the policy changes in those four years. Studies since then have continued to emphasise the vulnerability of the elderly, especially women (who formed a greater proportion of the very old), largely reflecting the impact of War on the French population.[48]

Launay underlined this point vividly in 1970: 'In ten years the age-group 65–69 will total nearly 900,000 less than today – they were young in 1940 – while the number in their eighties will increase by 700,000.' Four and a half of the seven million over 65 in the 1968 census were women, and nearly half of them widows. The War may also help to account for the very large proportion (43 per cent) of people living alone among households headed by an old person in 1970: and as a result these people had no direct access to the benefits of wage earners.[49]

The point made earlier about the general failure of occupational and earnings-related benefits to prevent poverty if the minimum levels are too low applies particularly to the retired. In 1972 nearly 7 per cent of 'trend' GDP was spent on pensions in France, leaving her fourth of the seventeen nations in the OECD report. But the minimum annual pension of 3,650 F, was only 45 per cent of the standardised poverty line used in that report. Only the USA had as low a benefit, and most of the other countries were much higher. As a result, one estimate is that only 18 per cent of pensions go to the poorest 20 per cent of the retired population. As another indicator, the minimum pension in 1972 was only 50 F above the minimum wage in 1962, despite the inflation over the intervening decade.[50]

The improvement of pensions, and the proliferation of many separate schemes for different industries and occupations, have taken more and more old people off the inadequate non-contributory grant to retired manual workers (AVTS) which provided some form of a minimum to workers provided that they had worked at least 25 years. The total receiving AVTS dropped by three-quarters from nearly two million in 1955 to a quarter of a million in 1970, while social security pensions increased by nearly two-and-a-half times to over three million.[51]

But even the changes and improvements in the 1960s often with inadequate supplements grafted on to limited and inadequate schemes, still leave many retired people well below the measure used to indicate poverty in work. In 1970 a widow received only one-half of the husband's basic pension – at 60 if she could show she was unable to work, but otherwise not until she was 65. Pensions are now based on the ten best years, not the last ten, which worked against those forced into poorer-paying jobs through declining health, disability or redundancy, but they remain very low for the lowest-paid workers.[52]

For the very poorest there are the 'bureaux d'aide sociale' but their effectiveness is difficult to establish. Writers such as Launay report that those without enough income from other sources still 'have to write each month to the mayor of their commune to ask him to be good enough to make them a gift' of a few dozen francs. The Petits Frères des Pauvres and others organise mass signings of stencilled letters for the elderly, with the result that all the local public assistance may be used up. There are also reports of wide-spread ignorance of entitlement or very great reluctance to apply, with minimal take-up rates. One of the apparently very few studies found that applications were made by only a very small percentage of those apparently eligible in one Paris arrondissement for 360 F a month for single people and 540 F for couples in the late 1960s. There are also reports of starvation among old people: a study of old people in the regions of Marseilles and Saint-Etienne found 10 per cent of men and 19 per cent of women existing 'in a state near to famine'.[53]

Discussion, let alone research, tends to omit or overlook the 350,000 old people living in residential homes and institutions. Most of the residents are among the oldest and poorest, many living in decaying 'homes': 'really public institutions for the dying', in Launay's phrase. The segregation from the rest of the community of these occupants and many other retired is indicated by a CNRS survey when 8 per cent of adults had no idea whether either parent was still alive, and another 27 per cent preferred not to answer the question.[54]

Inequalities among the retired widen with age, as needs may become greater with deterioration of physical strength and health. The risk of poverty is therefore sharply increased for the older retired, and this exacerbates the already poorer position of single widowed and divorced women as they grow older. The marked incidence of poverty among the retired in France and the considerable inequality in the range of pensions, let alone other resources for this group of the population, become even more disturbing when the marked variation in mortality rates means that many fewer of the poor are likely to reach retirement age. The literature on mortality rates is rich with detail, well illustrated by the title of an article in *Economie et Statistique*: 'At thirty-five schoolteachers still have 41 years to live, labourers only 34'.[55]

The unemployed

France has not been immune from the sharp increase in unemployment which has hit most western industrial societies since the early 1970s. The rise in the numbers looking for work has been particularly marked in France. Only a small part of the sixteen-fold increase in the thirty years from 1946 can be due to improvements in income support and employment services, encouraging more of the unemployed to register and so appear in the official statistics. The more than six-fold increase in the decade up to 1976 may even conceal the full extent of the increase among some groups.

Analysis of the scale of problem by standardised international definitions may be helpful, given the prolonged statistical and highly volatile political debate in France over the variety of official sources and their accuracy. France has averaged 2.3 per cent unemployment from 1962 to 1975, compared with 3.2 per cent for the UK and 5 per cent for the USA, rising to 4 per cent for 1976, with 6 per cent in the UK and 7.5 per cent in the USA. Over the first three quarters of 1977 the total increased faster than in the UK, and in the USA there has been a clear drop in the numbers out of work.[56]

By the French official figures 1,175,000 people were registered unemployed in September 1977. This is at best in line with the gloomier predictions of the VII plan of 'a permanent pool of one million unemployed by 1980, possibly as many as 1.4m'. In February 1976 the French unions walked out of the planning commission 'claiming the government was in league with the bosses to create permanent joblessness and break the power of organised labour'.[57]

Major improvements in income support for the unemployed over the last decade may have helped to reduce or at least restrain the number of unemployed experiencing poverty, given the marked rise in those out of work, especially since mid-1974. The insurance system, first introduced by collective agreement for about a quarter of the work force, was made compulsory in 1967, but until the emergency decisions of 1974 and 1975 it provided protection for only 40 per cent of the labour force. Redundancy payments were raised in 1975 as unemployment reached its highest post-war level and 'in mid-1976 about one out of every eight persons registered as unemployed' was receiving the highest rate.[58]

As with all benefits, those for the unemployed may vary dramatically. In their case the highest is the special lay-off payment of 90 per cent of previous gross earnings up to a monthly maximum of 11,376 F per month in 1976, almost eight times the average SMIC equivalent for that year. The lowest scheme is the basic public aid, with a grant of 372 F per month for those at least three months out of work, which is reduced by 10 per cent each year to a minimum of 37.20 F per month for a single person.

The basic support scheme (ASSEDIC) is an earnings-related contributory supplement to the unemployment assistance scheme. The latter is paid without a means test for the first three months and then other resources are generally taken into account more strictly and comprehensively than in Britain. Under these two schemes the average wage-replacement is 35 per cent or 40 per cent for the first three months. In March 1976, 58 per cent of those registered for work received one or more of these payments, with more recipients of public aid than the basic insurance scheme. Jane Marceau concludes that 'the income levels of many of the unemployed were desperately low . . . and still low even when a person was eligible for both' benefits.[59]

As in other countries, the impact of unemployment is of course very unequal. With schemes mostly dependent on previous earnings and particular industrial or occupational attachment, those most vulnerable to prolonged or repeated unemployment appear much less likely to receive adequate protection than in Britain. Those entering the labour force, or re-entering after a long absence, may also be particularly vulnerable to poverty before they find a job.[60]

Disability

Compared with Britain but in common with many countries on the European mainland, France has borne and continues to bear much greater costs from the wars of 1914–18 and 1939–45 in terms of disability and shattered human relationships, leading to misery, desolation and deprivation – a burden carried by civilian and military together. The much greater destruction of the country (homes, hospitals, schools, road, rail and other services, as well as workplaces) meant an immediate diversion of post-war resources to reconstruction and a willingness to compensate those directly disabled by the war. But the long-term social costs of war are less easily and certainly picked up.

Even today the war-disabled form a very large proportion of all handicapped, especially men. But those injured at work also form a large group: 'a much greater social plague than cancer or road accidents'. My impression is that this may be a worse problem than in Britain, but it may simply be that there is a greater awareness of it. Another writer describes war and alcoholism as the major causes of disability and illness among men. To what extent disability or hardship is associated with poverty is less easy to establish. The term 'handicapped' is applied very broadly in many of the books to cover a range of socially handicapped or marginal groups who are included in the totals of the poor, but I have failed to locate any detailed analyses of low income among those who are either disabled or temporarily ill. In his survey of Folie-Mericourt, however, Pierre Aiach found that workers and their families were more likely than salaried workers to have poor health and to be poorly protected against any financial loss.[61]

Poor housing

Poverty and poor housing seem much more closely related in France than in Britain, more comparable perhaps to at least certain areas of the USA. In 1965 Maurice Parodi drew attention to the housing problems of the poor and the ways in which these were compounded by official policy and practice in the allocation of accommodation, which required a certain minimum level of income and imposed quotas on particular groups such as migrants.

In November 1969 part of this picture was confirmed by the Minister of Housing's own estimate that one family in five in the Paris region was ineligible for social housing because their income was too low. In adding that this proportion would have been even worse in the poor 'quarter' of Folie-Mericourt in 1975, Willmott and Aiach report that only 17 per cent of 'priority' allocations could go to immigrants. In these respects there seems to have been little change; as Launay observes, housing 'remains the most important problem for the French' since the end of the War.[62]

The marked acceleration in economic and industrial change in the generation since the War, together with the sharp rise in the birth-rate till the 1970s and the increasing immigration of the 1960s, resulted in 'a radical geographical redistribution of the population into urban centres, and thus the creation of· urban social problems on a massive scale'. For many the housing problem has become particularly linked with the debates on social problems and 'inadaptation' in the shanty-towns and temporary camps ('bidonvilles' and 'cités d'urgence'), on which the literature is now considerable. Various urban renewal programmes with the demolition of established neighbourhoods have often only succeeded in accelerating a downward spiral to high-rent slums or the shanty-towns on the urban fringe. It is not known how many live in these areas, but it is believed that they are on the increase because of the continuing inadequacies in housing programmes. The major centre for research into the 'bidonvilles' has been the Bureau de Recherches Sociales of Aide à Toute Détresse, particulary at Noisy-Le-Grand, which consists predominantly of French families forced out of the cities, contrary to the popular impression reflected in some of the literature that such areas are occupied only by immigrants.[63]

Studies in the 'bidonvilles' have particularly focused on the structure of the family, and this has been related to discussion of the culture of poverty. Labbens argues that cohabition 'without benefit of clergy' merely reveals the economic or legal marginality which constitute a temporary or permanent obstacle to legal marriage among the poor; but marriage remains the ideal, and unmarried families are not predominant. He uses the term 'culture of poverty' to underline his belief that poverty is inherited. The inhabitants of the 'bidonvilles' are mostly born and bred in poverty in the urban industrialised areas of France, and he refers to symptoms of cultural backwardness: 'The victim of poverty has inherited behaviour and attitudes corresponding to a general social environment which no longer exists today.' In particular the predominant attitude is one of dependence and submissiveness, which prevents them from becoming too frustrated or from coming into conflict with the outside society.[64]

The general belief is that the worst poverty can be found in these camps; but research concentrated in some of the worst city slums has revealed a very similar picture. Although the very low-paid, the old and especially the migrants were most likely to be in the worst housing, many manual workers were likely to be poorly housed. There was some reduction in the housing shortage after 1960, but even in 1970 'one in five dwellings was overcrowded. Very many more were without some or all of the elements of "comfort",' especially in the rural and inner-city areas of the north and west. Despite promises of reform and a relative housing boom, the percentage of 'principal dwellings' provided by social housing stood at 11 per cent in 1973, no higher than in 1963. What new accommodation there was had to be erected on the outer suburban fringes, increasing sharply the time and money spent on travel to work, restricting the net income of many poorly-paid, and often cutting them off from their families.[65]

The literature reviewed suggests that the marked link between low income and poor housing found in Folie-Mericourt by Willmott and Aiach as opposed to Lambeth in 1973 to 1975 could be more widely applied. Housing problems both create and add to poverty in France; there is little evidence that the new housing allowances are significantly changing this picture. Despite the radical reform of these in 1971, take-up is probably still very poor; and various restrictions on the scheme continue to work against larger families and those in sub-standard housing.[66]

Geographical inequalities

Wide inequalities have persisted for a long time among the different parts of the country and are still very evident. Traditionally the west and the south-west have been the most deprived areas of France, with least industrial development, a large agricultural sector and much rural poverty. In the north-east, the poverty of industrially declining areas can still be described in Zolaesque terms.

In 1974 there was not only a much greater concentration of low pay in the west, especially Limousin, but a very marked difference between

Paris and the rest of the country. Only 17 per cent of wage earners re-ceived less than 1500 F net in the metropolitan area: the lowest pro-portion outside Paris was 34 per cent. The historical and cultural divide symbolised by the use of 'la Province' to indicate the whole of France outside Paris is reinforced by the distribution of earnings. Of course, there are well-paid workers in other parts of the country and very low-paid ones in the capital. The variation within regions can also be seen within the general area of Paris. Unlike London and the major British cities, Paris 'within-the-walls' is generally regarded as better-off, but its suburban ring lacks services, decent jobs and working conditions and sufficient and adequate housing.[67]

Rural poverty and agriculture

A major cause of poverty remains the very low return to those working in the agricultural sector. Despite rationalisation of the industry with a drop of one-quarter in the agricultural labour force from 1954 to 1962, it was still estimated then that over half the farms were in economic difficulties. On data based on the early 1970s the OECD report still picked out the considerable poverty in 'the relatively large agricultural sector' as a major factor accounting for the overall high rate in the whole country. Most indicators point to considerable rural poverty, which is likely to be increasing with the departure of the younger and more skilled or qualified to the towns and cities in the areas of greatest industrial growth, and particularly to the region of Paris.[68]

The urban influx, accelerated by the migrants from outside France, means that over three-quarters of the total population is expected to be urban in 1985, compared with little over half at the end of the War. The needs of the remaining rural population have tended to be over-looked by contrast with the problems created for, or by, the homeless, temporarily housed and shanty-town dwellers descending on the larger cities. But the one in three remaining in rural areas in 1968 contained a disproportionate number in the groups generally most vulnerable to poverty: the very young, especially in larger rural families; the elderly, including many single persons of 'les classes creuses' (the empty classes) who survived the 1914–18 war; the disabled; the unskilled; or the rural worker with no skills readily applicable to more technological industry.[69]

There is little evidence of any attempt to arrest the decline in many social and other public services that generally accompanies such a rural exodus, let alone any effort to reduce the inequalities that already existed between the larger cities with a better and greater range of ser-vices, and with larger employers who tend to provide higher pay and more fringe benefits.

While discussion flourishes about the 'socially maladjusted' who are believed to throng to the cities, there is also talk both in the regions and the centre of the need to preserve the linguistic and cultural identity of, for example, Brittany. While sophisticated Parisians may speak of the rest of the country as 'la Province' and the provincials with all the disdainful connotations that the term implies in English, those outside stress the universe of cultural differences and the variety of historical heritage in the different 'départements' of France.

One result appears to be the reinforcing of historical inequalities among and within regions, because these have become legitimated by traditional differences. The persistence of social hierarchies that leaves the fisher families, small farmers and smallholders, labourers and small craftsmen deprived becomes in some way rationalised in the resistance, by those with significant power among both liberal and traditional groups, to uniformity and the suppression of regional or local identities.

Corsica is perhaps the clearest example of rural poverty, comparable in many ways to the persistent structure of inequalities revealed in the work of Danilo Dolci in Sicily. But there are many other areas where a separate local identity and rural poverty have become closely interlinked: the fishing villages of Brittany and parts of the west coast; the poor farming land of the south-west.[70]

Far from revealing the poverty, tourism has almost disguised it in the travel agents' sentimental glossary of charm, culture and tradition. The growing proportion of the better-off businessmen, administrators or professionals with a second holiday home in the country also works against the rediscovery of the hardship of rural poverty and its fractured life chances. The Midi, for example, becomes the place of escape from the urban problems. An acknowledgment of rural poverty would also involve an admission of its functionality to the tourists, and even more the holiday home-owners, in terms of cheaper, better and often deferential services. The most that is noted is the backwardness and 'simplicity' of rural people, which is sufficient to explain any worrying inequalities in a society which would like to see itself as more technically-oriented and slowly more meritocratic.

The lack of evident concern in the literature closest to poverty may in part be because in these areas the local community with its traditional structures of control and support are assumed to prevent the 'inadaptation' that is the central focus of such studies and the debates that surround them. Indeed, in very crude terms, one might suggest that many of those engaged in research, administration and policy are concerned to recreate such community life and relationships of solidarity in the shanty-towns, temporary quarters and other 'insalubrious' areas of overcrowded cities that in many ways are only now having to cope with the urban explosion that hit New York, Boston or Chicago half a century ago, and London, Birmingham or Manchester over a century ago.

Inequality and poverty

The fusion, if not confusion, of much of the literature and debates on poverty, low incomes and 'maladaptation', 'inadaptation' or marginal populations has already been emphasised. In consequence much of the discussion of poverty in the context of wider structural inequalities seems to have been prompted by external studies, if only in rejecting or criticising them.

The main recent study by OECD on income inequality has already been mentioned. In France two main objections have been raised to this: the effect of the underestimates of income, and the use of tax returns for the French material rather than household surveys as in most of the other countries. INSEE's correction for the first factor in the dispersion of net incomes after taxes and benefits results in changes to INSEE's own data, which generally bring it closer to the distribution by deciles published by OECD. This adjustment does not change the ranking among countries but is carefully established in an article in *Economie et Statistique* over a number of pages with detailed tables.[71]

The failure to use French household surveys is presented in the summary preceding the article as much more significant. Yet only two paragraphs and no table is given to 'an example' of the difference this might make. By unpublished INSEE data from 1971 pre-tax incomes, France would apparently have moved away from being amongst the most unequal with the USA and Canada to a position much closer to Germany, showing a distribution 'appreciably less unequal' ('sensible-ment moins inégalitaire') than the tax returns. The ratio between the top and the bottom decile, it is stressed, would drop from 20.7:1 to 14.6:1.[72] In fact, according to my calculations, it would not change the ranking by pre-tax income at all: France would remain third, although at the top of the middle group rather than at the extreme with the USA and Canada.

Even if one accepts these criticisms of the OECD study, the extent of income inequality in France remains significant. As one critic himself points out, this is due in part to the large size of the French self-employed sector, where income inequality generally tends to be much greater than among employees. But he continues by admitting that the distribution of wages is also wider in France than in countries such as Germany or England (sic).[73]

The OECD study reports 'a general trend away from inequality during the 1956–70 period', even though improvements in the bottom decile may be partly accounted for by changes in definition over time. But 'all the measures of inequality indicate a decline in inequality', and 'much of this has probably been the result of the declining size of the agricultural sector.' Similarly, the OECD analysis of income maintenance reported a decline in poverty in France up to 1970, even though it still remained above the other countries studied.[74]

TABLE 4.3   *Income distribution by deciles as percentage, France 1970*

Deciles	Income before tax			Income after tax & contributions		
	without contributions	with contributions				
	INSEE	INSEE	OECP	INSEE	OECD	INSEE distribution corrected
1st decile	1.1	1.1	1.5	1.1	1.4	1.5
2nd decile	2.7	2.7	2.8	2.9	2.9	2.9
3rd decile	4.2	4.2	4.2	4.6	4.2	4.4
4th decile	5.6	5.8	5.7	5.9	5.6	5.7
5th decile	7.0	7.1	7.1	7.5	7.4	7.0
6th decile	8.2	8.8	8.7	9.5	8.9	8.4
7th decile	10.0	10.5	10.4	11.0	9.7	9.9
8th decile	13.2	12.8	12.6	13.3	13.0	12.2
9th decile	16.6	16.5	16.0	16.4	16.5	15.8
10th decile	31.4	30.5	31.0	27.8	30.4	32.3
Ratios:						
10th decile/1st decile	28.5	27.7	20.7	25.3	21.7	21.5
9th & 10th deciles/ 1st & 2nd decile	12.6	12.4	10.9	11.1	10.9	10.9

The full extent of inequality is clearly concealed by the lack of both comprehensive and detailed data on France for any one point in time, let alone over any period. The writers who pursue the theme of inequality and avoid confusing it with the social problem literature tend to note the data deficiency and then use material from many countries other than France, particularly the USA. However, the picture of inequality and poverty presented by international organisations has been supported by internal studies of the inequality of income and wealth. In April 1976 CERC published a report showing that incomes varied as much then as twenty years ago: the differential had widened till 1968 and then narrowed because the trade unions led by the Confédération Générale du Travail (CGT) forced the employers' groups to accept the need to help the very poorest by marked increases for the 'smigards'.[75]

The emergence of other reports on wealth and fortunes in 1976 showed that any general narrowing of earnings between manual and non-manual workers since 1968 was likely to be more than offset for professionals and middle management by their increased wealth. In one study the professions held on average seventy-five times as much wealth in bonds, stocks and shares as manual workers and twenty times as much as middle management. Yet this INSEE analysis did not attempt to allocate 40 per cent of wealth among the different groups, and *Le Monde* reports that most experts believe that this had the effect of concealing the full inequality of wealth. Certainly inheritance and general intra-family transfers are seen as the most important factors accounting for the concentration of wealth, with the economic power accruing to the professional a significant, though by no means comparable cause. The opposition in 1976 to the President's announced intention of introducing a capital gains tax, let alone a more rigorous wealth tax, suggests that there is likely to be little immediate change, even the proposed scheme would exempt 'inherited Capital and items held "for a long time" '.[76]

In 1977 the pattern of persistent and indeed growing inequality was underlined by the findings of a study of savings and wealth for 1975, which showed that inequalities had doubled over the previous twenty-five years. Wealth was estimated to be twice as unequally distributed as income in France with 10 per cent of households owning half the wealth and the 33 per cent at the bottom having only 0.5 per cent of the nation's wealth. The ratio between the median of these two groups was 330:1. France was judged to have much greater inequality in wealth than 'the other developed countries'. The authors of the report have drawn attention to the fact that many of the factors contributing to a slowing-down in the growth of inequality since 1968 are now becoming less important: 'the era which is starting seems less favourable to a reduction in the distribution of wealth'.[77]

At CREDOC Victor Scardigli and Pierre-Alain Mercier have given particular importance to the meticulous examination of the relation between poverty and inequality. Much of their subsequent work has yet to be published, but summary reports bear out, and indeed reinforce, their original hypotheses in 1972 that the persistence of very deprived groups is not simply an accident of the development of advanced industrial societies but is an integral and essential part of the mode of production which is dependent upon inequality and poverty to produce an increase in material wealth; and the cumulation of handicaps of every type sharply restricts the chances of upward mobility for those from poverty-stricken backgrounds.[78] But they do not explain the reasons that the proportion in poverty, the extent and form of their deprivation, and the vulnerability of particular groups may all vary among market societies. These issues deserve particular analysis on a comparative basis within the framework suggested.

As one illustration, the greater concern among the French than the British with social injustice was mentioned at the start of this paper. A study of oil refinery workers in the two countries underlines the importance of relating such perceptions to the objective position of groups in each society. Duncan Gallie found that most of the French workers 'were dissatisfied with their standard of living', while 'over 90 per cent of the British workers said that they thought it was very or pretty good'. Yet post-tax incomes were on average 38 per cent higher for these French workers and they 'were very much better-off than the British in relation to average manual worker wages in their region'.

A wider comparative study of inequalities, the population's awareness of them and the reference groups used for the evaluation of one's own position might help to account for differing patterns of poverty and the extent or lack of policy concern for the deprivation of particular groups.[79]

Conclusions

On the basis of external studies there is considerable poverty in France. This conclusion is supported and often vividly illustrated by French publications but they generally lack the clear definitions and rigorous analysis which permit a more detailed comparison of poverty among different groups and in different areas. The political debate on low pay maintained by some of the trade unions has led to recurrent, though scarcely persistent, attention to the minimum wage. The 'Accords de Grenelle', which increased SMIG to help the lowest-paid, resulted from the sharp political tensions of 1968.

In 1978 party after party had come to offer a 37 per cent increase to the four million native and foreign 'smigards' in the election manoeuvring. This would bring the minimum wage to 2,400 francs a month on a 40-hour week and again reduce income differentials – and, some claim, increase unemployment and bankruptcies. Low pay, the most publicly-debated aspect of poverty in France, remains very much a political issue, particularly kept alive by groups on the left, and any major improvement appears very dependent on the outcome of events such as the national elections.[80]

Other issues of poverty have not received the same political attention, even on an irregular basis. However, improvements in the minimum wage, combined with an explicit family policy, despite a traditionally greater emphasis on horizontal rather than vertical redistribution, have provided support for families on low incomes. In consequence family poverty appears to be more effectively prevented or reduced in France than in other groups. More recent evidence from the preliminary findings of a pilot survey for the EEC suggest that 'in comparison with people at other stages of life, families with children are less often poor in France than in Britain or Germany'.[81]

Despite the gains from the reforms of the 1970s, there does not appear to be any well-informed and firmly-established lobby or official body to prevent the poor falling behind again, as they did with the complacent assumption of effective family policies against poverty that Parodi and Schorr criticised in the mid 1960s.

As for the old, the immigrant and the agricultural worker whom Maurice Parodi believed to be most vulnerable then, there is little clear evidence of major improvements for them now.[82] Any presumption of gradually diminishing poverty and inequality, as recent reforms are implemented and take effect, seems at best optimistic in its equation of promise, or even proposal, with performance. The long-entrenched resistance to major changes that would help those most vulnerable to poverty encourages gloomier forecasts of widening inequalities and greater poverty.

Notes

Some of the preparatory work for this chapter has been uncomfortably like looking through the wrong end of a telescope. Reporting on a country in which he is living, a writer may check for himself claims that appear mistaken or oversimplified before deciding whether to accept or reject them; unlike most of the authors in this volume, I have not been able to do this. As someone who has been involved in the first-hand study, however limited, of poverty in some three countries, as well as attempting comparative reviews of the literature over the last dozen years, I am particularly conscious of the need to caution the reader.

Because of these problems I am all the more grateful to those people who helped me by collecting and providing data and by advising me on their interpretation. I owe a particular debt to Duncan Gallie, who responded very capably to many questions and, both encouragingly and frustratingly, stimulated many more; to Jennefer Brown for her thoughtful and thorough research assistance; and to Jean Smith who dealt with the secretarial tasks more efficiently than I deserved. I would also like to thank for their particularly helpful advice Paul Paillat, Jane Marceau, Gaston Banderier and Peter Willmott.

References

1 Malcolm Sawyer, *Income Distribution in OECD Countries*, Economic Outlook Occasional Studies, OECD, Paris, 1976; and OECD, *Public Expenditure on Income Maintenance Programmes*, Studies in Resource Allocation no. 3, OECD, Paris, July 1976. Both tend to be described in the French literature as 'OECD reports', in the same way as the regular annual country reports are described. Data on France in the reports of the Royal Commission on the Distribution of Income and Wealth (see for example Reports 5 and 6) have been mainly taken from Sawyer's study, but for discussion of this see their Background Paper no. 4: T. Stark, *Distribution of Income in Eight Countries*, HMSO, December 1977.

2 *Le Monde, 1976: l'Espoir Déçu*: 'L'Année Economique et Sociale', Paris, January 1977, containing articles published in 1976 but not precisely dated, written mainly by Gilbert Mathieu; pp. 117 and 127; pp. 122 and 120.

3 Commission of the European Communities, *The Perception of Poverty in Europe*, Brussels, March 1977, especially pp. 66–72.

4 Jane Marceau, *Class and Status in France: Economic Change and Social Immobility 1945–1975*, Oxford University Press, 1977, p. 185: a valuable source book and basic reference for anyone attempting to analyse part of the French social structure.

5 Pierre Laroque, introduction to *La Sécurité Sociale en France*, La Documentation Française, Paris, 1975, pp. 5 and 6.

6 Reported to the author at the time by Alwine de Vos van Steenwijk of Aide à Toute Détresse; Alvin Schorr, *Social Security and Social Services in France*, Department of Health and Welfare, Washington DC, 1965, p. 5.

7 Paul-Marie de la Gorce, *La France Pauvre*, Bernard Grasset, Paris, 1965. The influence of Michael Harrington, *The Other America*, Macmillan, New York, 1962, is clear, and the book is dedicated to 'the Other France' (p. 25).

8 Jules Klanfer, *L'Exclusion Sociale*, Bureau de recherches sociales, Paris, 1965, is based on this conference and contains some of the papers. See also the publications of A. à T. D. in the mid-1960s, *Familles Inadaptées et relations humaines* and *Familles Inadaptées, leur logement, leur travail*, Bureau de recherches sociales, Paris; and their journal *Igloos*.

9 Maurice Parodi, 'France', *Low Income Groups and Methods of Dealing with their Problems*, Papers for a Trade Union Seminar 1965, OECD, Paris, 1969.

10 Jean Labbens, *Le Quart Monde*, Aide à Toute Détresse, Paris, 1969.

11 Pierre-Alain Mercier, *Les Inégalités en France*, CREDOC, Paris, January 1974, is the major summary of this work to date. Shorter papers by Victor Scardigli are cited below, see references 21 and 38.

12 Jack Hayward, *The One and Indivisible French Republic*, Weiden-feld & Nicolson, London, 1973, pp. 82 and 178.
13 For exceptions, see note 21. The annual report of the VII National Plan is to include changes in the net resources of different family types among its social indicators to allow a better assessment of the impact of family policy on the distribution of family incomes: Alain Charraud, 'Les ressources des familles types de salariés', *Economie et Statistique*, 89, May 1977, pp. 3 and 5 note 3.
14 Marceau, op. cit., p. 4.
15 René Lenoir, *Les Exclus: Un Français sur Dix*, Editions du Seuil, Paris, 2nd edition, 1974, Annexe II, p. 153, with data, excluding the physically and mentally handicapped, from a study on the pre-vention of 'inadaptation' (maladjustment) undertaken in 1972 for the Minister of Public Health.
16 Correspondence with Gaston Banderier, September 1977.
17 Arnold J. Heidenheimer, Hugh Heclo and Carolyn Teich Adams, *Comparative Public Policy: The Politics of Social Choice in Europe and America*, Macmillan, London, 1976, p. 239. See also Parodi, op. cit., pp. 36–40.
18 OECD, op. cit., p. 72.
19 Ibid., pp. 64–67, Tables 26 and 27.
20 Ibid., p. 65, citing Lenoir, op. cit., though he clearly says 'one in ten, some five million' but 'at least fifteen million still live in con-ditions of poverty and deprivation,' basing this on his analysis of a CREDOC study of income in 1968 (pp. 27–8), a calculation com-parable to Launay's estimate. See also Lionel Stoleru, *Vaincre la Pauvreté dans les pays riches*, Flammarion, Paris, 1974, p. 52; Jules Klanfer, *Le Sous-développement Humaine*, Les Editions Ouvrières, Paris, 1967, p. 120; Jean-Pierre Launay, *La France Sous-développée: 15 millions de pauvres*, Dunod-Actualité, Paris, 1970. Table 1 appears in Stoleru, op. cit., p. 52.
21 OECD, op. cit., pp. 64 and 67. This and the following section draw particularly on Nicole Borel, 'Les bas salaires en juillet 1974', *Economie et Statistique*, 62, December 1974; Marceau, op. cit., ch. 3, 'Access to Rewards'; René Padieu, 'Les bas salaires', *Economie et Statistique*, 39, November 1972, pp. 17–29; and Victor Scardigli, *Social Policies and the Working Poor in France*, CREDOC mimeo, Paris, 1970.
22 Launay, op. cit., p. 1.
23 Borel, op. cit., pp. 5 and 4.
24 *Le Monde*, op. cit., pp. 120–1, quoting a study by CERC (Centre d'étude des revenus et des coûts), published in April 1976.
25 Borel, op. cit., pp. 7ff.
26 Ibid., p. 10.
27 Scardigli, op. cit., p. 3.
28 Klanfer, op. cit., 1967.
29 Scardigli, op. cit., p. 55.
30 De la Gorce, op. cit., ch. 6.

31 *The Guardian*, 11 May 1973; for more detailed discussion of earlier data, see Launay, op. cit., ch. 8.
32 Elisabeth Vlassenko and Serge Volkoff, 'Les salaires des étrangers en France en 1972', *Economie et Statistique*, 70, September 1975, pp. 47–54.
33 *The Guardian*, op. cit., and *Sunday Times* Business News section, 14 March 1976.
34 Launay, op. cit., p. 113.
35 R. Lawson, 'Social Security, Employment and the Single-Parent Family' in A. Samuels (ed.), *Social Security and Family Law*, Oceana Publications, London, 1980. See also Marceau, op. cit., pp. 173–5 and 167; Barbara N. Rodgers, 'Family Policy in France', *Journal of Social Policy*, 1975, 4:2, pp. 113–28; and Schorr, op. cit.
36 Marceau, op. cit., pp. 59–60.
37 Mercier, op. cit., pp. 60–2, and quoting Paul Paillat, 'Influence du nombre d'enfants sur le niveau de vie de la famille – Evolution en France de 1950 à 1970', *Population*, June 1971.
38 'Developments and Trends in Social Security, 1974–1977', *International Social Security Review*, XXX:3, 1977, pp. 312–13.
39 Frank Field, Molly Meacher and Chris Pond, *To Him Who Hath: A Study of Poverty and Taxation*, Penguin Books, Harmondsworth, 1977, p. 222 and Table 38, p. 223.
40 Charraud, op. cit., pp. 3–4, Tables 5 and 10.
41 Ibid., Table 10, p. 18.
42 Scardigli, op. cit., p. 55; and *International Social Security Review*, op. cit.
43 Gaston Banderier and A. Charraud, *Données Statistiques sur les Familles*, les collections d'INSEE, Paris, M 48, November 1975, pp. 24–6, Table 58, and p. 69.
44 Lawson, op. cit.; and *International Social Security Review*, op. cit., p. 313.
45 Lawson, op. cit.; Claude Ameline et Pierre Verdier, 'L'Aide Sociale à L'Enfance', *Revue Française des Affaires Sociales*, 1977:1, January-March, pp. 66 and 59; see also on social aid and other means-tested benefits in France, Cindy Stevens, *Public Assistance in France*, Bell, London, 1973.
46 Hélène Roze, 'Impôts directs et transferts sociaux: effets sur l'échelle des revenus, de 1962 à 1970', *Economie et Statistique*, 59, September 1974, Table 7 and Graph 1; Marceau, op. cit., pp. 187ff.; A. Beattie, 'France', *Pensions, Inflation and Growth: A Comparative Study of the Elderly in the Welfare State*, ed. Thomas Wilson, Heinemann, London, 1974; see also J.J. Dupeyroux, *Evolution et Tendances des Systèmes de Sécurité Sociale*, CECA, Luxembourg, 1966.
47 Paul Paillat, 'Old People', *Low Income Groups and Methods of Dealing with their Problems*, Papers for a Trade Union Seminar 1965, OECD, Paris, 1969, Tables 1 and 2, p. 180.
48 Pierre Laroque, *Politique de la Vieillesse: Rapport de la Commission*

d'Etude des Problèmes de la Vieillesse, La Documentation Française, Paris, 1962; Parodi, op. cit., p. 41; Marguerite Perrot, Gaston Banderier and Serge Volkoff, *Les Revenus des Personnes Agées,* les collections d'INSEE, Paris, M. 52, March 1976; and Mercier, op. cit., p. 379.

49 Launay, op. cit., p. 68.

50 OECD, op. cit., Table 3, p. 22; Table 31, p. 76; and p. 75.

51 Perrot *et al.,* op. cit., part I; and Sawyer, op. cit., p. 26, footnote 50.

52 Launay, op. cit., p. 71.

53 Ibid., pp. 69–70; and studies cited by Henri Bartoli, *Economie et Création Collective,* Economica, Paris, 1977, pp. 436 and 435. Without any apparent source, he adds 'several thousand old people die of hunger in the Paris region every year'. On the gap-filling functions of social aid and other schemes, see Stevens, op. cit.

54 Launay, op. cit., pp. 74 and 77, giving no date or fuller reference to the survey cited.

55 Perrot *et al.,* op. cit., p. 87; Guy Desplanques, 'A 35 les instituteurs ont encore 41 ans à vivre, les manoeuvres 34 ans seulement', *Economie et Statistique,* 49, October 1973 – data from 1955 to 1965.

56 *National Institute Economic Review,* November 1977, Table 4, p. 32; Joyanna Moy and Constance Sorrentino, 'An analysis of unemployment in nine industrial countries', *Monthly Labor Review,* April 1977, Table 2, p. 15, show French unemployment rising from 2.8 per cent in 1970 to 4.3 per cent in 1975 with the data adjusted to US concepts, compared with a rise from 1.7 per cent to 4.1 per cent in the official French rate.

57 *Bulletin Mensuel de Statistique,* 10, October 1977, Table 2, p. 10. *Sunday Times,* Business News Section, 14 March 1976.

58 Marceau, op. cit., p. 68; Moy and Sorrentino, op. cit., p. 19.

59 *Economie et Statistique,* 86, February 1977, p. 60; Marceau, op. cit., pp. 68 and 188–9.

60 François Michon, *Chômeurs et Chômage,* Presses Universitaires de France, Paris, 1975.

61 Launay, op. cit., pp. 84 and 95. Pierre Aiach, *Vivre à Folie-Mericourt: étude des processus cumulatifs d'inégalités,* Institut National de la Santé et de la Recherche Médicale, Le Vesinet, July 1975, p. 181.

62 Parodi, op. cit.; Peter Willmott and Pierre Aiach, 'Deprivation in Paris and London', *Sharing Inflation?*: Poverty Report 1976, ed. Peter Willmott, Temple Smith, London, 1976, p. 174; Scardigli, op. cit., pp. 35–40; and Launay, op. cit., p. 25.

63 Marceau, op. cit., p. 38; and pp. 69ff. Among the studies of Noisy-Le-Grand, see Jean Labbens, *La Condition Sous-prolétarienne*; L'Héritage du Passé, Paris, 1965.

64 Labbens, op. cit., 1965; and 'Reflections on the concept of a "culture of poverty" ', Working Paper of the International Committee on Poverty Research, Paris, 1966.

65 Marceau, op. cit., pp. 70 and 192 and sources quoted there. See also

Labbens, op. cit., 1969 on temporary camps, and ch. 9 on those poorly-housed in the XVIII arrondissement of Paris.

66 Willmott and Aiach, op. cit., pp. 171ff; Roger Lawson and Cindy Stevens, 'Housing Allowances in West Germany and France', *Journal of Social Policy*, 3:3, 1974, pp. 230-2.

67 Borel, op. cit., p. 12; Mercier, op. cit., p. 364.

68 OECD, *Low Incomes in Agriculture*, Paris, OECD, 1964, p. 172; and Parodi, op. cit., p. 42; OECD, op. cit., 1976, p. 67.

69 Marceau, op. cit., pp. 36-7, and Launay, op. cit., ch. 7.

70 Britanny and also Corsica, according to the data for the late 1960s quoted by Mercier, op. cit., p. 365.

71 Jean Bégué, 'Remarques sur une étude de L'OCDE concernant la répartition des revenus dans divers pays', *Economie et Statistique*, 84, December 1976, pp. 97-104: Table 3 is taken from p. 101.

72 Ibid., p. 104.

73 Ibid.

74 Sawyer, op. cit., pp. 26 and 27.

75 Quoted in *Le Monde*, op. cit., pp. 120-1.

76 Sources for this paragraph are given in *Le Monde*, op. cit., pp. 122 and 124; see also pp. 129-30 for a discussion of wealth tax; Marceau, op. cit., p. 192, and on ignorance of the extent of inequality, p. 185.

77 From reports by Gilbert Mathieu in the *Sélection Hebdomadaire du journal 'Le Monde'*, 1 to 7 December 1977 and 20 to 26 April 1978; see also Marie-Françoise Masfety-Klein, *Regard sur l'actualité*, Documentation Française, Paris, October 1977.

78 Pierre-Alain Mercier and Victor Scardigli, 'Contribution à l'étude des causes individuelles et collectives de pauvreté: Rapport d'avancement des travaux au 1 Oct. 1975', CNRS, Paris, 1975, pp. 1-2.

79 Duncan Gallie, *In Search of the New Working Class*, Cambridge University Press, Cambridge, 1978, p. 58: see also W.G. Runciman, *Relative Deprivation and Social Justice*, Routledge & Kegan Paul, London, 1966.

80 *The Guardian*, 1 March 1978.

81 Letter from Peter Willmott, January 1978; report to be published in Peter Willmott, Phyllis Willmott and Linda McDowell, *Poverty and Social Policy in Europe: Pilot Studies in Britain, Germany and France*.

82 Parodi, op. cit., pp. 56-61; and Schorr, op. cit., pp. 37-38.

5 Poverty and inequality in Ireland

Séamus Ó Cinnéide

Summary

Compared with other EEC countries, Ireland has a high dependency ratio and a low GNP per head of population. For these if for no other reasons poverty is likely to be a more serious social problem in Ireland than in these neighbouring countries. However, we know very little about poverty in Ireland. It has been the subject of research and discussion for only a decade: the 'rediscovery of poverty' in Ireland happened around 1971. Even still the most basic information is missing. There are no comprehensive statistics on income distribution in Ireland. It is possible to build up a picture of income distribution using data from a variety of sources. In 1971 it was estimated in this way that at least 20 per cent of the population were poor. In this chapter an attempt is made to update this estimate to 1975. There seems to have been some positive redistribution in the meantime, but the conclusion as to the extent of poverty in Ireland at present (or in 1975 which is the most recent date dealt with here) must remain very tentative. The greatest deficiency in existing incomes data is that there is no information on low wage earners. With regard to the wider aspects of inequality, such Irish data as are available show the expected association between low income (or low social class) and lack of household facilities, and health and education problems.

Background

Poverty, whatever it is, however it is defined, is enmeshed in the particular social structure and economy to which it belongs in a highly complex kind of way: it can hardly be discussed in isolation. At the outset then it is necessary to highlight some distinctive features of the Irish background which affect poverty and the discussion of poverty in Ireland.[1]

First of all, the structure of the population of Ireland is different from that of other EEC countries because of demographic trends which

124

have made Ireland unique in the past and which are still very much at variance with those elsewhere. The distinctive Irish population trends were a high level of emigration, low marriage rate, high average age at marriage and high fertility. With regard to total population the Irish experience has recently been summarised as follows:[2]

> In the second half of the last century, Ireland suffered an enormous population decline, from 6,529,000 in 1841 to 3,322,000 in 1901: in the first half of this century the fall continued, almost without interruption, but at a slower rate – by 1961 the total population had fallen to its lowest level of 2,818,000. However, after 1961, with the onset of greatly increased industrial and general economic growth (stimulated by the First Programme for Economic Expansion) the Irish population began to show consistent increases. The 1966 Census recorded a population of 2,884,000, some 66,000 higher than the 1961 level and the next Census in 1971 yielded a total population of 2,978,000, representing a further increase of 94,000. At this time a further watershed in the Irish demographic scene was reached when, for the first time in well over a century, the tide of emigration was turned. Since 1972 the annual estimates of net migration have indicated small but consistent net inflows.

With regard to marriage rate, age at marriage and fertility rate, the Irish statistics have changed dramatically over the past fifteen years so that they are now nearer European norms; but vital differences remain. In the past the combined effect of low nuptiality, late marriage and high fertility was a birth-rate which was in line with that in other countries. The fact that now more people are getting married earlier has not been offset by a matching decline in fertility, which means that the birth-rate is significantly higher than that in other EEC countries. The birth-rate for Ireland for 1971 was 22.7 per thousand; in other countries it ranged from 12.7 in Germany to 17.2 in France and the Netherlands. Despite a dramatic decline in fertility in recent years, because of the composition of the population the birth-rate is expected to remain high in the foreseeable future.

The significance of these features and trends is most clearly seen by reference to the present composition of the Irish population. The Irish population is particularly young (31 per cent under 15 years of age, 55 per cent under 30) and the overall dependency ratio is high, with obvious implications for public expenditure, particularly on social infrastructure. The most recent population projections (Keating, 1977) postulate a decline in the dependency ratio – but not a dramatic one – to 71.2 in 1981 and 68.9–69.1 in 1986. It is worth mentioning too that a very high proportion of the population in Ireland, 48 per cent, live in rural areas and towns of under 1,500 people; and about a quarter of the work force is engaged in agriculture (including forestry and fishing); this latter figure is the highest for the EEC countries.[3]

The pattern of employment is at once a demographic feature and a feature of the economy. But more needs to be said about the Irish economy as compared with that of the other EEC countries. Taking GNP per head as an appropriate measure, Ireland is by far the least wealthy of the nine EEC countries. In addition:[4]

> [it] can be seen that Ireland's rate of growth of product and of product *per capita* was rather lower than in most of the other EEC countries. Nevertheless, it is notable that the Irish growth experience was considerably better than that of the UK despite the close trading and other relations between the two countries. However, if Ireland is to close the income gap with its EEC partners, a far higher growth rate of GNP *per capita* will be required.

It is against the background of the Irish demographic and economic conditions outlined in this brief conspectus that the discussion from here on must be read.

Rediscovery of poverty

Any attempt to collect and collate data on 'poverty' in Ireland will reveal that there is very little material from before 1970 or so; what exists, which is little enough, dates mainly from the period between then and now. It would seem that at the beginning of the 1970s a rediscovery of poverty took place in Ireland.[5] Perhaps it is not surprising that this happened at a time when Ireland was more prosperous than it had ever been in its recent history.

During the nineteenth century, when Ireland was governed from London, poverty in Ireland was the subject of numerous British parliamentary enquiries and reports by philanthropic bodies and individuals. Many of them centred on the proposal to establish a Poor Law system of workhouses, which proposal was implemented in 1838, and on the subsequent operation of the Poor Law.[6] The nadir of the welfare of the population of Ireland, at least in the social and economic sense, is probably marked by the Great Famine of 1847, when a million people died and a million people emigrated within five years.[7] There is ample documentary evidence of the widespread extent of poverty in Ireland, both in the countryside and in the cities in the last century and at the beginning of this century.[8] The teeming slums of Dublin, in which a quarter of the people of that city lived, are a recent memory; an acute sense of shared material deprivation is part of the mental equipment of the large proportion of Irish people who were brought up on small farms until comparatively recent times.[9]

When these images were beginning to fade, new impressions of poverty were being projected by objective observers. The main way this began to happen was in assertions about the inadequacy of income maintenance payments. Even in 1945 the chairman of the National Health Insurance Society, the social insurance agency, reported that '[everyone] realises how inadequate the sickness and disability benefits are, and how necessary it is to increase them'.[10] In 1964 Kaim-Caudle, in what was the first independent examination of social security provisions in Ireland, concluded that '[the] present rates of social assistance appear to be inadequate'.[11]

The 112,000 old age pensioners over 70 received in 1963 (£1.63) per week without any additional allowance for rent. . . . It requires little imagination to realise that these pensions are quite inadequate by mid-20th century standards. Yet the (£1.63) received by an old age pensioner must appear princely to the unemployed with one adult dependant who in a rural area receives (£1.73), i.e. (£0.87) per adult per week in assistance payments. Such a man, if he were to purchase nothing whatsoever, not pay anything for rent, fuel and electricity could not buy enough food to maintain himself on a prison diet. It is extremely difficult to understand how ten thousands of people can manage to exist on unemployment assistance at all. They have to rely on help from some quarter - neighbours, emigrants' remittances, family, religious orders, food centres or charities.

In 1963 social insurance payments were about 40-50 per cent higher than the corresponding assistance rates; i.e., an unemployed worker who was properly insured got 40-50 per cent more than an unemployed worker who was not properly insured and whose eligibility for income maintenance depended on a means test. But even those receiving social insurance benefits were badly off.[12]

While the rates are certainly not liberal and hardly adequate, people receiving social insurance benefits and pensions may possibly exist without help from other sources. Still the difficulties would be enormous. . . . It would require a woman well above average intelligence, virtue and industry to make ends meet on such an income. There would be no margin for luxuries such as cigarettes, beer, holidays, entertainment; all clothing purchased would have to be second-hand and household goods could not be replaced. If the parents were more ordinary average kind of people the family would get into debt, live in squalor and suffer from malnutrition.

Although there had been improvements in the meantime Geary and Hughes were sounding the same critical note six years later:[13]

We have calculated, by reference to occupational distribution, that if the people out of work in a week in December 1967 were at work at wages ruling at the beginning of the year, their re- numeration would be £414,000. Actual payment of unemployment benefit and unemployment assistance was about £135,000, equal therefore to 32 per cent of their working pay. In the classical works of the unemployment Acts a person qualified for aid when 'able and willing to work but unable to find suitable employment'. That such people, through no fault of their own, should find their earnings reduced by 68 per cent to a level which must be near sub- sistence, is an affront to natural justice and a burden on the cons- cience of citizens in general.

Apart from these comments on the social security system, there was little else. In a report dated 1973, 'An Agenda for Poverty Research', a working group established by the directors of five research institutes engaged in social science research presented what was intended as an exhaustive reference list of published material on poverty in Ireland. The only items dating from before 1970 were an article on the distri- bution of non-agricultural incomes, the report on a manpower survey, and reports on studies done in a poor urban area and in two under- developed rural areas, as well as the work by Kaim-Caudle already mentioned.[14] 1970 saw the publication of an analysis of non-agricul- tural unemployment cited above,[15] an account of Home Assistance, the residual public assistance service,[16] and an attitude survey which referred to low pay.[17]

But undoubtedly the main event in the rediscovery of poverty was the Kilkenny Conference on Poverty held in November 1971. The con- ference was organised by the Council for Social Welfare, an advisory body established by the Roman Catholic bishops. It was attended by nearly 170 people, including representatives of the churches, religious orders, the political parties, government agencies, the social partners, the universities and voluntary bodies engaged in social services. Five papers were read at the conference and eight others were circulated for discussion.[18]

The conference attracted a good deal of attention at the time and led to further discussion and action which is still going on. In particular it seems to have influenced the Labour Party (which was the minority party in a two-party coalition government from 1973 to 1977),[19] the trade union movement,[20] the Roman Catholic Church[21] and social re- searchers. Its continuing influence can be seen most clearly in refer- ences to the major finding of the conference that at least 20 per cent of the population were (are?) poor. This was the conclusion of a paper on 'The Extent of Poverty in Ireland' presented at the conference.[22]

The figure of 20 per cent, and the numbers from which it was derived have been extensively quoted;[23] in fact they have taken on a life of their own, often being accepted as given without reference to their provenance, often being rediscovered and attributed to new authorities.[24] The validity of the findings, and how they are arrived at, will be referred to later.

The most tangible effects of the rediscovery of poverty were government initiatives. Six months after the Kilkenny conference, a leading member of Fine Gael, the then majority opposition party, made a major speech on poverty in the Dail (lower house of parliament). He had found the conference 'a profound experience, a spiritual experience' and pointed out that:[25]

the level of poverty in this country today in many sectors is something which is intolerable and which is causing social unrest which, if left to fester, could undermine our society.

Within a year the Labour Party, the minority opposition party, were drafting a report on *Poverty in Ireland*. Then in February 1973 there was a general election. The two opposition parties made a pre-election coalition agreement and published a joint policy statement, the *Statement of Intent* or *Fourteen Point Plan*. One of the fourteen points read:[26]

The elimination of poverty and the ending of social injustice will be a major priority in the next government's programme. It is conservatively estimated that under Fianna Fail a quarter of our people live in poverty. The social policy of the new government will bring immediate assistance to those in need and lay the foundations of long-term policy that will root out the causes of low incomes, bad housing and poor educational facilities.

In the event the National Coalition won a majority and formed the new government. The first Budget was presented shortly after they took office. It included exceptional provisions for increases in income maintenance payments, which were made possible, partly, at least, by substantial savings to the Irish Exchequer following Ireland's accession to the European Communities in January 1973. Speeches on the Budget represented a consensus on the desirability of helping the 'less well-off' and the figure of 20 per cent poor was quoted.[27]

Apart from the increases in income maintenance payments, of which the increases in Children's Allowances were the most dramatic, the major initiative of the 1973-7 National Coalition Government with regard to poverty was the establishment, in May 1974, of the National Committee on Pilot Schemes to Combat Poverty, although the results of this initiative have yet to be seen. The Social Action Programme of the European Communities, adopted the previous December, had included for the first time provision for the promotion of pilot schemes to combat poverty in member countries. In advance of EEC plans the Irish schemes were launched. The National Committee was in effect a new agency funded by the Irish Government and the EEC, but with freedom to plan its own activities. These activities are now in progress.[28] The period since the Kilkenny Conference in 1971 has seen the publication of a number of other reports on poverty. These will be referred to later.

This section was intended to convey that since 1970 there has been more analysis and discussion of poverty in Ireland than there was perhaps in the previous half century. Even in the past seven years efforts have been diffused, interest has not been consistently sustained, and a lot of the groundwork remains to be done, as this chapter will show.

An official poverty line?

There is no official poverty line in Ireland: there is no income which is officially regarded by the government, or any government agency, as being the cut-off point between poverty and non-poverty. An official poverty line is arrived at usually either as the result of research or by reference to the basic rate of income maintenance which is provided, on the understanding that it provides an 'adequate' living for the recipient. But there has been no officially sponsored research designed to establish what a minimum adequate income, or poverty line, would be; nor are the lowest incomes maintained by social security or public assistance payments in Ireland justified as being adequate or appropriate.

Income maintenance in Ireland, as in most countries, is a dual system comprising a variety of social insurance and social assistance schemes. The first government payments were introduced under the Poor Law in 1847; this was Outdoor Relief payable on an arbitrary basis to a very restricted range of destitute people. In 1923 the Outdoor Relief was renamed Home Assistance, and in 1977 this scheme was replaced by one called Supplementary Welfare Allowances.[29] The scope of the poor law provision was whittled away in two ways: by the building up of a social insurance system and by the introduction of special means-tested public assistance schemes for particular groups of beneficiaries.

The foundations of social insurance were laid in 1911 with the establishment of a scheme of sickness and unemployment benefits. A marriage benefit for women contributors was introduced in 1929, a contributory widows' pension scheme in 1935, and a contributory old-age pension in 1965. The first specific social assistance scheme was that for old-age pensions introduced in 1908; the general Home Assistance scheme was further eroded by the introduction of a scheme for Blind Pensions in 1920, an unemployment assistance scheme in 1935, a non-contributory widows' pension scheme in 1935, and provision for persons suffering infectious diseases and uninsured disabled people generally in 1944 and 1954 respectively. In more recent years schemes for deserted wives (1971), unmarried mothers (1973), the wives of prisoners (1974), and older single women below pension age (1974) have been introduced. Altogether there are now eleven separate social insurance schemes (not counting an occupation injuries scheme and a redundancy payments scheme) and eleven social assistance schemes. In addition children's allowances (family allowances, introduced in 1944) are payable in respect of children, regardless of the means or the insurance record of their parents.[30]

The rates of assistance applicable to a single person, a married couple, or any specific income unit, varies according to the scheme involved (the unemployment assistance scheme is the least generous), the person's place of residence if unemployed, and his age if he is an old-age pensioner. The corresponding insurance rates are in all cases higher by anything from 8 per cent to 28 per cent, depending on the other circumstances of the case. Table 5.1, which is based on 1975 rates, illustrates these variations; the categories represented are of course only a fraction of all possible categories.

Is the poverty line represented by the highest insurance rate or the lowest assistance rate; or is it somewhere in between; or is it outside that range altogether? Nobody has ever said, least of all any Minister for Social Welfare. But the question of the adequacy of the income maintenance rates generally can be examined further.

The lowest rates which obtain are those for Unemployment Assistance, both the urban rates and the rural rates. These rates have been increased from time to time, and in recent years every year, or twice a year as in 1976 and 1977, mainly to meet increases in the cost of living. But the rate which applies in any year is only compared to that which applied the previous year; its adequacy is judged accordingly and not by reference to any independent or objective standard. And yet if one goes back to the beginning when Unemployment Assistance was first introduced in 1933 the rates of payment were not said to be adequate. All the Minister could say was that the rates were the best the country could afford.[31]

Certain criticism has been offered concerning the rates of payment which it is proposed to make. The only answer to this criticism is that the total cost of the measure now before the Dail is estimated to reach the maximum limit of the amount which can be provided for this purpose. Any increase in these rates, any amendment of the Bill designed to secure increased expenditure, would defeat the whole purpose of the measure as it could not then be proceeded with.

We have to bear in mind what the possible cost of any suggested change is to be. If there were adequate money available there is not one here I am sure who would not be prepared to suggest an increase in these scales. But we have to bear in mind that any substantial increase in the burden of taxation might have results other than we desire.

One could imagine the Minister's successors saying the same thing if challenged ever after.

TABLE 5.1   *Income maintenance payments, 1975 weekly rates for selected categories of recipients*

Category of Recipient	Social Assistance Rate (£)	Social Insurance Rate (£)	Insurance Rate as % of Assistance Rate
Single Person			
Old-age pensioner, 80 and over	10.05	11.70	116
Old-age pensioner, under 80	9.30	11.05	119
Widow (basic rate)	9.30	10.00	108
Unemployed person (urban area)	8.10	9.90	122
Unemployed person (rural area)	7.75	9.90	128
Single person + 2 children (not including children's allowances)			
Widow (basic rate)	15.50	16.70	108
Married couple			
Unemployed person (urban)	13.95	16.35	117
Married couple + 3 children (not including children's allowances)			
Unemployed person (urban)	20.85	24.30	117

But people depending on income maintenance payments for a living knew they did not have enough. Two-thirds of a small sample of Home Assistance recipients (i.e., recipients of the residuary public assistance payments, most of whom would be getting them as a supplement to other welfare payments) interviewed in Dublin in 1967 said their income was inadequate by amounts which represented 7 to 80 per cent of their income; many said that they had to do without things they needed badly, like food and clothing and fuel.[32] Nearly three quarters

(125 out of 171) of a sample of low-income people, nearly all of whom were depending for a living on income maintenance payments, when interviewed in 1973 said that their income was inadequate; a quarter of them said they needed an extra 50 per cent or more, over and above their current income.[33] In a survey of 444 households done in 1974, 122 households had income maintenance payments as their main source of income; the respondents in 75 of them thought that the rates of payment were 'inadequate' or 'very inadequate'.[34]

These results are indicative but inconclusive. It could be argued that most people, whether depending on income maintenance payments or not, think that their income is inadequate, or at least that they could do with more; on the other hand, people who have got used to living on a very low income may come to accept it uncritically. Perhaps public opinion surveys, designed to establish what the 'poverty line' is, are more reliable.

The results of two surveys done in Ireland are available. The first is a postal survey of 'informed opinion' done in 1974. Questionnaires were sent to 445 social workers, 143 TDs (Members of Parliament) and 318 Assistance Officers, the public service officials who administer Home Assistance at a fieldwork level; questionnaires were completed by 216, 33 and 144 respondents respectively.[35] The second is a public opinion survey of a sample of 1004 persons done in 1976. This was part of a survey done in all EEC countries.[36] In the 1974 survey respondents were asked to state for various categories of family or income unit 'the minimum amount of money per week which [they] would require to cover food, fuel, gas, electricity, clothing, housing, medicines, education and entertainment in order to enjoy a non-poor way of life'. In the 1976 survey respondents were asked: 'In your opinion, what is the real minimum income on which a family of four persons. . .in this area can make ends meet?' Data were also collected for constructing a scale linking the income needs of income units or family units of different compositions. From these two surveys it is possible to calculate the 'poverty line' for four typical income units. The results are given in Table 5.2. For comparison the two sets of results have been given at 1975 prices and the rates of income maintenance payments under three schemes at that time are given too.

There is a remarkable agreement between the results of the two surveys, even though the samples were quite different. The estimates of the Assistance Officers are particularly interesting since they were the people who administered the income maintenance scheme of last resort and whose work involved them in assessing the incomes of poor people and awarding payments accordingly. The poverty line is estimated in nearly every case as being about twice the corresponding rate of official assistance.

TABLE 5.2   *A comparison of minimum income levels for different income units at 1975 weekly rates*

Row no.	Derivations of minimum income levels	Category of income unit			
		(1) Single person (£)	(2) Single parent + 2 children (£)	(3) Couple (£)	(4) Couple + 3 children (£)
	EEC Survey: Irish Public Opinion				
1	"absolute minimum income to make ends meet"	20.88	32.76	30.50	48.38
	Informed opinion survey				
	All informed opinion				
2	'Poverty line' for old-age pensioners	20.24		30.19	
3	'Poverty line' for others	22.23	26.66	32.58	52.19
	Assistance Officers Opinion				
4	'Poverty line' for old-age pensioners	17.93		27.27	
5	'Poverty line' for others	19.24	31.58	28.63	47.09
	Income maintenance Payments (non-contributory + children's allowances)				
6	Old-age Pension (Under 80)	9.30	15.56	18.60/ 13.95	23.22
7	Widows' Pension	9.30	16.86	–	–
8	Unemployment assistance (urban)	8.10	14.61	13.95	23.22

Note: A forthcoming study by E.E. Davis of the Economic and Social Research Institute on 'Public Attitudes towards Poverty and Related Socio-Economic Issues' based on a nationwide sample survey of 2359 respondents in December 1976 will include *inter alia* further data comparable to those at rows 1–5 above.

Sources: Row 1: *The Perception of Poverty in Europe,* Commission of the European Communities, Brussels, 1977; p. 19. The original incomes are given in European Units of Account per month. They have been taken to relate to May 1976 (the time of the survey in Ireland) and have been recalculated at November 1975 prices accordingly.
Rows 2–5: Julian MacAirt, 'The Causes and Alleviation of Irish Poverty', *Social Studies* (Maynooth, Ireland), forthcoming. This is the report of a postal survey of 216 social workers, 33 TDs (members of Parliament) and 144 Assistance Officers (public assistance fieldworkers) done in June 1974. Again the figures have been adapted to November 1975 prices.
Rows 6–7: *Report of the Department of Social Welfare,* The Stationery Office, Dublin, 1976.

In deciding what the poverty line was in 1975 another approach is to up-date the income level accepted as such at the Kilkenny Conference on Poverty in 1971. This is a very safe approach. People who afterwards accepted and quoted the estimate of the extent of poverty arrived at by applying that poverty line did not always advert to the way the poverty line was decided on. However, the estimate was presented as a minimum estimate and none of the wide variety of people who took part in the conference contradicted it or challenged the way it was calculated. To that extent at least it was a poverty line which was accepted as valid.

For the present purpose 1975 has been selected as the year to which to up-date the 1971 poverty line, because it is the most recent year in respect of which a wide range of demographic and incomes data is available. The updating exercise is set out in a schematic way in Table 5.3.

TABLE 5.3   *Calculation of 1975 poverty line for four categories of income unit (weekly rates)*

		Category of Income unit			
Row no.	Description of rates given	(1) Single person	(2) Single parent + 2 children	(3) Married couple	(4) Couple + 3 children
	1971 poverty line				
1	weekly rate, current prices	£5.77	£9.62	£9.62	£15.38
2	as % of 1971 Unemployment Assistance (urban) rates	146%	159%	136%	153%
	1971 poverty line 1975 prices				
3	weekly rate	£9.87	£16.45	£16.45	£26.30
4	as % of 1975 Unemployment Assistance (urban) rates	122%	113%	118%	114%
	1975 poverty line				
5	Unemployment Assistance (urban rates) + 50%	£14.81	£24.68	£24.68	£39.45
6	UA (urban) rate for single person; other rates according to 1976 survey scale	£14.81	£23.24	£21.63	£34.32
	Comparison				
7	'absolute minimum income' (1976) survey	£20.88	£32.76	£30.50	£48.38

The 1971 poverty line as it applied to four categories of income unit is given in row 1, and its relationship to the rates of Unemployment

Assistance which obtained in 1971 are given in row 2: the poverty line was 36 to 59 per cent higher than the Unemployment Assistance rates. If one expresses the 1971 poverty line in 1975 prices the results are as given in row 3. These rates are only 13 to 22 per cent higher than the corresponding Unemployment Assistance rates (row 4), depending on the category of income unit involved, because in the meantime rates of Unemployment Assistance have increased in real terms.

Poverty is relative in that a definition of the poverty line must depend on the levels of incomes generally. It does not, then, seem justifiable to retain the 1971 poverty line in absolute terms: a higher poverty line is suggested for 1975. It must be remembered that the 1971 estimates of the poverty line were proposed as minimum estimates; they have been referred to as conservative estimates.[37] They were made at a time when there was less information available on the adequacy of income maintenance payments and on what people thought the poverty line should be, information which is now available, for example, from the EEC public opinion survey referred to above. The poverty line which emerged from those results was about 100 per cent higher than unemployment assistance rates. In order to err on the side of conservatism the 1975 poverty line which is proposed here is only 50 per cent higher than those rates. Such a poverty line is given in row 5 of Table 5.3. A question remains about the relative weighting of the poverty line for the different categories of income units. In this case it is suggested that the estimates in row 5 can be improved by applying the weighting which is calculated from the results of the EEC public opinion survey. In row 6 the poverty line which has been arrived at for a single person has been retained, and the estimates for the other categories of income unit have been adjusted. Row 6 of Table 5.3 is presented as a reasonable, though conservative, estimate of the poverty line in Ireland in 1975. This amounts to from less than £15 for a single person to just over £34 for a couple with three children. What a sample of the public in Ireland thought were the absolute minimum incomes to make ends meet in 1976, when expressed in 1975 prices, were much higher, as can be seen from row 7. Another useful comparison is that the average weekly industrial earnings for an adult male worker in the transportable goods industries in September 1975 was £45.86.[38]

How many are poor?

In the ordinary way the number of people who are poor would be calculated by analysing income distribution data and determining how many have an income below the poverty line however that is arrived at.

But Irish data on incomes distribution are not adequate to that purpose. The following is a 1976 account of Irish sources of incomes data and a criticism of their limitations.[39]

The data published to date on this topic have been extremely patchy and have been collected and published for purposes other than giving a picture of income distribution. The main sources are the 1965–66 Household Budget Inquiry (urban household incomes); the Farm Management Survey reports (farm enterprise income from farming); computer returns from the Revenue Commissioners' income tax files (income of individuals above the tax threshold); and the earnings surveys in the Census of Industrial Production discontinued since 1968 (individual employee earnings in industry). The Department of Health's uniform national income standard for medical cards means that national and regional figures of the numbers below this standard are available, but the degree to which people's incomes are below is not known. None of these data sources cover the whole population, and, as this was not their main purpose, they do not satisfactorily show the distribution of income.

Since that was written the results of the 1973 Household Budget Survey, which for the first time covered all households both urban and rural, have become available. Apart from the fact that the HBS was intended as a survey of expenditure patterns and not of incomes, the main limitations of the published statistics are that they relate to households rather than family units, or basic income units (as defined below), and that separate information is not given for each size and composition of household.

In estimating the extent of poverty, or indeed in talking about incomes generally, a basic choice has to be made: what is the appropriate unit to consider? The solution adopted here is that each individual person is regarded as a separate income unit unless he/she belongs to the income unit of the husband or parent. This means that there are four kinds of basic income unit. (1) a single person i.e. a person who does not have a wife or a dependent child; (2) a single parent with one or more dependent children; (3) a married couple; and (4) a married couple with one or more dependent children.

None of the sources of data on incomes uses the above classification. However, before commenting on the inadequacy of the data, it is proposed to analyse the population statistics with a view to relating the incomes data to sub-groups within the population. The most recent estimates of the composition of the total population are derived from the Labour Force Survey of 1975.[40] Table 5.4 gives a breakdown of the total population in 1975 (3,104,000) by composition of basic income unit and status within income unit (rows 12–19). It is estimated that there are 1,451,000 basic income units altogether made up as follows (numbers are thousands):

866 comprised of a single person
22 comprised of a single parent + child (ren)
191 comprised of a married couple
372 comprised of a married couple + child (ren).

Out of the 567,000 married women in the population, 563,000 (equal to number of married men) are regarded as belonging to income units headed by their husbands, while the other 4,000 comprise or head in-

TABLE 5.4 *Estimated distribution of basic income units, 1975, by composition and by economic status of head and of total population by income status and composition of corresponding basic income unit*

Composition of basic income unit

Row No.	Economic status of heads of basic income units	(1) Single person (000's)	(2) Single parent + children (000's)	(3) Married couple (000's)	(4) Married couple+ children (000's)	(5) All Units
1	Farmers	71	2	23	68	164
2	Other employers & self-employed	25	1	14	40	80
3	Assisting relatives	38	–	2	–	40
4	Employees	406	2	69	207	684
5	*Total at work*	540	5	108	315	968
6	Unemployed	51	1	11	39	102
7	Retired	108	–	67	–	175
8	Engaged in home duties	99	15	–	–	114
9	Other	68	1	5	18	92
10	*Total not at work*	326	17	83	57	483
11	*Basic income units*	866	22	191	372	1451
	Total population categories					
12	Heads of basic income units	866	22	191	372	1451
13	Dependent married women	–	–	191	372	563
14	Dependent children	–	45	–	1045	1090
15	*Total population*	866	67	382	1789	3104

Source: Labour Force Survey, 1975, First Results, Dublin, 1977.

come units of their own. There are 982,000 children under fifteen in the population; the total of 1,090,000 children given in Table 5.4 also includes an estimated 108,000 children aged under 18 who are in full-time education. Table 5.4 also shows estimates of how the 1,451,000 basic income units are distributed according to the economic status of the head. Two-thirds of them are headed by persons who are at work, while the remaining one-third, 483,000 basic income units, are headed by persons who are not at work.

Of the four categories of persons at work (rows 1–4) there are no data on the income distribution of three of them; the exception is the farmers. With regard to the categories of persons not at work, it can be assumed that the first three of these (rows 6–8) correspond to categories of income maintenance recipients. Of the remaining 92,000 basic income units 68,000 are single persons and 44,000 of them (nearly two-thirds) are students aged 18 and over who are in full-time education.

In attempting to estimate the number or proportion of income units with an income below the poverty line there is not much to go on: there are just three sources of relevant information. Income distribution data relating to farmers are available from the Farm Management Survey of 1975; second, as far as recipients of income maintenance payments are concerned (and they account for most if not all of the persons 'not at work') rates of payment and statistics of recipients are available from the Department of Social Welfare; third, Department of Health records on eligibility for free medical care provide crude data on income distribution. These sources are dealt with below one by one.

Farmers represent 11 per cent of all basic income units, and (assuming 2 children on average to single parents with children and 3 on average to married couples with children), about 15 per cent of the total population. There is no information available on the income distribution of basic income units involved in farming, but there are data on farm incomes from the Farm Management Surveys. The most useful concept which is used in presenting the results of these surveys, for the present purposes, is 'labour income per labour unit'. Labour income refers to all labour, not just family labour. . . . [It] is calculated as family farm income plus wages paid, minus an estimate for a return on the investment made by the farmer and/or his family in the farm business'.[41] As the relevant report points out, 'income estimated in this way is compared and contrasted with the average income earned outside farming, which when related to the farming sector is often referred to as the comparable income'.[42] Table 5.5 gives the distribution of farms by size and by labour income per labour unit. In order to compare these figures to our 1975 poverty line this latter can be expressed in annual rates as follows:

140   Séamus Ó Cinnéide

	£
Single person	770
Single person + 2 children	1,208
Married couple	1,125
Married couple + 3 children	1,785

TABLE 5.5   *Percentage distribution of farms by size and by labour income per labour unit, 1975*

	Income range (£)									
	0	0–299	300–499	500–699	700–999	1000–1499	1500–1999	2000–2499	2500–2999	3000	All
Size (acres)	% of population									
5–30	5.2	13.7	9.1	6.4	4.0	2.5	1.2	.4	.1	.1	42.8
30–50	1.8	3.0	2.6	2.2	3.6	4.2	3.0	1.5	.6	1.0	23.5
50–100	1.9	1.4	1.4	1.8	2.1	4.8	3.8	2.4	.9	1.4	21.9
100–200	.7	.6	.4	.2	.6	1.3	1.4	1.0	.9	2.0	9.1
200 +	.4	.3	.1	.2	.2	.3	.2	.2	.1	.8	2.6
All	9.9	18.9	13.6	10.8	10.5	13.2	9.6	5.5	2.6	5.3	1000

Source: An Foras Taluntais (Agricultural Institute), *Farm Management Survey,* 1972–5 (February 1977).
Notes: (1) The above distribution is based on results from a sample of 1,554 farms; (2) 1 acre = 0.405 ha; 1 hectare = 2.471 acres.

From Table 5.5 it can be seen that approximately 55 per cent of farms give a labour income per labour unit from farming, one could say a farming wage of less than the poverty line for a single person; conversely less than 20 per cent of farms in 1975 provided a farming wage above the poverty line for a married couple with 3 children. The main deficiency in these data is that they relate to income from farming only: they do not take account of income from employment outside the farm or from income maintenance payments. It is also impossible to relate the data to basic income units. However, the existence of such low income from farming is a strong indication that some farmers have altogether quite low incomes.

With regard to income maintenance recipients, Table 5.6 gives the estimated numbers of recipients and their dependants at the end of 1975. Nearly one-third of the total population (32 per cent) were recipients of income maintenance payments or the dependants of recipients at that particular point in time; this represents 36 per cent of all income units, 25 per cent of all dependent wives and 30 per cent of all children. How many of them have incomes below the poverty line?

A starting point for answering the question is to assume that most recipients of income maintenance payments are poor, that those who are not poor are the exceptions. The basis of this assumption is the prior assumption that most recipients have no income other than their income maintenance payments. The poverty line for 1975 adopted in this chapter (Table 5.3) represents a higher income for each of the four categories of income unit than the basic income maintenance rates of payment under any of the corresponding social assistance or social insurance schemes (Table 5.2). Therefore all those who are relying on basic income maintenance payments for an income are by this definition poor. Some recipients of unemployment benefit and sickness benefit (both social insurance schemes) get more than the basic rates because they are eligible for pay-related supplements under a scheme introduced in 1973. The scheme is financed solely by way of employers' and employees' contributions, which are a proportion of pay up to a fixed ceiling. Forty-three per cent of recipients of unemployment benefit were receiving pay-related supplements at a recent date;[43] the percentage of recipients of sickness benefit similarly eligible is 24 per cent (Department of Social Welfare statistics). The pay-related supplements do not bring some recipients over the poverty line, either because they are too low or because of the application of the 'wage-stop' provision whereby nobody can get an income of more than £50 per week from pay-related supplements and nobody can get income maintenance payments in excess of 85 per cent of their previous take-home pay.

First of all recipients divide between those who receive insurance benefits and who could in theory have other unlimited income (52 per cent of recipients, representing 50 per cent of recipients + dependants), and those who are receiving means-tested assistance benefits and whose other income could only be very low or non-existent. An exception are those receiving smallholders' assistance (Table 5.6, row 5) since their means are assessed on a nominal basis (i.e., their means are calculated by assuming a certain income related to the official valuation, now out of date, of their land). (This group is made up of small farmers, and the data presented above would suggest that there are many people with low incomes in the farming sector).

The only kind of additional income to recipients about which reasonable assumptions can be made is income in the form of earnings; income from other sources is not considered here. In order to be able to have such income, recipients would need to be able to work; this excludes people who are too old, people who have to look after children, and people who are genuinely sick. Recipients of insurance benefits who are able to work, since they are not means-tested, can retain their earnings as an addition to their income from benefits; recipients of means-tested assistance benefits can only increase their income by earning if they cheat and do not declare their earnings. The estimates

TABLE 5.6   *Estimated number of recipients of income maintenance payments at 31 December 1975*

Row no.	Category of need in respect of which payments made (I = Insurance scheme, A = Assistance scheme)	Direct recipient (000's)	Adult dependant (000's)	Child dependant (000's)	Total recipients (000's)
1	Old age, retirement: I	77	25	6	108
2	A	131	11	5	148
3	Unemployment: I	54	25	58	138
4	A	45	20	87	151
5	Occupancy of smallholding A	29	22	60	112
6	Sickness, disability: I	81	29	63	173
	A	21	7	17	45
8	Widowhood: I	61	–	21	82
9	A	13	–	7	20
10	Desertion I	1	–	3	4
11	Single parenthood A	6	–	7	13
12	Other lack of means A	5	2	2	9
13	*Totals*	523	142	336	1,002
14	*Total population, Ireland, 1973,* of which:				3,104
15	Adults, except married women	1,451			
16	Married women		563		
17	Dependent children under 18			1,090	
18	*Recipients as percentage of corresponding population group*	36	25	30	32

Notes:
The estimates at Rows 1–13 above are derived from Tables 8.7, 8.7(a) and 8.9 (pp. 151–4) in *Towards a Social Report,* National Economic and Social Council (Report No 25), Dublin, 1976.
The income maintenance schemes included in each row are as follows:
1 Old-age contributory pension; retirement pension
2 Old-age (non-contributory pension)
3 Unemployment benefit
4 Unemployment assistance; single women's allowance
5 Unemployment assistance; smallholders
6 Disability benefit; invalidity pension

Table 5.6 (continued)

7 Disabled persons' maintenance allowance; infectious diseases maintenance allowance
8 Widows' contributory pension
9 Widows' non-contributory pension
10 Deserted wife's benefit
11 Deserted wife's allowance; unmarried mothers' allowance; prisoner's wife's allowance
12 Home assistance (= public assistance); orpahn's pension, contributory and non-contributory

below then (3 and 4) are based on assumptions about opportunity and ability to work and propensity and opportunity to cheat the system.

Taking account of the above considerations, the following categories of income maintenance recipients could have an income above the poverty line:

1 Recipients whose income from income maintenance payments alone is adequate. This could only apply to persons receiving insurance benefit in respect of unemployment or sickness (rows 3 and 6) who are getting a pay-related supplement as mentioned above and/or redundancy payments (social insurance) as well. Perhaps 30 per cent of the relevant groups have adequate incomes (i.e. above the poverty line).

2 Recipients of smallholders' assistance whose additional income from farming brings them above the poverty line. It is estimated that at the outside no more than 20 per cent of the group could have such income.

3 Recipients of unemployment assistance and unemployment benefit and recipients of sickness or disability benefit who are working and illegally concealing their income. It is impossible to know how many would be involved: say 10 per cent of the relevant groups (rows 3, 4 and 6).

4 Widows, deserted wives and retired people receiving insurance benefits who are also working: again say 20 per cent of the relevant groups (rows 1, 8 and 10).

The numbers in the above groups, and the estimates are very tentative, add up as follows:

1	30% of	135,000	=	40,500
2	20% of	29,000	=	5,800
3	10% of	180,000	=	18,000
4	20% of	139,000	=	27,800
				92,100

If 92,000 recipients of income maintenance payments have an income above the poverty line, then 431,000 recipients have an income below the poverty line. With dependent wives and children they represent about 825,000 people in all or 27 per cent of the total population. They do not include persons with incomes below the poverty line who are not receiving income maintenance payments.

A further indication of the extent of poverty can be acquired from health administration statistics. In Ireland primary medical care, in particular the services of a general practitioner, are available only to persons with a low income who pass a means test administered by the health authorities. The income limits (expressed as weekly incomes) which applied in 1975 were as follows:[44]

Single person, living alone	£19.00
Single person, living with family	£16.50
Single parent + 2 children	£24.00
Married couple	£27.50
Married couple + 3 children	£35.00

These income levels are from 2 per cent to 28 per cent higher than the poverty line as expressed in income levels for similar income units (Table 5.3 above). On 31 December 1975 603,000 income units, representing 1,162,000 persons, were eligible for free primary medical care.[45] It must be assumed that the number of people with incomes below the income limits set out above was something of that order, 37 per cent of the total population. Given that in some cases the administration of the means test would have taken place some time earlier, and that the incomes of people on the register could have risen in the meantime, the number and percentage would need to be corrected downwards.

The conclusion to all this must remain very impressionistic. If the poverty line presented in Table 5.3 is accepted as reasonable, the various estimates which can be made of the percentage of the population with inadequate incomes point towards the range 20–30 per cent. Since this was the conclusion of the exercise on the extent of poverty in 1971, it is all the more necessary to look at trends between 1971 and 1975.

Recent trends in incomes

This review of trends extends back beyond 1971 to 1966, because trends in the longer period are of interest in themselves and in particular in so far as they allow of comparison between trends at different times within the period. In some cases the data available here is sufficient for a comparison to be made between what happened in respect of incomes in the two periods 1966–71 and 1971–75. The earliest year, 1966, is used here because it is the first year in relation to which certain incomes data are available (those in Tables 5.14 and 5.16); it is also a census year.

In looking at trends in incomes it is necessary first to establish certain benchmarks or general standards with which particular types of income can be compared. In Table 5.7 two sets of data are given for this purpose. GNP per head of population is a very crude index of

TABLE 5.7 *Trends in GNP per head and in average weekly industrial earnings, 1966-1971-1975*

	Current prices			% Increase in real terms		
	1966	1971	1975	1966-71	1971-75	1966-75
1 GNP per head of population	£372.4	£641.00	£1178.04	24	8	33
2 Average weekly industrial earnings	12.4	21.08	45.86	25	27	59

productivity and, by extension, prosperity. The figures for average weekly industrial earnings given here are those which are most generally used as an index of trends in earnings; they relate to adult males employed in transportable goods industries but excluding the smaller enterprises.[46] Between 1966 and 1971 GNP per head of population increased by 24 per cent and increases in average industrial earnings more than matched this; between 1971 and 1975 economic growth slowed down but industrial earnings continued to increase at the rate already established. This resulted in an overall increase of 33 per cent in GNP per head of population for the nine years 1966-75, and an increase of 59 per cent in average industrial earnings in that period.

How do trends in the incomes of the poor compare with the above trends? The largest groups of poor people in respect of which we have incomes data are those who subsist entirely on income maintenance payments. In 1966 there were 170,000 recipients of social insurance benefits and 155,000 recipients of social assistance benefits, 325,000 recipients altogether (but not including dependent wives and children); by 1975 there were 274,000 recipients of social insurance benefits and 224,000 recipients of social assistance benefits, 498,000 altogether, an increase of 53 per cent from 1966.[47] The great majority of these recipients are unlikely to have other sources of income.

Table 5.8 gives the rates of benefit payable to recipients of social assistance, in four categories of household composition, under three assistance schemes and from children's allowances. Between 1966 and 1971 incomes of all recipients (taking account only of income in the form of income maintenance payments) increased substantially in real

TABLE 5.8   *Trends in income maintenance rates for various classes of recipients, 1966–1971–1975*

Classes of recipients	Current prices			% Increase in real terms		
	1966 (1)	1971 (2)	1975 (3)	1966-71 (4)	1971-75 (5)	1966-75 (6)
Single Person						
1 Old-age pension, under 80	£2.38	£4.65	£9.30	40	17	64
2 Unemployment assistance (urban)	1.70	3.95	8.10	67	20	100
Single Person + 2 children						
3 UA (urban) + children's allowances	2.70	6.06	14.61	61	41	128
4 Widows Pension + childrens allowances	3.59	6.91	16.86	38	42	97
Married Couple						
5 UA (urban)	3.13	7.05	13.95	62	16	87
Married couple + 3 children						
6 UA (urban) + children's allowances	4.78	10.03	23.22	51	35	104

Note: The deflators used are the increases in the consumer price index from November 1966 to November 1971 (39.10%), and to November 1975 (137.84%).

Source: Reports of the Department of Social Welfare 1967–71 (published 1973); and 1972–75 (published 1976).

terms, and to a greater extent than average industrial earnings. The main difference between the categories of recipients is that persons receiving assistance, no matter what their family composition, fared much better than other recipients. Again, between 1971 and 1975 incomes of recipients increased in real terms, and in most cases more than average industrial earnings did. In this period the major difference is between those with children and those without children: single persons and married couples without children got real increases which were less than the increase in average industrial earnings; single parents with children and married couples with children got real increases higher than the increase in average industrial earnings. Overall, between 1966 and 1975 the incomes of typical social assistance recipients increased by something between 64 per cent and 128 per cent; in relative terms unemployed persons with children did best and single old age-pensioners did worst. Two things have happened: the rates of benefit to unemployed persons and others have converged, and in recent years families with children have been given special attention. This latter was evidenced especially by the increases in the rates of children's allowances made in the Budget of 1973: for families with two children the children's allowances were increased from £2 to £5 per month on that occasion, and for families with three children the increase was from £4.25 to £8.75 per month.[48]

TABLE 5.9 *Social insurance payments as percentage of assistance rates in 1966*

Category of recipient	Insurance rate as % of assistance rate
Single person	
Old age pensioner	129
Widow	114
Unemployed person (urban area)	155
Unemployed person (rural area)	188
Single person + 2 children (not including Children's Allowances)	
Widow	123
Married couple	
Unemployed person (urban)	148
Married Couple + 2 children (not including Children's Allowances)	
Unemployed person (urban)	146

Table 5.9, giving data on income maintenance payments in 1966, can be compared with table 5.1. The comparison reveals that between 1966 and 1975 there was a convergence between different social assistance rates which applied to recipients in the same family composition category, and a convergence between social assistance rates and social insurance rates generally. In 1966 an old-age pensioner under 80 was getting 37 per cent more than an unemployed person, when both were benefiting under social assistance schemes; by 1975 the differential had narrowed to 15 per cent but a new higher rate of benefit had been introduced for the small number of pensioners aged 80 and over. In 1966 social insurance rates were from 14 per cent to 88 per cent more than the corresponding social assistance rates; by 1975 the differentials had in all cases narrowed and were in the range 8 to 28 per cent.

If in the nine-year period 1966 to 1975 income maintenance recipients improved their incomes position *vis à vis* that of the average industrial worker, how did workers at different levels of income fare in relative terms? Because of the lack of income maintenance data referred to above, this question cannot be answered in a comprehensive way or with any assurance. However, two exercises have been done on income trends which give some indication as to what happened within the period under review.

In the first, done by the National Economic and Social Council, the incomes of seven prototype workers, covering a wide range of income levels, were considered. The prototype workers were comparable with regard to family composition, each having a wife and four children, and their disposable income was considered as well as their gross income. The results are given in Table 5.10.

TABLE 5.10   *Trends in real disposable income for seven prototype workers, 1965–66 to 1974–75*

Prototype Workers		Gross earnings per annum (current prices)		% increase in real gross earnings	% increase in real net income
		1965–66 (1)	1974–75 (2)	(3)	(4)
		£	£		
A	Senior administrative	4,750	9,022	−4.8	−15.3
B	Middle management	3,045	5,785	−4.7	−12.1
C	Executive	1,600	3,188	−0.1	−9.1
D	Clerical	1,120	2,435	9.0	−2.9
E	Skilled worker	921	2,330	26.9	14.0
F	Unskilled worker	745	2,030	36.7	26.5
G	Agricultural worker	491	1,345	38.3	33.9

Notes:
1 The table is based on data taken from a previous report of the Council (no. 11) *Income Distribution: A Preliminary Report.*
2 For the first four prototype workers (A,B,C and D above) 'the incomes shown are based on public sector salary rates for comparable grades in the tax years 1965–6 and 1974–5. For the last three (E F and G above) the incomes 'are based on published statistics and assume that the full amounts due under the National Agreement were paid during 1966 to 1974'. Each prototype worker is assumed to have a wife and four dependent children. Net income (col. 4 above) is calculated by taking account of direct and indirect benefits and direct and indirect taxes as appropriate in each case.
3 The deflator used is the average increase in the consumer price index of 99.4% between 1965 and 1974.

Source: Report on Public Expenditure, National Economic and Social Council (Report No. 21) 1976; Table 3.1, page 17.

The table shows that workers whose gross earnings in 1965–6 were over £1,000 per annum suffered decreases in their real gross earnings in the nine years to 1974–5 and even greater decreases in their net earnings;

the higher their earnings to begin with, the greater the decreases they suffered. Conversely those who started in 1965-6 with gross earnings under £1,000 experienced increases in their real gross earnings in the period to 1974-5 and smaller increases in their real net earnings. Again, there was an inverse relationship between earnings in 1965-6 and percentage increase. For those whose earnings are represented by the prototype scales of earnings there was a real distribution of income between 1965-6 and 1974-5. The main weakness in these data is that they relate to prototype workers and not to the total labour force. The scales of earnings for the top four prototype workers are based on those in the public service, and similar information is not available for the private sector.[49]

TABLE 5.11 *Increases in basic rates of pay of workers under National Pay Agreements, 1970-75*

		Weekly basic rate of pay at end 1970 (£)	Weekly basic rate of pay after 1975 Agreement (£)	Increase/Decrease in real terms (%)
Men	10		28.02	+41
	15		35.18	+18
	20		43.07	+8
	25		50.95	+2
	30		59.28	−1
	40		75.49	−5
Women	10		27.02	+36
	15		34.36	+15
	20		42.20	+6
	25		50.46	+1
	30		58.78	−2
	40		75.00	−6

Notes:
The pay increases taken into account above are the standard increases only and do not include what some workers got following negotiations under the anomaly, productivity and related clauses in the Agreements. The 1970 National Pay Agreement covered 18 months beginning 1 January 1971; the 1975 Agreement covered 12 months ending on 31 March 1976. The deflator used is the increase in the consumer price index from November 1970 to February 1976 (91%).

Source: Irish Congress of Trade Unions, *Trade Union Information*, nos 217-9 (July-September 1976 p. 3).

The second exercise on trends in basic pay was done by the Irish Congress of Trade Unions and relates to the period 1970 to 1976. In this case the basic pay of six prototype workers was considered, but only the standard increases negotiated under the National Pay Agreements between the social partners were taken into account: the figures relate to basic pay only; i.e., excluding any element in earnings which resulted from anomaly or productivity agreements under the National Pay Agreements or from changes in the amount of overtime worked. The results are given in Table 5.11.

The results are very much in line with the results of the NESC exercise: there is an inverse relationship between level of earnings and the percentage increase in earnings in the 5¼-year period 1970-6, with workers in the two highest categories of income suffering decreases in real terms within the period. In other words, there was a redistribution of (gross) earnings among workers represented by the six prototype levels of earnings within the period 1970-6. In each of the categories of earnings women did not fare as well as men.

The above data relate to employed persons, who account for only three-quarters of those at work (see Table 5.4). The only other substantial group in respect of whom we have a time series of incomes data is farmers. These data are derived from farm management surveys of a representative sample of farms, and the surveys were conducted by An Foras Taluntais (the Agricultural Institute). Table 5.12 gives data

TABLE 5.12   *Trends in average farm incomes, by size of farm, 1966-75*

Size of Farm	Average family farm income			Increase in average income in real terms		
	1966-67 £	1972 £	1975 £	1966-72 %	1972-75 %	1966-75 %
1 All sizes	465	1173	1656	68	−11	50
2 200 + acres	1391	4012	6016	92	− 5	82
3 5-15 acres	127	239	355	25	− 6	17

Note:
The deflators used were the increases in the consumer price index from November 1966 to November 1972 (50,57%), and to November 1975 (137.84%).
Source: An Foras Taluntais (Agricultural Institute) Farm Management Surveys.

for the financial year 1966-7 (ending March 1977) and for 1972 and 1975. Average family farm incomes increased substantially between 1966 and 1972, and certainly more than the average industrial earnings or the earnings of any of the prototype employees considered above did; however, the very largest farms experienced an increase of 92 per cent in the average farm income compared with only 25 per cent for the very smallest farms. (The smallest farms, consisting of 5 acres or more, but under 15 acres, account for 17 per cent of all farms). Between 1972 and 1975 average farm incomes fell. The trends for the nine years 1966-75 show that the average farm income for all farms increased more than that of employees (from the evidence presented in Tables 5.10 and 5.11), but that there was no redistribution of incomes within the sector.

Taking account, then, of all the time series data on incomes which is available, the following pattern emerges: in the nine years 1966-75 income maintenance recipients, lower wage earners (employees with lower earnings) and farmers generally improved their positions as regards incomes; on the other hand, the position of employees in the higher earnings categories and small farmers worsened in absolute terms and as compared with the other categories. It is not being too rash to say that in the period under review there was considerable redistribution of income and that a substantial number of poor people, if not them all, improved their relative position in the population. However, the data is so inadequate that no statement can be made, for instance, comparing the percentage increase in the average income of the lowest decile or the lowest quartile of the population from 1966 to 1975 or from 1971 to 1975 with the percentage increase in the average income of the highest decile or highest quartile, or of the population as a whole. The evidence suggests that the extent of poverty, the number of people who were poor, diminished between 1966 and 1975 and even between 1971 and 1975, but this conclusion begs the question of how the poverty line for 1966 should compare with the poverty line for 1971 and that for 1975; and a correct estimate of the number of people poor in 1975 is as elusive as ever.

While the final draft of this chapter was being prepared, a new paper on income distribution in Ireland became available. The paper is based on an analysis of data from the 1973 Household Budget Survey and from the Revenue Commissioners. The data relate to 'households' and 'tax units' respectively, and there is no breakdown of the households or tax units by size or composition: for that reason the analysis does not produce any estimate of the number of households or tax units which have an income below any particular level. Nevertheless, the results are of interest in that the income distributions are comparable to those in other countries. The conclusion arrived at using Lorenz curves and Gini coefficients is that, compared with nine other OECD countries, 'inequality in Ireland is found to be definitely greater than that of only three of the nine, and is definitely less than in two of the nine countries'. Second, using Household Budget Survey data relating to urban households (the 1973 survey was the first to cover both urban and rural households), the author describes the trend in the distribution of household incomes from 1965-6 to 1976. (The available data relate to

1965–6 and the four years 1973 to 1976.) The conclusion is that in terms of gross income there was a decrease in inequality from 1965–6 to 1974, and then an increase in inequality to 1976. This conclusion is consistent with the findings presented above. The most recent year to which the tabular data discussed above relate is 1975, and in this chapter there has been no discussion of trends from year to year in recent years.

The wider aspects of inequality

There is general agreement that poverty is not just a matter of in-adequate income, that there are other types of deprivation which are usually associated with inadequate income. To what extent are poor people in Ireland deprived in other ways? There have been no compre-hensive surveys which could give relevant and precise answers to the question. (The census of population does not collect information on incomes, and only a limited amount of cross tabulations of socio-economic status – which is related by income – by other characteristics is published). Most of the data on the relationship between poverty and other forms of deprivation come from limited surveys concerned with specific questions. The most relevant and the most readily avail-able data are summarised in this section. They relate to three topics: household facilities, health, and education.

Data on household facilities by household income are available from the Household Budget Survey of 1973. Five facilities are covered: telephone, washing machine, refrigerator, full central heating and one or more cars. For each of these facilities the percentage of households with the facility increases, as one would expect, with increasing house-hold income. Comparing the highest income bracket with the lowest, a person in the former category is four times more likely to have a fridge, eight times more likely to have a telephone or a car, nine times more likely to have a washing machine, and 15 times more likely to have full central heating, than a person in the latter category. Households which depend on income from certain income maintenance schemes have a low incidence of all the facilities. (There is no information available on the relationship between income and standard of housing.)

With regard to health, the best available relevant information comes from specific studies of limited samples. The two given here are studies of Dublin children. Between 1964 and 1966 the Medical Research Council of Ireland analysed over 1,200 cases of children of less than two with gastro-enteritis, and compared them with a control group of 1,339 children selected from the healthy infant population. One of the items considered was family income, and the distribution by family in-come of the two groups is given in Table 5.13.

TABLE 5.13   *Gastro-enteritis and family income*

Weekly family income	Gastro-enteritis	Control group
	%	%
Under £10	49.7	28.9
£10 – £20	46.5	68.8
£20 +	3.8	2.3
	100.0	100.0
	n = 1,157	n = 1,339

Source: The Medical Research Council of Ireland, *Dublin Gastro-enteritis Study*, 1967.

Family size and home conditions were found to be significantly related to incidence of gastro-enteritis. R.C. Geary and C.O. Muircheartaigh *Equalisation of Opportunity in Ireland: Statistical Aspects* (1974) comment on the overwhelming significance of these results.

In 1971 a study was done on the influence of a number of social factors on certain growth and development parameters based on an investigation of 412 Dublin city children aged between four and seven years. The main development parameters which the study dealt with were height and weight, and they related these to the occupation of the father, among other things.[50]

The results show that in the case of the information for height there is a fairly strong association between father's occupation and the level of physical development, in that children belonging to families in the less well-off social categories exhibit a level of development considerably worse than in the higher social groups. The proportion of children classified to the lowest quadrant (less than the twenty-fifth percentile) was roughly one quarter for the two highest socio-economic groups but it rose to 34 per cent for the next lowest category (other non-manual workers) and increased sharply again to about 42 per cent for the two final groups covering skilled and unskilled manual workers. At the other end of the percentile scale the proportion of children in the uppermost quadrant remained very steady at about 20 per cent for the first three social groupings but then dropped significantly to about half of that level in the cells relating to skilled and unskilled workers. The data for the weight measurements show a very similar pattern.

The volume of the 1971 census report dealing with education has not been published at the time of writing, and the published data on the 1966 census did not relate educational attainment to social group.

The most comprehensive analysis of education in Ireland was published in 1965 and the statistics, which related to 1963, are now out of date.[51] That study examined participation rates in education and showed that they were related to social class.[52] There are no comprehensive up-to-date data on the relationship between educational attainment or educational participation and socio-economic group or social class in Ireland, not to talk of data relating education to income level.

The findings of three more limited studies may be cited as straws in the wind, showing that Ireland conforms to the pattern of relationship between educational inequality and social inequality generally which is found in most countries. A study of 120 educationally retarded children in an Irish town in 1966, which was published in 1969 includes the following commentary.[53]

> The findings of this survey substantiate existing evidence of a relationship between social class and educational performance. Only two per cent of educationally retarded children came from professional or managerial homes while 55 per cent of the former compared with only 10 per cent of the latter came from homes of semi or unskilled manual workers. Explaining the problem of differential performance in terms of genetically determined ability does not account for the disparity between measured ability and actual performance and is obviously inadequate. It is more probable that educational retardation is the result of a multiplicity of determining conditions, some of which are associated with or summarised by the concept of social class, so that social class would tend to be a good indication of the probable educability of the child.

At the other end of the educational spectrum, data on participation in third-level education by social group in 1966 are available. These are given in Table 5.14. The table shows that the proportion of potential students who actually registered at Irish universities for the first time in 1966 was only 5.5 per cent, but this percentage varied greatly according to the social group of the parents: the participation rate for the sons and daughters of 'higher professional' parents was eighteen times that of the sons and daughters of 'skilled manual' parents, and the sons and daughters of 'unskilled' parents were hardly represented at all.

The most recent survey which produced data on education and social class was a survey of a representative sample of 2,271 Dubliners done in 1972–3.[54] It gives a breakdown of educational achievement by a seven-stage ordinal occupational scale adapted for Ireland from the Hall and Jones scale. The author concludes that

> [t] here is a marked correlation between educational achievement and occupational status. *Unskilled* and *semi-skilled* respondents are

TABLE 5.14 *Number of first-year university students in each social group (in 1966) as a percentage of the number of potential students in Ireland*

Social Group	Number of potential students	Number of first-year students in Ireland	Number of students in each social group as percentage of potential students
12 Farmers	14,906	553	3.7
1 Agricultural Workers	4,328	14	0.3
2 Higher Professional	1,137	423	37.2
3 Lower Professional	1,245	359	28.8
4 Managerial and Executive	2,238	575	25.7
5 Senior Salaried Employees	1,236	246	19.9
6 Intermediate Non-Manual Workers	5,679	651	11.5
7 Other Non-Manual	5,603	90	1.6
8 Skilled Manual	9,011	190	2.1
9 Semi-Skilled	4,495	26	0.6
10 Unskilled	5,952	14	0.2
11 Persons who cannot be allocated to above groups	2,725	58	2.1
Totals	58,554	3,199	5.5

Source: Monica Nevin, 'A Study of the Social Background of Students in the Irish Universities', *Journal of the Statistical and Social Inquiry Society of Ireland*, vol 24, part 6, 1967–8, Table 4, p. 224.

predominantly without formal certification in education while *executive* and *higher professional* respondents are predominantly of leaving certificate [i.e. on completion of 5-year secondary school] and university degree standards.

The data in this section are fragmentary, but they all point in the same direction: that there is a relationship between incomes inequality, or class inequality which is a proxy more often available, and inequality of other kinds, in particular with regard to possession of household facilities, healthy development and the incidence of illness, and educability and participation in education. The nature of the relationships, positive or negative, is not in doubt, but the strength of the relationships between factors already dealt with and the nature of the relationships between them and other factors have yet to be established by more extensive research.

The future

Poverty is a serious social problem. The statistical data presented here show that it is an extensive problem; major interest groups, including political parties, recognise it as a problem; a considerable proportion of 'ordinary people' perceive the problem too. Of all the EEC countries Ireland is undoubtedly one of the countries, if not *the* country, with the highest incidence of poverty. In some respects poverty is the same in all EEC countries, but there are also significant differences. There are distinctive Irish features associated with the population structure and the dependency ratio and the structure of the economy; there is a high level of unemployment, an exceptionally high level of dependency on income maintenance by the state and an income distribution among farmers which means that a large number of them are poor.

However extensive poverty is today, it is probably less so than it was a decade ago. In the meantime a number of things have happened: the numbers engaged in agriculture have decreased, negotiated increases in earnings for employees have been redistributive, and there has also been increased redistribution in favour of people who depend on social insurance and social assistance payments. It is impossible to say how these changes came about; the only clue is that in the period in which they occurred more information on poverty in Ireland became available and there was more discussion of the problem among politicians, among social service personnel and in the mass media. Some observers would hold that the Kilkenny Conference on Poverty in 1971, and in particular the simple statistics which it produced, made a sensational impact on public opinion, an impact which is not yet spent.

Will the trends of the past decade continue? The decline in agricultural employment has a dynamic of its own, but the other trends are influenced by public opinion. What will the public want or what will the public tolerate? There are no ready answers to these questions. The most recent public opinion survey on poverty can be read in different ways: 50 per cent of respondents felt that 'the authorities' are doing too little for people in poverty, and about three-quarters of them said they were willing to give time and money to combat poverty themselves.[55] On the other hand, poverty was seen as being more attributable to personal failings or bad luck than to society and social injustice.[56]

In general terms poverty must be tackled in two ways: first, by allowing for greater participation in the labour force and eliminating discrimination within it; second, by redistributing income through taxation and the social services from those in the labour force to those outside it. The government and the public have been alarmed at the need for new jobs in the near future, as shown in population projections. At the moment the emphasis is on job creation for the successive annual waves of school leavers and for people made redundant in declining sectors of employment; so much so that less attention, hardly any attention, is devoted to the question of redistribution.

In the future the key to what happens may lie in the area of research and public education. The work of the National Committee on Pilot Schemes to Combat Poverty will be coming to fruition within the next few years and could have a great impact. In any case, since the issue of poverty has been put on the political agenda, it should be more difficult to ignore it.

References

1 In this chapter 'Ireland' refers to the 26 counties of the Republic of Ireland; it excludes Northern Ireland, which is part of the UK.
2 W. Keating, 'An analysis of Recent Demographic Trends with Population Projections for the years 1981 and 1986', paper read before the Statistical and Social Inquiry Society of Ireland, 3 March 1977.
3 K.A. Kennedy and R. Bruton, *The Irish Economy,* Commission of the European Communities (Economic and Financial Series, no. 10), Brussels, 1975, p. 12.
4 Ibid., p. 9.
5 For a discussion of the nature of and reasons for the rediscovery of poverty in various countries see: A. Sinfield, *Poverty Research in Britain and Europe,* Conference on Poverty Research, 1967; A. Sinfield, 'Poverty Rediscovered', in J.B. Cullingworth (ed.), *Planning for Change,* Allen & Unwin, London, 1973; A. Sinfield, 'A Comparative View of Poverty Research', *Social Studies,* vol. 4, no. 1 (Spring 1975), Maynooth, Ireland.
6 References in S. Ó Cinnéide, 'The Development of the Home Assistance Service', *Administration,* vol. 17, no. 3, 1969.
7 See: E.R.R. Green, 'The Great Famine', in T.W. Moody and F.X. Martin (eds.), *The Course of Irish History,* Mercier Press, Cork, 1967; and C. Woodham-Smith, *The Great Hunger: Ireland 1845-9,* London, 1962.
8 See, for instance, A.M. MacSweeney, 'A Study of Poverty in Cork City', *Studies,* vol. IV (1915), Dublin.
9 See, for instance, the literary works of Peadar O'Donnell, Patrick Kavanagh, and Eugene McCabe.
10 Most Rev. J. Dignan, *Social Security – Outline of a Scheme of National Health Insurance.* Champion Publications, Sligo, 1945, p. 15.
11 P. Kaim-Caudle, *Social Security in Ireland and Western Europe,* Economic and Social Research Institute, Paper no. 20, Dublin, 1964, p. 24.
12 Ibid.

158   Séamus Ó Cinnéide

13 R.C. Geary and J.G. Hughes, *Central Aspects of Non-Agricultural Unemployment in Ireland*, Economic and Social Research Institute, Paper no. 52, Dublin, 1970, p. 26.
14 L. Reason, 'Economics of the Distribution of Non-Agricultural Incomes and Incidence of Certain Taxes', *Journal of the Statistical and Social Inquiry Society of Ireland*, vol. 20, part 4, 1959–61, 1959; An Foras Taluntais, *West Cork Resource Study*, 1963; An Foras Taluntais, *West Donegal Resource Survey*, parts 1–4, 1969.
15 Geary and Hughes, op. cit.
16 S. Ó Cinnéide, *A Law for the Poor – A Study of Home Assistance in Ireland*, Institute of Public Administration, Dublin, 1970.
17 H.A. Behrend, Knowles and J. Davis, *Views on Pay Increases, Fringe Benefits and Low Pay*, Economic and Social Research Institute, Paper no. 56, Dublin, 1970.
18 Published in full in *Social Studies*, vol. 1, no. 4, August 1972.
19 See, for instance, the Labour Party, *Poverty in Ireland – A Report Prepared by the Labour Party*, Dublin, (stencilled) 1973.
20 'The inadequacy of existing social welfare services, especially in regard to the rates of benefits and pensions paid to social welfare recipients, is abundantly evident not least in the revelation of a paper prepared for the Kilkenny Conference on Poverty in November 1971 that, on a conservative estimate, more than one-fifth of our people are below the poverty line, this again being assessed conservatively'. *Discussion Document on Economic and Social Development* prepared for the Fourteenth Annual Delegate Conference of the Irish Congress of Trade Unions, July 1972 (stencilled).
21 See, for instance: Council for Social Welfare, *A Statement on Social Policy*, 1973, p. 1; and Irish Catholic Bishops' Conference, *The Work of Justice Irish Bishops Pastoral*, Veritas Publications, Dublin, 1977, p. 53.
22 Ó Cinnéide, op. cit., 1970.
23 See notes 24–7.
24 'The estimate given by the Minister for Labour at the weekend of the number of persons in the 26 Counties who, as he put it, live below an acceptable level of income and general welfare, was a depressing 640,000, nearly a quarter of the population.' Editorial, *Irish Press*, 26 March 1974.
25 Dr Garret FitzGerald, *Dail Debates*, vol. 260, cols 1481, 1484, 3 May 1972.
26 *Statement of Intent*, 7 February 1973 (stencilled).
27 E.g., by the Minister for Health and for Social Welfare, Brendan Corish: *Dail Debates*, vol. 265, cols 1620, 1621, 22 May 1973.
28 A brochure *Combat Poverty – an introduction to the Working of the National Committee on Pilot Schemes to Combat Poverty*, published by the committee in May 1975, gives an account of activities projected at that time.
29 For a history of Home Assistance see: Ó Cinnéide, op. cit., 1969.
30 For an account of the development of all the income maintenance

services see: Department of Social Welfare, *First Report 1947–49*, Stationery Office, Dublin, 1950; and D. Farley, *Social Insurance and Social Assistance in Ireland*, Institute of Public Administration, Dublin, 1964. More recent developments are covered in Department of Social Welfare reports: *Report, 1963–66*, Stationery Office, Dublin, 1967; *Report, 1967–71*, Stationery Office, Dublin, 1973; *Report, 1972–75*, Stationery Office, Dublin, 1976.

31 S. Lemass, Minister for Industry and Commerce, *Dail Debates*, vol. 49, cols 1664, 1774, 27 September 1933.

32 Ó Cinneíde, op. cit., 1970, p. 93.

33 M. Sheehan, *The Meaning of Poverty*, Council for Social Welfare, Dublin, 1974.

34 J. Mac Airt, 'Irish Urban Poverty: A pilot study contrasting 444 working class and middle class area families in 10 towns', *Social Studies* (forthcoming) Maynooth, Ireland, 1978.

35 J. Mac Airt, 'The Causes and Alleviation of Irish Poverty', *Social Studies*, Maynooth, Ireland, 1977.

36 H. Riffault and J.R. Rabier, *The Perception of Poverty in Europe*, Commission of the European Communities, Brussels, 1977.

37 See note 20.

38 Irish Statistical Bulletin, vol. 51 no. 1, March 1976.

39 National Economic and Social Council, *Statistics for Social Policy*, Report no. 17, Stationery Office, Dublin, 1976 (i), p. 43.

40 Central Statistics Office, *Labour Force Survey, 1975, First Results*, Stationery Office, Dublin, 1977.

41 J.F. Heavey et. al., *Farm Management Survey 1972–75*, An Foras Taluntais (Agricultural Institute), Dublin, 1977, p. 72.

42 Ibid.

43 See J. Murray, 'Summary of Paper delivered to the Unemployed Workers Support Group of the LGPS Union' (stencilled), 18 January 1977.

44 *Relate*, 1975.

45 Department of Health, *Statistical Information Relevant to the Health Services, 1976*, Stationery Office, Dublin, 1977, Table D 1, pp. 62, 63.

46 The detailed statistics appear in the *Statistical Bulletin* published quarterly by the Central Statistics Office.

47 National Economic and Social Council, op. cit., pp. 149, 151; recipients of certain locally administered schemes (home assistance, disabled persons maintenance allowances). Infectious disease maintenance allowances, included in Table 5.10, are *not* included here.

48 Department of Social Welfare, *Report, 1972–75*, Stationery Office, Dublin, 1976, p. 97.

49 In January 1976 the aggregate number employed in the public service, including teachers, the army and the police was 240,000, 35 per cent of all employees: *1977 Administration Yearbook and Diary*, published by the Institute of Public Administration, Dublin, p. 273, and Table 5.8, p. 146 above.

50 M.P. Kent and J.J. Sexton, 'The Influence of Certain Social Factors on the Physical Growth and Development of a Group of Dublin City Children', *Journal of the Statistical and Social Inquiry Society of Ireland*, vol. 22, part 5 (1972–3), 1973, p. 198.
51 *Investment in Education*, Stationery Office, Dublin, 1965.
52 Ibid., Table II.
53 K. Cullen, *School and Family*, Gill & Macmillan, Dublin, 1969, pp. 126, 127.
54 M. Mac Greil, *Educational Opportunity in Dublin*, Catholic Communications Institute of Ireland, Dublin, 1974.
55 Riffault and Rabier, op. cit., pp. 77, 78.
56 Ibid., p. 72.

6 Poverty and inequality in Italy

David Moss and Ernesta Rogers

By article 38 of the 1948 Constitution the Italian Parliament was empowered to introduce laws to guarantee a minimum level of subsistence to all citizens.

> Every citizen unable to work and without the necessary means of subsistence has the right to maintenance and social assistance. It is the right of workers to have the means adequate to their necessities of livelihood foreseen and provided for in the case of injury, sickness, disablement, old age and involuntary unemployment.

The right to assistance and social insurance is here framed in terms of needs and necessities, concepts which require empirical specification in cash or kind if the benefits conferred by this right are to be implemented and their scope assessed. Yet since this declaration of principle thirty years ago parliament has neither defined a minimum acceptable standard of living nor created a national agency to provide the basic assistance pledged in the Constitution. There is nothing in Italy comparable to the Supplementary Benefits Commission whose nationally-applicable scales of aid embody a conventional and adjustable definition of need; and there can therefore be no official count of the numbers whose resources fall below such a level and who claim, or who can be reckoned to be entitled to claim, assistance – a statistic which might have served, as it has served in other countries, as a starting point for assessing the numbers of Italians effectively in poverty. As a conventional category created by official definition 'the poor' do not exist in Italy.

This obstacle to the investigation of poverty might be overcome by detailed empirical studies of social and material deprivation. Such accounts have held a central place in Italian political debate since the late nineteenth century, whether initiated by parliament – the Jacini Inquiry into Agriculture (1885), the Lorenzoni Inquiry into the Conditions of the Southern Peasantry (1909), and the Parliamentary Commissions of Inquiry into Poverty and Unemployment (1953) – or undertaken by private citizens: the best-known of these contributions have been the writings of the *meridionalisti* on the Southern Question.

161

Paradoxically, however, this tradition has almost dried up with the political institutionalisation in post-war Italy of the two dominant cosmologies (Catholicism and Marxism) both of which give a central, though naturally different, place to the notion of poverty. In their distinct ways both approaches hamper the term's use in empirical research and therefore as a satisfactory focus for political debate.

That ideas of spiritual and material poverty are fundamental to Christian doctrine scarcely needs saying. What is relevant here is the Catholic understanding of poverty in contemporary Italy, since that understanding, in the hands of those Catholics who have governed the country uninterruptedly since 1945 from within the Christian Democrat Party, has profoundly influenced the form of the Italian welfare state.

First, who are the poor? Confronted by developing industrial societies, Catholic social thought has modified its traditional view which roughly identified the poor with wage earners, those whose only resource was their labour and who were consequently reduced to destitution when they were unable to work.[1] Today the poor are more broadly defined and more widely distributed in society:[2]

> In affluent societies poverty is not only measured by income level or standard of living. . . . Poverty is not only economic but also ill-health, loneliness, professional failure, the lack of social relations, physical and mental handicaps, family misfortunes and all the frustrations which derive from the inability to integrate oneself into the nearest human group.

Clearly such a definition is so extensive and contains so many heterogeneous and vaguely circumscribed categories that it quite excludes any possible or significant count of 'the poor'. By eliminating any single characteristic of the poor as a category, it precludes a single mode of combating poverty and encourages the creation of many different sorts of institution to deal with poverty's various aspects.

Second, what can be done about poverty? The reply is unequivocal:[3]

> For those who adhere to the Christian conception of life the problem of poverty becomes particularly serious, since in their eyes it is eternal. A Christian cannot believe in the possibility of totally eliminating poverty. It is an aspect of suffering and as such accompanies Man from the Garden of Eden to the Last Judgment. One can reduce it, and one must make every attempt to do so, but only those magicians who even in the field of social science do their best to bewitch the public can think of eliminating it.

What form should the attempt at relief take? For Catholics the alleviation of poverty through individual care and action brings out the deepest bond of *caritas* which unites man to man, and man to God, independently of any purely social tie. Therefore it must not be the task of the state to assume all responsibility for welfare and to suppress the role and institutional framework in which private concern, lay or religious, can express the cardinal human virtue. 'Catholics distinguish themselves from, and generally oppose, those who want a total and exclusive monopoly by the state'.[4] The consequences of such a monopoly are darkly drawn:[5]

> The prevalence of public assistance over private assistance has a
> severe defect: it helps, but it does not show love. . . it allows the
> rich man to lose his sense of duty towards the poor, but it lets the
> poor man acquire the feeling of a right to be helped and this makes
> him less patient, more intolerant, more arrogant and demanding.

Apart from the diffidence towards the right to assistance, such principles support a further fragmentation of welfare interventions. Not only should the services be sufficiently differentiated to meet the wide range of needs which define poverty, but within each service a place alongside state intervention must be found for private initiatives. In practice – and the Catholic Church has had the power to translate its claims into practice – the welfare system has been made immeasurably more complex, besides permitting each single institution to deny sole responsibility for a given problem in the name of the healthy constitutional directive of welfare 'pluralism': some of the consequences will be sketched more fully in the final section of this chapter.

Marxism's contribution to defining and chronicling poverty in Italy has scarcely been more satisfactory. Profoundly influenced by idealism, Italian Marxists have failed, and have acknowledged their failure, to produce detailed empirical research. The Communist Party's leading authority on welfare has spoken of the 'disdainful lack of interest in empirical research and in specific analyses of social reality: the traditional vice of Italian Marxism and of many intellectuals'.[6] He attributes the particular failure in the field of poverty to the predominance of the concept of 'class' over 'individual need', and to the traditional distaste of the working-class movement for the problems of the disorganised, often politically hostile, sub-proletariat.[7] No doubt because the very word 'poverty' has been so closely associated with Christian thought, Marxists have preferred such terms as 'emargination' and 'social decomposition', which, while situating deprivation in the context of their wider critique of capitalist Italy, scarcely provide the analytical thrust to distinguish its varying causes and manifestations. Also, their recent accounts of Italian society have devoted far more attention and intellectual effort to the middle classes than to the poor, thus reflecting current political strategy.

Among social scientists who do not owe their primary allegiance to Catholicism or Marxism, poverty has often provided the background, but rarely the foreground, of research. Economists have been broadly concerned with the overall inequalities which have characterised post-war Italian development; sociologists have devoted their attention to the political control of development and welfare agencies rather than to the relationship of these agencies with their clients; anthropologists have studied communities in the most backward and deprived parts of Italy without in general focusing directly on the basis and incidence of local poverty or comparing their conclusions. The most recent national survey that this chapter can draw on remains the report of the Parliamentary Commission of 1953, compiled at a time when Italy was deeply rural, its population largely dependent on agriculture, and with very variable access to the rudimentary social services. Our account therefore begins with this report, in order to emphasise the dimensions of poverty facing post-war governments and to provide a sense of perspective for subsequent changes. We then describe the current distribution of deprivation in rural and urban areas, identify some of the processes which create and maintain that deprivation, and conclude with a brief summary of how the changing welfare services have failed adequately to alleviate it. The description is intended to bring out the fragility of Italian development, to point to the numbers who, although not perhaps the object of welfare interventions at any given moment, are nevertheless very insecurely protected against the threat of poverty. Considerable space is therefore given to inequality rather than to the more narrowly-defined poverty. In any case, the evidence to do otherwise - to furnish precise and reliable details of the numbers and characteristics of households at very low levels of subsistence - simply does not exist.

Poverty in 1952

The evidence collected by the Parliamentary Commission in the course of 1952 offers immediate and awful witness to the extent of mass poverty. According to their definition of poverty in terms of standard of living - housing, nutrition and clothing - the commissioners estimated, on the basis of a national sample and a set of detailed local monographs, that 24 per cent (2,702,000) of Italian households were in conditions sufficiently wretched to justify the intervention of the state to assist them: half (1,357,000) were classed as 'destitute' (miseri), and the remainder (1,345,000) as 'in hardship' (disagiati). The bulk of this deprivation was concentrated in the south and islands, where it accounted for no less than one in every two households, but it was by no means unknown elsewhere: 6 per cent of households in north Italy and 15 per cent in central Italy fell into these two categories.[8]

Living conditions were indeed appalling. One in every four Italians was living in a dwelling either unfit for habitation or overcrowded, where 'unfit for habitation' referred to caves, cellars, attics and shacks (2.8 per cent of the population), and 'overcrowded' indicated more than two persons per room (21 per cent of the population). Not surprisingly, adequate hygiene and sanitation were, if not luxuries, almost signs of privilege in certain areas. Fewer than half (48 per cent) of homes in the south had running drinkable water, and barely more (57 per cent) had a lavatory, as against the national figure of two-thirds and three-quarters respectively. Sharing a dwelling with animals, and a bed, mattress or simple floor space with siblings or parents was a common necessity in rural areas, while in the larger cities the decaying centres and expanding peripheries sheltered the nuclei of urban poverty. A random sample of 100 families in a central quarter of Palermo turned up a total of 576 people sharing 91 rooms, 14 of the families having running water (cut off in summer in favour of the municipal fountains), 1 a lavatory and the remainder making do with an open drain beside their kitchens.[9] Much of the literary and cinematic neo-realism of the period was directed to the revelation of this Italy.

The profile of these two and three-quarter million households, containing roughly 12 million people, showed the distribution of poverty in the familiarly vulnerable categories: large families, the old and disabled, agricultural workers, and the unemployed. The larger the family, the more likely it was to be poor; so that while 16 per cent of all families of two persons were destitute or in hardship, the proportion rose directly with family size to reach 41 per cent of all families with eight or more members. Where the family head was disabled or retired, one-third and one-quarter respectively of such families were in poverty; where he or she was employed in agriculture or unemployed, the incidence was still greater, at 41 per cent and 47 per cent.[10]

The principal determinant of poverty was lack of work, analysed by the Parliamentary Commission on Unemployment of 1953 and the target of the economic proposals by trade unions (the CGIL Work Plan of 1950) and government (the Vanoni Plan of 1954). Official statistics – those enrolled in labour exchanges – revealed 1,715,710 people in search of work in 1951, equal to nearly 9 per cent of the work force. But this figure, implying a misleadingly simple demarcation between the employed and the unemployed, conceals the severer problem: the numbers of people underemployed and holding precarious jobs, who were provided with neither a sufficient livelihood nor security for the future and who were to be found in all sectors of the Italian economy.

Nearly half the labour force (44 per cent) worked in agriculture, appropriately in a country where 57 per cent of the population lived in small, mostly rural, settlements of less than 20,000 inhabitants. The terms on which men derived a living from the land were strikingly varied within and between different parts of Italy, yet for the most part uniformly inegalitarian. According to the cadastral survey of 1946, 1 per cent of landed properties held 45 per cent of all privately-owned land, while more than half the properties (54 per cent) consisted of dwarf holdings of less than 0.5 ha., covering a mere 4 per cent of private land and quite inadequate to provide each owner with more than a fraction of his livelihood.[11] In competition with the wholly landless rural proletariat for tenancies, sharecropping contracts and day labour was a mass of peasant smallholders who worsened the bargaining position of employees *vis-à-vis* landowners and drastically reduced the number of days per year for which each man could find work. In Sicily, for example, day labourers were estimated to find work for no more than 150 to 160 days each year, and peasants were scarcely better off at 180 to 200 days.[12]

Strategies for making ends meet were born of this desperately restricted and irregular demand for labour. In Alpine and Apennine villages adult family members sought work by seasonal migration to lower altitudes. In Piedmont and the Lombard plain the putting-out organisation of the textile industry drew in the underemployed rural households. In the deep south and Sicily, where there were few alternatives to extensive grain cultivation, men gathered sticks, fennel and chicory for petty sale or a meagre supplement to diet.[13] If the local economy was sufficiently diversified, agricultural workers also took on unspecialised jobs in the industrial and service sectors, where the prevalence of casual labour in the building industry, small workshops and tiny retail enterprises hardly offered a more satisfactory living. To make up the family income children were despatched at an early age to the fields or menial jobs, thereby forcing their withdrawal from school and curtailing their chances of escaping from an apparently eternal poverty.[14]

Contemporary inequality

The pattern of Italy's economic development since 1952 provides ammunition for those who wish to emphasise its benefits and for those who wish to expose its failures. Christian Democrats, under whose governing aegis this quarter-century lies, can point to the standard indicators of advance: an annual GNP growth rate of *circa* 5 per cent between 1951 and 1971; the trebling of average *per capita* income in real terms; the spectacular improvement in living conditions and consumption patterns. Today the national average of persons per room in occupied dwellings has come down from 1.3 to 1.0 since 1951 (and from 1.8 to 1.2 in the south), and only a tiny fraction of families (0.3 per cent) do not have access to running water or a lavatory in their homes. The proportion spent on food in household budgets has been considerably reduced: surveys carried out in the immediate post-war years recorded that industrial workers (in Trieste) and peasants (in Calabria) were spending roughly two-thirds of their income on food, close to the national average of 58 per cent.[15] The most recent data show a fall in the national figure to 42 per cent (which is still high by comparison with other European countries) as against the figure for the south of 46 per cent.[16] The increased income thus made available has been used to purchase the luxuries of two decades ago: a mere 3 per cent of households owned refrigerators, and 1 per cent washing machines, in 1955, while by 1975 the respective figures stand at 94 per cent and 76 per cent. Two-thirds of all homes now possess cars.[17]

These improvements cannot be gainsaid, but they tell only half the story. Against them can be marshalled a formidable array of failures: an unemployment figure which has fallen below one million in only two years since 1951; the persisting inequalities in life-chances, on almost any indicator, between those born in the south and those born in the north; the continuing migration to other parts of Italy and abroad in search of work, with its accompanying rural dislocation and urban chaos; the extent of insecure and poorly-rewarded employment in agricultural, industrial and service sectors. The relevance to poverty of these facts will be discussed in the following sections.

Neither the steady increase in GNP nor the growth in *per capita* income appear to have made serious inroads into the overall range of economic inequalities in Italian society. The data on which Table 6.1 is based are extremely shaky: they derive from surveys carried out in different ways by different agencies, according to a variety of definitions and criteria, disarmingly admitted by their compilers themselves to be neither more than a rough guide nor easily comparable with even their own previous surveys. Nevertheless, these statistics are the only ones available, and they have not been impugned as presenting a wholly false picture.[18]

With the caution demanded by the qualifications expressed in the note to Table 6.1, it seems likely that the pattern of post-tax income distribution has remained strikingly stable since 1948. While there may be a shift in the proportions of income going to the highest and middle income households, the share of the bottom 30 per cent is the same as that of thirty years ago: within that group the poorest 10 per cent of households received 2.8 per cent of total income in 1948 and 2 per cent in 1975. Any improvement belongs to the period 1948–58 – before the economic 'miracle' – and has since been lost.

TABLE 6.1   *Household income distribution after tax, 1948-75*

Groups of income recipients	Share of total income				
	1948	1958	1966	1972	1975
	%	%	%	%	%
Top 10%	33.9	30.6	28.4	28	30
10–20%	14.4	14.9	15.3	16	15
20–40%	20.3	20.3	23.2	23	22
40–70%	20.4	20.7	22.4	23	22
Bottom 30%	11.0	13.5	10.7	10	11
Total:	100.0	100.0	100.0	100	100

Sources: 1948, 1958, 1966: Roberti (1971), Table 4.1, p. 824;
1972: Barberis (1976), Table 2, p. 70; 1975: Banca d'Italia (1977),
Table 1.4, p. 174.

An alternative and more detailed appreciation of current inequalities between households is provided by Table 6.2, which plots income distribution by occupation of household head and by income class:

TABLE 6.2   *Income distribution by occupation of household head, 1975*

Occupation	% Households per income class*							Av. income*
	0–1	1–2	2–3.5	3.5–5	5–8	8+	Total	
Employees								
Managers	–	–	–	–	0.5	0.8	1.3	11.9
White-collar	–	0.1	3.3	5.5	6.5	3.1	18.5	6.1
Agriculture	0.2	0.6	0.9	0.4	0.3	–	2.4	2.9
Other sectors	0.5	2.7	9.9	9.5	6.7	1.5	30.7	4.3
Self-employed								
Agriculture	0.3	0.8	2.2	1.1	0.6	0.3	5.3	3.6
Other sectors	0.3	1.3	3.2	2.6	3.0	2.0	12.4	5.7
Professional	–	0.1	0.3	0.3	0.5	1.0	2.2	9.4
Unoccupied+	3.9	8.4	7.4	3.4	2.8	1.3	27.2	3.1
Total	5.2	14.0	27.2	22.8	20.9	10.0	100.0	4.6

Notes:
* million lire. In 1975 £1 = 1446 lire, so L. 1 million = £692
+ *condizione non-professionale*

Source: Banca d'Italia (1977), Table 1.5, p. 176.

Four-fifths of the poorest households – that 5.2 per cent of all households, with net annual incomes of less than £692 (£13 per week) – were headed by men and women *in condizione non-professionale*, for the most part pensioners. This category also provides the majority of the next lowest class, with incomes of between one and two million lire, so that those households whose senior member was retired, sick, disabled, a student, a housewife or a widow were substantially over-represented among the poorest groups: their average annual income was only two-thirds of the national average. Equally poorly placed were those homes whose head worked in agriculture and whose incomes, both for the self-employed and the employees, were again substantially below the national average. While the lowest income groups were to be found among all occupations, their weight was greatest in the agricultural sector, where approximately one-quarter of households headed by a farmer, peasant or labourer received annual incomes of less than two million lire. In terms of actual numbers of households, the lowest income category (5 per cent of the 15,981,172 households recorded for Italy in the 1971 population census) contains roughly 800,000 households, and the 1–2 million lire category approximately 2,400,000.

Such broad figures, and the structure of income distribution they identify, are hardly startling. The weakest social categories in Italy are also the weakest in other western industrial societies, although with 16 per cent of the labour force still employed in agriculture in 1974, the absolute weight of the lowest-paid sector remains greater in Italy than elsewhere in Europe. Where Italy is distinctive, however, and where the achievements described as the economic miracle seem most precarious or deceptive, can best be brought out through the comparison of these household data with the distribution of personal incomes set out in Table 6.3.

The precarious position of agricultural workers and the unoccupied is again emphasised by these figures, which show one in three and one in two people respectively in these categories in receipt of incomes of less than one million lire. But two further facts stand out: the very large number of very low incomes, and the wide range of income inequalities within each sector.

First, while only 5 per cent of households had annual incomes of less than one million lire, one-quarter of all individual incomes fell into the lowest class, and nearly one-half of all incomes failed to reach two million lire per annum. The juxtaposition of household and personal income figures strongly suggests that considerable numbers of homes are maintained above the lowest level only by the summation of the separate incomes of two or more members. As Table 6.3 shows, many such incomes are exceedingly low, a level associated with the irregularity and uncertainty of the employment which generates them. Consequently

TABLE 6.3   *Distribution of personal income by occupational category and income class, 1975*

Occupations	% Individuals per income class*							
	0–1	1–2	2–3.5	3.5–5	5–8	8+	Total	Av. income*
Employees								
Managers	–	–	3.1	15.2	36.3	45.4	100	9.9
White-collar	4.1	8.7	40.1	27.2	15.1	4.8	100	3.9
Agriculture	33.3	29.2	28.1	9.4	–	–	100	1.7
Other sectors	8.6	22.6	45.4	19.2	3.5	0.7	100	2.7
Self-employed								
Agriculture	15.5	32.5	36.6	9.1	4.0	2.3	100	2.5
Other sectors	10.4	15.4	29.3	18.3	17.2	9.4	100	4.4
Professional	4.2	6.8	19.5	11.8	21.2	36.5	100	8.0
Unoccupied	56.3	28.0	11.2	2.3	1.2	1.0	100	1.4
Employees								
Managers	–	–	–	0.9	4.5	11.4	0.9	–
White-collar	3.6	8.4	26.5	37.6	43.9	27.3	20.1	–
Agriculture	3.6	3.6	2.4	1.6	–	–	2.6	–
Other sectors	10.9	32.3	44.5	39.2	15.1	6.4	29.9	–
Self-employed								
Agriculture	2.6	6.1	4.7	2.4	2.3	2.6	3.9	–
Other sectors	4.3	7.2	9.4	12.1	24.3	26.1	9.7	–
Professional	0.3	0.6	1.0	1.2	4.8	16.3	1.6	–
Unoccupied	74.7	41.8	11.5	5.0	5.1	9.9	31.3	–
Total	100	100	100	100	100	100	100	
Total personal income	23.5	20.9	30.3	14.7	7.0	3.6	100	2.8

Note: * million lire.

Source: Banca d'Italia (1977), Tables 1.8 and 1.9, pp. 180–1.

the loss of any one of these several contributions to household subsistence may push a family immediately to a lower, and perhaps the lowest, income group: as we shall illustrate below, precisely because such low incomes are most at risk and because the welfare system intervenes quite inadequately in support of incomes lost through unemployment, sickness or retirement, the margin which separates from hardship many more families than the figures for distribution of income by household reveal is a thin and erratic one.[19]

Second, not only is the spread of incomes wide, but the proportions of incomes at the lowest level in all sectors is substantial. 8.6 per cent of dependent workers and 10.4 per cent of the self-employed in industrial and service occupations had total incomes of less than one million lire in 1975: together, and excluding the unoccupied, they constituted the decisive majority of low personal incomes. These figures, however, include both full-time and part-time workers and all sources of income (rents, interest payments, social security and welfare transfers in addition to earnings), and they do not distinguish income earners by sex. Nevertheless, consideration of net occupational earnings only for employees (managers, white-collar and wage earners) draws attention to the extent of low (relative to average) pay: 11.1 per cent of all employees earned less than one million lire annually, less than one-third of the average net occupational earnings for full-time employees and the self-employed which stood at 3.1 million lire. By sectors the less than one million lire category accounted for 48.9 per cent of all agricultural employees, 8.5 per cent of industrial workers and artisans, and 15.4 per cent of all those in service activities (excluding the public sector).[20]

The significance for poverty of these perhaps rather undiscriminating figures is to underline the fact that the flow of men and women out of agriculture since 1951 – 5,530,000 by 1974[21] – into industry and services has by no means been a straightforward shift from low to higher income levels for the individuals and families concerned. While it is a commonplace that the economic miracle of the years 1958–1963 was founded on cheap labour, these figures on the continuing extent of poorly-rewarded industrial employment are a salutary reminder that the consequences of that development have not been so widespread as to eliminate its enabling conditions.

Poverty in rural areas

Since 1952 rural Italy has become directly embedded in the national and international economies. Within these complex distributive systems – destructive of confident generalisation and prediction – the hinterland has benefited from the redistribution of wealth generated elsewhere and channelled by public and private decision to rural areas. Apart from social security benefits, the principal transfers have been of two kinds: first, government investment programmes administered by the Land Reform Boards and the Southern Development Agency (*Cassa per il Mezzogiorno*), supported by directives to parastate and private industries, and supplemented by the EEC agricultural price support scheme and the Regional Fund; second, the sums earned by migrants in industrial Italy or abroad and remitted to their home communities to support parents, wives and children who remain behind. In spite of this very considerable flow of resources – which in the first post-war decade amounted in the south to one of the highest levels of external assistance in the world – rural areas, and particularly the south, have remained poor both absolutely and relative to the north. The index for average earnings in villages with less than 5000 inhabitants, which still account for one-fifth of Italy's population, stood at 88 in 1975, compared with 126 in towns of over 200,000 inhabitants. In the south average household incomes in 1975 were only 80 per cent of those in the north, the same differential as in 1971.[22] While the south has a high (though steadily falling) proportion of its labour force employed in agriculture, it has an increasing share of the total national agricultural labour force (43 per cent in 1951 and 52 per cent in 1974) and of agricultural wage-workers (53 per cent in 1951 rising to 75 per cent by 1974).[23] Thus its growing share of the lowest-paid sector and of the lowest-paid category within it (see Table 6.3) drags down the south's average personal and household incomes and points to the extent of near-subsistence livelihoods. The immediate cause of these continuing disparities between south and north, and more generally between rural and urban Italy, lies in the failure both to create sufficient industrial employment in these poor areas and to convert peasant agriculture into modern farming.

In the case studies of industrial development projects no researcher has been able to ignore the political context and content of development. Power at the centre to allocate, and at the periphery to obtain, resources has been the stuff of Italian politics, creating ties between patrons and clients which permeate all levels of political and administrative organisation and which control the outflow of every kind of state benefit. But this mode of distributing funds intended to relieve poverty and unemployment has had consequences inimical to that aim: not only have the large sums spent on development often not led to a sustained advance but also some of the poorest communities, and the poorest groups within each community, have been excluded from the benefits that do accrue.

First, the *ad hoc* bargaining to secure funds has resulted in a widely dispersed and feebly co-ordinated set of initiatives, frustrating any concerted attack on a particular problem or area: the overall economic benefits of each project are thus severely reduced where they are not simply wasted. Second, the politics of resource allocation have produced quite inappropriate types of investment. This is especially clear in the case of the factories set up by the major state holding corporations,

ENI and IRI, which, because an increasing proportion of their funds are voted by Parliament, are particularly vulnerable to political pressures.[24] The kinds of plant that such modern corporations establish – the steel and petrochemical factories of Taranto, Bagnoli, Gela, Pisticci, Manfredonia and Ottana – have been technologically advanced, capital-intensive and wholly unrelated to the existing local economies. Consequently their labour demands have been small and often for skilled labour from elsewhere, while the plants have been far too big to stimulate local satellite industries and thus create more jobs.

Indeed, the main consideration in relieving poverty – the extent and nature of likely employment – is rarely raised in the debates over specific investments. In the town of Manfredonia, for example, local political leaders, concerned to exaggerate their control over job opportunities in order to attract supporters, encouraged or at least failed to deny the much publicised but wildly inflated figure for labour requirements at the future ENI petrochemical plant. The ENI management, itself anxious for good relations with these same community spokesmen, never disabused the population of the hollowness of their claims. As an issue for public discussion and a focus for the mobilisation of the poor and unemployed the effective role of the project in promoting employment was scarcely raised.[25]

Third, because these modern firms can offer higher wages and better security than are usually available locally, applications for jobs there are much oversubscribed and by no means restricted to the unemployed and underemployed: the entire occupational hierarchy of the community is revalued so that those who are already earning a (comparatively decent) living, feeling their status threatened by the distribution of new resources to their erstwhile inferiors, apply for such jobs.[26] Given that these resources are political currency and that their allocation generally takes account of what the beneficiary can himself offer to the mediator or politician who controls them, the poor groups in each village, with little to offer and no prestige to guarantee it, are often excluded from a share in the benefits of this type of development; more accurately perhaps, the benefits only accrue coincidentally to those who stand in the greatest need.

In some communities – frequently the poorest, where such funds are especially valuable and therefore most bitterly contested – the incorporation of development plans into political debate, in which potential but uncertain economic growth is only one consideration, has led to the rejection of state resources. In Sicily the very considerable advantages in controlling funds has paradoxically tempted politicians into refusing to apply for them, lest the delay in their approval, due to the lengthy bargaining and common administrative dilatoriness, should allow the funds to reach the village when the original applicant has been voted out of office: only his political opponents will benefit.[27] At the other end of Italy, in a Piedmontese mountain village, the inhabitants associate the intervention of the state with the decline of their formerly peasant community, and react by refusing to elect men who publicly profess their ability to harness the state's resources for the community's benefit in favour of those who reject this kind of development.[28] In both communities loss of such funds renders the population increasingly marginal and impoverished, and therefore weaker in bargaining for future resources; the seeming destination of these villages is a spiral of greater absolute and relative poverty.

Failure to generate alternative employment to agriculture over much of Italy has been accompanied by exacerbation of the already grave problems within the agricultural sector itself. The impact of land reform, which by 1962 had distributed 628,030 ha. (2 per cent of Italy's agricultural and forest land) to 113,064 assignees, was restricted; and the provision of irrigation, credit, marketing facilities and technical assistance, initially to the reform's beneficiaries and later to all farmers, has never been sufficiently co-ordinated or regular to enable smallholders to meet the competition of expanding agri-businesses within the EEC. With the exception of capitalistically-farmed enclaves, plots remain predominantly small, unconsolidated and devoted to increasingly less profitable extensive crops; incomes are consequently low. In 1970 farms of less than 5 ha. covered one-fifth (21.7 per cent) of Italy's agricultural land, only a slight fall in the figure for a decade earlier (25 per cent) and by far the largest peasant sector among the EEC countries.[29] Labour requirements on these holdings continue to be low, scarcely guaranteeing full-time work for their owners or tenants and still less providing secure employment for the landless. An estimated 300,000 peasants and labourers in the north and 600,000 in the south have insecure, insufficient and inadequately rewarded work in agriculture.[30] The refusal of young men to tolerate such conditions has steadily driven up the average age of the work force until today more than one-third of the agriculturally-employed are aged over 55 and less than one-tenth under 25. The consequences of this demographic shift described for an Alpine village where 40 per cent of all holdings are managed by couples aged over 60 – that productivity, incomes and innovative zest have declined sharply – could be generalised for many hill and mountain villages: this process is certainly destined to continue.[31]

The major supplement to local incomes is the remittances earned by migrants to the industrial centres of Italy, Europe, America and Australia. Migration and emigration are not new: indeed no single postwar year can match the losses sustained in the peak years of the period 1900-14. But whereas the effects of previous migrations have been to alleviate the pressure on valued local resources, today such movements have become depopulation, when the home community can provide neither decent subsistence nor desired life-styles. Between 1951 and 1971 more than four million people left the south at least temporarily, and this drain is reflected on a less massive scale in the rural hinterland of central and northern Italy. The traditional migrant has been a single adult male, but over the past decade the outflow of brides seeking urban spouses and of the dependants of earlier migrants has become substantial.[32] Some migrants represent a direct drain on village resources: the wealthy, whose agricultural rents and incomes are consumed in cities to purchase education and houses, and brides, whose departure may be accompanied by a dowry. However, the majority of migrants – peasants turned industrial workers – maintain their wives' or parents' or both households with a large part of their earnings elsewhere.

Remittances have certainly provided Italy with useful foreign currency. Their official value (excluding all cash brought back personally) has risen from 176 milliard lire to 359 millard lire in the period 1963–73 at current prices:[33] in 1973 remittances from West Germany were equivalent to 14 per cent of the value of Italy's import bill.[34] This flow has certainly benefited consumers of the imports obtained with this foreign exchange, but its long-term benefits in the migrants' home communities are harder to establish. Indeed, it should be said that no village study has investigated or compared the economic consequences of different patterns of migration according to the proportions of local migrants in more or less highly-paid sectors of different national economies and therefore to the varying amounts remitted, the full period of remittance and the range of kin and affines assisted. No account of household or community poverty can be complete without some such assessment.[35]

Studies carried out in the early 1960s often claimed that 'through emigration the peasant has broken the formidable bonds of his secular poverty'.[36] If taken restrictively to refer to basic living conditions improved by private initiative rather than state action, this claim is largely justified: every local report and survey shows that the priority expenditure for remittances has been home improvement and purchase and the acquisition of consumer durables, and the national figures for living conditions quoted above reflect these priorities. But if the claim implies that within each community migration itself does not generate problems of poverty and inequality, then two points must be stressed.

First, as many migrants are drawn from the middle-ranking peasants as from the poorest groups: 40 per cent of emigrants from one village studied in Calabria held an average of 4 ha. of land each, in a community with a sizeable landless proletariat. While the deprivation of those who remain is made more conspicuous by the improvements in the lot of their immediate superiors, the departure of smallholders whose farms might have offered at least casual work and whose remittances are not for the most part productively invested has frustrated the creation of extra employment and may even have reduced the total demand for labour. Evidence from the same Calabrian village, although grounded in an imprecise use of 'poverty', shows that one development coeval with migration has been the trebling of the locally-defined 'poor', from 5 per cent of the population in 1900 to 15 per cent in 1960.[37]

Second, the old, the orphaned and the handicapped become increasingly unprotected through the departure of men and families who in the past would have provided them with subsistence. These categories took their place in traditional peasant communities in various ways. Where few peasants owned land, in the sharecropping areas of north-east and central Italy, the aged and the orphaned were often welcomed into households for their labour contribution in home or field, which might earn the group access to larger resources.[38] In villages where rights to land were widely distributed and highly prized, the elderly could compel their children to support them in retirement through their control of land. Today the threat of disinheritance is, if not empty, substantially weakened through the undesirability of agricultural livelihoods, so that while sons and daughters may support their elderly parents with cash gifts, fewer will work the land for them; the basic security of domestic food production is disappearing.[39] Men who do stay on the land find it increasingly difficult to attract brides, so that the present generation of agricultural workers will have fewer descendants to support them when they can work no longer. Here the provisions of social insurance and welfare will be essential.

To conclude this section with more speculative generalisation: the geographically restricted industrial growth and the persistence of a backward peasant agriculture has left rural communities 'poor' with respect to Italy's major urban areas. Within those villages material inequalities are at least as great as a quarter of a century ago, and they are relatively greatest in the most backward areas. Such a conclusion is hinted at in the Gini coefficient for income distribution which shows income in the south to be more unequally distributed (0.42 in 1975) than in the north (0.37). It is possible, although hardly certain in the face of such shaky evidence, that the most recent trend is towards an increase in these internal inequalities: in 1971 the top 3 per cent of southern households received 14 per cent of total southern income, against 21 per cent in 1973; the corresponding proportions for the top 3 per cent of northern households were 12 per cent and 15 per cent.[40] As national ideas of a decent livelihood, generated by growth in one part of the country, are diffused in the rural hinterland, these material inequalities serve to fix more sharply the category of those locally construed as 'poor' and to emphasise the extent of their exclusion from the newly-valued occupations, goods and services.

Poverty in urban areas

Post-war growth in Italy's urban population has been explosive. This is true not only in the industrial centres of Liguria, Piedmont and Lombardy – where Turin and Milan have absorbed increases, based largely on immigration, of 63 per cent and 36 per cent respectively between 1951 and 1971 – but also in the administrative cities of south Italy where immigration has added to a persistently high birth-rate to show growth most notably in Rome (69 per cent), Cagliari (61 per cent), Palermo (58 per cent) and Bari (44 per cent) over the same two decades.[41] Expansion on such a scale would have created social problems even if the public authorities had planned and carried out provision of housing, welfare and urban utilities. In fact, the demand for those services has been met everywhere no more than partially, for the most part privately, and in some cases not at all.

Housing is the most serious failure. The public sector has managed only a steadily falling share of total housing expenditure (14 per cent in 1962, a trivial 3.7 per cent in 1972), so that cheap subsidised houses for the new urban work force are in very short supply.[42] The consequences of abandoning public initiative, and in many cities even effective supervision of development, can be seen in almost any urban periphery, where speculation in land and buildings has combined with the continuing demand for housing to produce at best a chaos of high-density and exorbitantly expensive dwellings with poor access to services, and at worst the re-creation of shacks and shanty-towns which provide a temporary, but too often permanent, urban foothold for immigrants. The worst case, Rome, is the best described, with an officially estimated 16,506 families (62,351 people) living in shacks in 1968 and a very much larger number in the *borgate*, the settlements on the outskirts first established to house the population forcibly removed from the city centre in the 1930s and enormously swollen by recent migrants. The (officially tolerated) chaos of Roman housing, and the resulting evasion of minimum housing standards and access to services, can be imagined from the calculation that in 1974 between one-quarter and one-third of the city population (roughly 830,000 people) were living in unauthorised dwellings.[43]

At both local and national levels urban planning has been a central focus for political conflict. The government's failure to mediate between the powerful and heterogeneous interests involved with its promised reforms of rent control and security of tenure has led the trade unions into campaigning directly for more, better and cheaper houses. The issue is especially acute in large cities, where – in towns of more than 200,000 inhabitants – only 26 per cent of families own their dwellings.[44] Some of the bitterest urban violence of recent years has been generated around occupations and evictions from empty flats. The tenuous hold that many rural migrants have on access to urban goods and services reflects the same category's insecure position in the industrial structure created by Italy's idiosyncratic pattern of development. The chaotic urban periphery mirrors the complexities and privations of work.

The full extent of poorly-paid and irregular industrial and service work has recently been 'rediscovered' in the search for an explanation of Italy's low and still falling official participation rate: in 1973 only 36 per cent of the population were recorded as active, 69 per cent of males and 24 per cent of females aged over 15.[45] Early accounts suggested that the fall was the product of an increasingly wealthy society: higher wages enable households to have single breadwinners and to prolong children's education, while better pensions permit earlier retirement. This view has collapsed in the face of detailed investigations, which show that the official participation rate is quite misleading in so far as it simply fails to record the casual, underpaid and exploitative employment once thought to be characteristic of insufficiently developed areas and now revealed as an integral part of that development itself. What attentive analysis of Italy's industrial structure has shown is that alongside stable, well-paid industrial work there exists for male family heads a wide range of lower-paid and relatively insecure jobs which seem to be offering perhaps a growing proportion of new employment opportunities. For other household members – the young, the female and the elderly – there are a large number of semi-clandestine jobs with low or very low wages and little or no security: these are nonetheless acceptable since, as indicated above, they enable families to make up their joint incomes to a satisfactory, if precarious, level.[46]

Disparities between wage rates in different industries in Italy are very wide, indeed unique in the EEC. In 1970, on a base of 100 for the average industrial wage, the range of wages extended from 72 in the building industry to 238 in the gas, electricity and water industries; this spread of 166 points contrasts sharply with 26 for West Germany and 41 for France.[47] Many of the unskilled migrants from rural areas find jobs precisely in the lowest-paid and seasonally variable sector, the construction industry. Studies in Milan and Rome have shown how in each city the early migrants built their own homes in the periphery and recruited later migrants to take up the trade full-time.[48] Not only is this the poorest-paid industry in the secondary sector, but it also offers the fewest chances of professional mobility.

Within each sector there are very considerable inequalities in earnings and conditions of work, related principally to plant size. One of the distinctive characteristics of the Italian economy is the continuing presence of very small technologically backward firms and workshops, which account for the overwhelming majority of all industrial plants and a significant proportion of the work force. Between 1961 and 1971 the numbers employed in firms of less than 10 employees in the secondary sector remained constant at about 4 million: in the manufacturing industry in 1971, for example, 23 per cent of the work force was employed in tiny plants with up to 10 workers, and a further 31 per cent in plants with 10-99 employees.[49] The relevant characteristics of these small enterprises are their relatively low wages (both hourly and monthly earnings in plants of less than 50 employees are *circa* 50 per cent below those in plants with more than 1000 workers) and comparative job insecurity (turnover in small plants is roughly three times that in the largest firms). Unionisation is low, giving little protection to wages or jobs. Moreover, while recent union policy in collective contracts has been to support wage claims reducing differentials between and within industries, its efforts have been in part undone by the growing importance of plant-level bargaining; gains here are made by organised workers in large firms, while for the fragmented labour force in tiny plants local bargaining is insignificant.[50]

Finally, below the official statistical horizon but widely, and perhaps increasingly significant, are a mass of *lavoratori neri*, clandestine workers whose position remains irregular and insecure and who make up a heterogeneous set of categories largely excluded from stable industrial employment, dominated by adult males. Although statistical evidence can only be indirect, a 1974 sample estimated that there were roughly two million men and women clandestinely employed in all sectors, while an earlier survey suggested a figure of two million for industry and tertiary workers alone. The same 1974 report showed that 28 per cent of the officially unemployed, 12 per cent of pensioners, 10 per cent of housewives and 10 per cent of the disabled were in fact working in the week of the survey.[51]

These workers consist mainly of young people, pensioners working to supplement their pensions but reluctant to have them reduced by declaring their work, and housewives who take on domestic work for manufacturing industries, especially clothing and textiles. Pay is low: a survey for Modena revealed that for a 6½-8-hour day the average monthly earnings of female homeworkers in the wool, clothing and leather industries totalled between L. 58,000 and 78,000 in 1971; the hourly wage rate was equivalent to only 60 per cent of the average rate in the manufacturing industry as a whole. Insurance contributions are rarely paid – only 3 per cent of the Modena sample were included in insurance schemes – and there is no security of work, no mobility, no holidays, no sickness or redundancy pay and no career prospects.[52] It is not certain that all clandestine workers are from households which would be at very low levels of subsistence without their incomes; but, given the reluctance to allow wives and daughters to take on manual work and the knowledge that the fullest possible education is desirable for the life-chances of the young, households in which resort to these categories' labour is made are more likely to be poor than not.

Neither the economic nor political reasons adduced for the persistence of low-paid and clandestine employment give any hope for its elimination in the near future. Economists point to the expanding percentage of trade between Italy and its EEC partners, and conclude that successful competition in these markets will require capital-intensive, technologically advanced production which will restrict the demand for labour and render it more selective. The more integrated the EEC economy, the more difficult it will be for the already marginal groups in Italy to find secure jobs. Furthermore, in large enterprises the high labour costs, forced up by union strength and social security levies (see below) have been plausibly identified as a motive for 'decentralising' production to smaller firms and plants where such pressures can be more easily evaded. Small firms will remain small or clandestine, and in some sectors strengthened by decentralisation, to render their businesses viable. The opportunities which this evolving industrial structure presents to the steady outflow of men and women from agriculture and rural areas can only reinforce the weight of those in lower-paid and insecure occupations.[53]

The political advantages which have created this economy have not been ignored. The flood of laws to protect the market position of small firms, to ensure access to credit and to reduce their liability to social security contributions have been traded against political support for the governing parties, especially the Christian Democrats, which have deliberately ensured the survival of these firms. At a time when its hegemony is under sustained attack, the DC is unlikely to abandon the support which derives from the conservative entrepreneurs, petty bourgeoisie and their politically volatile marginal employees.

In sum, while the widespread multiple deprivation of 1952 has been drastically alleviated, there are still enough households at very low income levels, and many more dependent on precarious sources of income, to render crucial the role of the social welfare services. For those homes in which the senior members are unable to work, or in which illness, injury or unemployment remove one of the essential sources of income, the intervention of welfare and social insurance organisations will be decisive to establish a minimum security against hardship or destitution. We now turn to the form and content of this intervention.

Social welfare institutions

Italy's social welfare institutions have rarely elicited anything but a cry of despair from those who have sought to understand, assess and improve them. Their structure is complex to the point of incomprehensibility, and they are in general hopelessly ill-adapted to take account of economic and demographic changes in the population they serve. Although the exact figure is not known, the number of agencies in the social insurance and welfare field is estimated at 41,500: this includes national agencies for particular categories of client or misfortune, all regional, provincial and municipal authorities with statutory responsibility for various types of social assistance, and all other institutions recognised by the state and accountable to it in return for fiscal privileges. In addition there is a mass of private organisations, lay and religious, in the welfare field, calculated at 3491 in 1967, and a further 13,027 ecclesiastically-controlled institutions providing a range of broadly social services.[54]

The longevity of public agencies is remarkable: 50 per cent of national agencies set up before 1900 were still in existence in 1974, alongside 80 per cent of those created between 1922 and 1943. Rather than replacing its predecessor, organisation has simply replaced organisation in a haphazard and unco-ordinated way, so that some areas of intervention have long been served by a variety of agencies while others have only recently or poorly been covered: of the 129 national agencies which deal with specific categories of client, fully 23 concern state employees and 20 serve military personnel.[55]

The political *raison d'être* of this development is notorious: public funds have been channelled to these organisations to reward politically-important categories, to create (largely unproductive) employment, and to provide funds for local use in the establishment of patron-client ties. Consequently the administrative costs, reinforced by the generally high salaries of functionaries, can represent a higher proportion of the agency's expenditure than the assistance it provides for clients: the Municipal Relief Agency (ECA) in Rome, for example, spends 60 per cent of its budget on administration, and its counterpart in Venice absorbs 55 per cent.[56] The political function of these agencies at local level is neatly illustrated from an Apulian town where the School Board (*patronato scolastico*), with powers to spend its funds on clothes, meals and school equipment for the local poor, in fact devoted its resources to creating jobs for the unemployed intelligentsia in the

expectation of subsequent political support from the beneficiaries.[57]
The overall pattern of social welfare intervention is similar to that described above for development: fragmented and unco-ordinated funding,
a structure peculiarly responsive to political considerations, and the
failure of funds to reach many of those really in need.

Two general points about social welfare institutions can be made
before our particular descriptions. First, their complexity penalises the
client as heavily as the researcher. The plethora of agencies is not only
costly in its duplication of bureaucracies and tasks at the expense of
actual provision of help, but also in so far as the client, confronted by
an often impenetrable jungle of different organisations with varying
criteria of eligibility and types of benefit, may fail to secure his or her
due through ignorance. Second, the fragmentation of services in fact
covers gross inequalities in the assistance provided for different categories of client. This is marked in the field of social insurance; but it is
also evident in the organisation of welfare, where the extensive role of
private agencies – encouraged in principle by the Catholic Church and
de facto by the poor services offered by the state – enable major disparities to persist. Indeed, precisely those inequalities in life-chances
created and entrenched by the marked economy, which it might be
thought are the target of social welfare intervention, are in many cases
closely mirrored there. The north, with higher average incomes and less
inequality, has more welfare agencies and more funds than the south;
similarly, the poorest assistance and the meanest benefits go to the
lowest-paid workers and the unemployed, not merely as a matter of
empirical fact but as of right.

Social insurance

As in other European countries, the first social insurance schemes were
introduced in Italy from the beginning of this century. The earliest
insurance against industrial accidents was established in 1898, disability pensions and unemployment insurance in 1919, insurance
against tuberculosis and occupational diseases between 1922 and 1929,
and family allowances for most categories between 1934 and 1937. The
direction of Fascist schemes, however, was against unitary, standard
protection and in favour of voluntary, sectoral schemes to provide each
category of worker with its own scale of contributions and benefits.
The plea to introduce some order into this confusion, voiced by the
D'Aragona Commission in 1947, went unheeded, largely because the
suggested reforms were so costly as to be then impracticable: since then
the numbers and disparities of insurance schemes both between and
within sectors have scarcely been reduced and most probably increased.

The plight of pensioners – the majority of whom fall into the lowest income category – has been noted above. Although the coverage of pensions has been vastly extended since 1951, both in terms of the numbers covered (from 3,671,104 in 1951 to 15,169,143 in 1974) and in terms of the proportion of GNP devoted to pensions (1.5 per cent in 1952: 5.6 per cent in 1970[58]), the benefit which each single pensioner draws is scarcely adequate to provide subsistence. The numbers and cash value of the various types of pensions covered by INPS (schemes for dependent workers, the self-employed and various other special categories, representing *in toto* 75 per cent of all pensions) are set out in Table 6.4.

TABLE 6.4   *INPS pensions: numbers and average values,* 1965–75*

Year	Old-age No.	Av. value	No.	Disability Av. value	No.	Survivor Av. value	Social pensions† No.	Av. value
1965	3,512,000	273,600	2,138,000	248,300	1,179,000	222,200	–	–
1970	4,634,000	366,700	3,416,000	338,100	1,550,000	290,000	766,027	153,927
1975	4,175,095	986,000	4,958,595	814,000	1,303,175	633,000	840,002	499,000

Notes: * in lire.
† introduced in 1969, payable to all citizens over 65 not included in a contributory scheme.
Source: Annuario Statistico Italiano, relevant years.

In terms of its average value each pension puts its beneficiary firmly into the lowest income class, yet there are also striking inequalities between categories of beneficiary. Survivor pensions, which are more commonly drawn by women, reach barely two-thirds of the value of the old-age pension; the social pension, which is likely to benefit those whose working lives have been spent in marginal, poorly-paid occupations without contributory coverage, reaches little above one-half of the old-age pension, amounting to £333 per annum. The weak position of women and marginal workers in the labour market is here repeated in the assistance provided for them when their husbands die or they are no longer able to work.

Because many of the schemes are recent, and the period for contributions correspondingly short, many pensions – up to a peak of two-thirds for disability pensions – are at the minimum level.[59] In 1977 the value of the minimum old-age pension stood at L. 79,650 (£53) per month for a wage earner and at L. 74,350 (£49) for a self-employed person. Since 1976 pensions have been linked to the average industrial wage, so that increases are now automatic. Nevertheless, in times of high inflation which characterise present-day Italy, when increases in wages generally fail to match the rise in the cost of living, the position of pensioners is far from securely protected. It is hardly surprising that the low absolute level of pensions forces a number of pensioners to go on working unofficially (see above). Where pensioners live in a household with other wage earners, their pension is generally considered a valuable asset in the total budget; when they live alone or with a dependent spouse, it is insufficient to provide a decent subsistence. The trend towards smaller households and the departure from rural areas of younger families which would formerly have supported the elderly is therefore likely to underline the poverty of many pensions.

Protection against the consequences of unemployment and underemployment, and compensation in the case of an accident causing it, is equally insufficient, and it also establishes clear inequalities between industrial and agricultural workers. Not only is the ordinary unemployment benefit tiny (L. 1200 = 80p. per day) but, in contrast to industrial workers who collect their benefit from the eighth day after the interruption of work, agricultural workers receive their payments only at the end of the year, calculated on the basis of the difference between the (conventional) full working year of 270 days and the number of days actually worked. In order to qualify for unemployment benefit at all, they must show at least 102 days work in the previous two years; this tends to exclude the most marginal seasonal workers whose precarious employment on peasant farms is also the most poorly rewarded. Such workers are also excluded from the complex system of additions to wages reduced by short-time working (*cassa integrazione*) since they must show 180 days worked on the same farm. Finally, the pensions for disabling accidents sustained at work tend to favour industrial workers over agricultural employees: although the method of calculation is complex, a 10 per cent disablement for a person on a (conventional) minimum wage will amoung to L. 74,151 (£49) per month for an industrial worker and nearly one-third less, L. 52,307 (£35) for an agricultural worker.

This brief summary of some social insurance schemes cannot do justice to their full complexity or ramifications. But it is important to emphasise that, while the average benefit is low – too low effectively to keep many of its beneficiaries out of poverty – and its distribution unequal, the mode of financing improvements in these schemes' extensions appears to have operated precisely to restrict the numbers of men and women covered. The main financial burden of social insurance falls on the employers, who must pay 70 per cent of his employees' total contributions, equal to 23.5 per cent of earnings, in addition to special contributions to insurance against occupational injuries and disease, and flat-rate family allowances.[60] This levy, estimated at between one-third and one-half of the total cost per unit of labour, is by far the severest in the EEC. In fact it has increased the cost of labour, particularly in industries where trade unions have been able to ensure substantial wage rises, to the point at which employers prefer not to take on extra labour or are said to favour decentralisation to small plants where the costs of social insurance contributions can be more easily evaded. When employment here, which in many cases is anyway precarious and low-paid, is interrupted, workers are not eligible for the protection of social insurance schemes. The gravity of such a situation will become apparent as we examine the basic assistance provided for those who have no claim to insurance or whose resources are inadequate for subsistence.

The welfare system

We define as welfare institutions those dispensing relief (*beneficenza*) and assistance (*assistenza*). The distinction between these two forms of help is a subtle one which cannot be pursued here, although the ambiguities of both terms have provided those who wish to resist the re-organisation of the welfare services with an ideal terrain for protracted terminological combat. No less ambiguous is the 'poverty' that their intervention must meet. According to the legal definition of 1923, 'a poor man is not he who lacks everything but he who lacks what he needs to live decently according to his individual and social conditions'. The relativity of such a definition harmonises neatly with the Catholic emphasis on the variegated nature of poverty, and it defies the fixing of an empirical subsistence level. Also, the institutional channels of assistance are so various that no *de facto* level of eligibility could possibly be extracted from their workings.

Responsibility for the finance and control of parastate agencies in the assistance field is fragmented among the entire range of ministries. Each has at least some funds to distribute, although the bulk of funds (two-thirds) are controlled by the Ministry of the Interior, one-fifth by the Ministry of Health, and one-tenth by the Treasury. Within the same ministry, however, separate agencies deal with distinct categories of beneficiary: the Ministry of Defence, for example, oversees three agencies for poor war orphans, according to whether their fathers were sailors, airmen or *carabinieri*. The multitude of private organisations operate their own systems of finance and accountability, but they may also accept responsibility for clients to whose upkeep the state contributes. Public and private agencies use a range of different criteria of eligibility and provide a variety, sometimes a choice, of benefit. All that can be said generally and with some confidence is that no single institution can do much more than offer the most temporary alleviation of its clients' poverty: it certainly cannot and does not provide a serious defence against market forces which create poverty in the first instance.

The only public agency established specifically to assist the poor *tout court* is the Municipal Relief Agency (*Ente Communale di Assistenza*). Created in 1937, regulated by the same law of 1890 which regulated its predecessor and controlled and financed by the Ministry of the Interior, each ECA deals with those vaguely defined as 'in poverty or need'. The statutory obligation to assist the poor is not matched by a complementary right of the poor to assistance. All awards are discretionary, and the funds – allocated by a committee elected by the local council – may be distributed in the form of financial assistance, food, clothing or medicines, as well as job creation and special grants to cover exceptional cases (flood and earthquake damage, for example). There is no reason, therefore, to revise the 1953 Parliamentary Commission's statement that 'in practice the determination of those eligible depends on the agency's discretion'; no standardised national criteria exist for assessing need or the type of benefit to distribute.[61]

Any suggestion that this local discretionality and statutory flexibility might lead to a more efficient response to need must be dispelled immediately by the scale of benefits offered. The numbers to whom all ECAs provide help at present are 1,431,000 (1973), a substantial figure but considerably lower than the 2,568,650 assisted in 1952. Yet the average value of assistance received by each beneficiary stands at exactly L. 17,547 *per annum*.[62] Although at such an insignificant level of help further calculations seem otiose, there are quite considerable differences in the overall geographical distribution of ECA funds: in 1973 the north appropriated 44 per cent of the funds to share among 31 per cent of the total numbers of those assisted, while the south with 54 per cent of those assisted accounted for only 42 per cent of the funds.[63] A similar picture appears if we consider all municipal expenditure in the welfare field: the northern municipalities spend an average of 1772 lire per inhabitant, the centre 1076 lire and the south 870 lire, less than half the *per capita* expenditure of the north.[64] The poorer half of Italy therefore, with a greater absolute and relative number of households in poverty, distributes fewer funds to more people than the richer north.

One local study brings out two interesting features of poverty relief. A sample of ECA's beneficiaries in the Veneto revealed that many were being helped not only by ECA but also by the municipality's other welfare services, and that in over half these cases neither agency was aware of the other's intervention. Moreover, exactly half the sample had been drawing ECA benefits for more than eight years.[65] A pale reflection of the pattern of household income described above can be seen in these facts: just as a range of households maintain themselves at a moderate livelihood by summing separate incomes from low-paid or precarious work, so at very much lower levels of subsistence do the poorest households preserve themselves from absolute destitution by combining the separately quite inadequate benefits from different welfare agencies. To judge from the lengthy period over which households in the Veneto sample draw benefits, they may reach a precarious equilibrium in this way. The opportunity to receive benefits from more than one source, combined with the discretionality and autonomy of each agency, has encouraged the activity of informal intermediaries who can selectively advise clients of possible claims and support them in their applications; the role and political context of these intermediaries has been usefully described for a small town in the Abruzzo.[66]

While ECA offers help generically to 'the poor', other agencies define their clients and tasks more narrowly. Each municipality has a statutory obligation to furnish medical, hospital and midwifery costs for the poor (of whom it keeps a register); the provincial administrations deal with the mentally ill and defective, illegitimate and poor children, orphans and the elderly in poverty; and at present the regional administrations (of which more below) are poised to assume a range of supervisory and relief tasks over the whole field of social services. In addition there is a jungle of parastate and publicly recognised agencies – the best-known being the (recently dissolved) ONMI (mothers and infants) and ENAOLI (for the orphans of workers) – which distribute public funds or the services which would otherwise need to be purchased in the market. They may either run these services themselves or sub-contract them to private, usually religious organisations, which receive contributions from the state or the beneficiary or both.[67] Because each agency's responsibilities are narrowly defined, a client may be successively assisted by different agencies for quite short periods: the illegitimate children of mothers in poverty, for example, were helped by the provincial administration till the age of 6, by ONMI (since 1975 the Regions) between the ages of 6 and 18, and by ECA until 21. A client may thus be required to satisfy distinct criteria of eligibility and may receive a different scale of benefit even though the need or handicap which entitles him to assistance remains the same.

The traditional form of agency intervention for the young and the old in poverty, from homes unable to provide subsistence or without a family at all, was placement in an institution, either separately from or together with the physically or mentally handicapped. Exactly how many people are in institutional care is not known. In 1970 their number was estimated at 340,532, of whom just over one-third (126,017) were classified as 'destitute elderly' (*vecchi indigenti*) and a further one-third (149,619) were 'normal minors' (*minori normali*: orphans, illegitimate or single-parent children, and children from the poorest homes).[68] As we might expect from the predominance of low-income groups in the south, children there are more likely to be placed in institutional care than in the north. They not only fill the homes in their own region but can be found, often in substantial numbers, elsewhere in Italy. From the available figures, however, it appears that while the numbers of the old in institutional care are slightly increasing, the numbers of children are falling rapidly: in 1961 there were 200,550 children in homes through poverty and neglect but in 1972 only 128,981. This fall reflects in part the improved (though still hardly adequate) benefits available to unmarried mothers (now at L. 50,000 per month), which enables them to keep their children at home, and in part the reversal of the policies of agencies and the developing emphasis on care within the community. This is the focus of the reorganisation of welfare and social services currently under discussion.

To summarise: it should be absolutely clear from this section that despite increased coverage and expenditure, the level of some social insurance benefits and most relief subsidies is inadequate to lift a family above a broadly defined poverty line. This failure is reflected in the size and composition of groups at very low income levels and deserves a few concluding remarks. First, the low level of each single benefit drives each claimant to spread his claims as widely as possible, especially in those areas where agencies' discretionary powers are greatest. Some types of pension and welfare benefit thus effectively become negotiable, where neither a clear right nor an obligation can be invoked. This is most obviously the case for disablement pensions, which constitute the largest category of pensions (with the fastest rate of increase: see Table 6.4), and which offer the widest scope for discretionary assessment. In the town of Latina, for example, an astonishing 9 per cent of the population was officially afflicted with greater or lesser disabilities.[69] Scope for discretion widens the range of intake of client and is thus likely to inhibit the perception of a broader common interest among those who draw any particular benefit. Clients depend, and see themselves to depend, individually on an intermediary or directly on the agency, and they do not necessarily see themselves as sharing a common set of life-chances with others in the same formal and narrow category of beneficiary.

Second, the fragmentation of intervention among a multitude of narrowly-defined agency responsibilities, and the consequent dependence of clients on perhaps several sources of benefit to alleviate need, serve powerfully to prevent evaluation of the success or failure of change in a single agency's policy. When intervention is limited and its scale is too small to pretend that it is alone sufficient for serious improvement, then among the several sources of support that a poor person may enjoy it is difficult, even impossible, to assess the consequences for clients of a deliberate change in the type of benefit of any one source. So, not only does the present confused structure of welfare intervention inhibit the potential for collective action by claimants to encourage change, but it also largely prevents any agency from evaluating its own contribution towards the relief of poverty and distress.[70]

What of the future? The reorganisation of welfare services is at present in what is euphemistically called a 'transitional period': that is, the defects of the services described above are generally recognised, but there is no agreement on the form of what should replace them. Changes in the provision of welfare are further complicated by their dependence on the devolution of legislative powers and administrative controls to the recently established Regions and on the long delayed reform of the health services. The legal and political implications of such widespread transfers of powers and functions between administrative levels, especially where regional and local politics do not reflect the national balance of power, eliminate any chance of an immediate and satisfactory solution.

For the Socialist and Communist Parties the work of destruction must begin with the dissolution of the national agencies of assistance and the publicly-recognised local institutions of relief and assistance; their tasks and patrimonies must pass to the Regions. The Christian Democrats insist on the continuing functions of central government through the amplified role of the Ministry of the Interior, and on setting clear limits to public assistance to protect private initiatives. But, whatever happens in the field of private assistance, the principal direction of public intervention is in the creation of local units of social security (ULSS), territorially based and serving populations of up to 200,000 inhabitants. Their emphasis is towards the provision of all, broadly defined, social welfare and health care, in which relief of poverty is only one aspect; overall administrative control lies in the hands of the Regions, but participation in the operations and decisions of each ULSS is designed for the political parties, trade unions and special categories represented in each catchment area. Stress is to be laid on preventive intervention, co-ordination between health and welfare services, and care for clients within the community – in contrast with the fragmented interventions and placement in homes characteristic of the past. The ideal structure of these ULSS has lent itself to widely different interpretations, however, likely to be entrenched in a variety of institutional practices.[71]

In the meantime, in the absence of agreement on the overall form of public intervention and control (a *legge-quadro*), some Regions have advanced directly into the social welfare field. Four Regions (Lazio, Emilia-Romagna, Tuscany and Umbria) have defined the ULSS and the general setting of social and health services in their territories; three others (Lombardy, Piedmont and Veneto) have begun to introduce legislation in the field of health alone; still others have intervened to assist categories already but inadequately helped under the existing state provisions, but without altering the fundamental structure of assistance. The regions of Trento-Alto Adige and Val d'Aosta now give benefits to the wholly and partially blind to supplement their state pensions, while the Umbrian Region offers supplementary grants to old people, children and the disabled.[72]

As this list indicates, most of these initiatives have been undertaken in the north and in central Italy, and they will be very hard to undo when the national framework for social security is finally agreed on. This suggests two final considerations, prompted by a guarded pessimism. First, the provision of services is likely to vary enormously with the powers and wealth of different areas and regions, so that the poor will receive very different benefits and services depending on their place of residence. If the criteria of eligibility for particular benefits vary locally or by region, then a geographically mobile, urbanising population may still find itself confronted by a range of criteria for assistance and scales of benefit, perceived as essentially arbitrary and hard to disentangle. Second, if the present trend is continued, then the services provided in the richer north will be better and more extensive than those in the south. In this case, the reorganisation of the welfare services would confirm one striking element of continuity over the last quarter of a century, that the poorest areas and social categories have received the least help in the relief of their poverty.

References

1 R.L. Camp, *The Papal Ideology of Social Reform*, Brill, Leiden, 1969, summarises the most authoritative pronouncements.
2 CEI (Conference of Italian Bishops) Document, *Inchiesta*, II, 7, 1972, pp. 64–5.
3 A. Fanfani, *Colloqui sui Poveri*, Vita e Pensiero, Milan, 1950, p. 9. It is worth pointing out that, in addition to his period as Prime Minister, Fanfani has also been Minister of Labour (1947–50) and Minister of the Interior (1953–4), two ministries with direct responsibilities for social welfare.
4 CEI, op. cit.
5 Fanfani, op. cit., p. 91.
6 G. Berlinguer and P. Della Seta, *Borgate di Roma*, Riuniti, Rome, 2nd edition 1976, p. 12.
7 G. Berlinguer, *Prefazione* to F. Terranova, *Il Potere Assisfenziale*, Riuniti, Rome, 1975, p. 8.
8 Commissione Parlamentare di Inchiesta sulla Miseria in Italia, *Atti* 1953–8, 13 vols, Rome: vol. 2, 1953, p. 42 and *passim*.
9 D. Dolci, *Poverty in Sicily*, Penguin, Harmondsworth, 1966, p. 77.
10 Commissione Parlamentare, op. cit., p. 58.

11 D. MacEntire and D. Agostini (eds.), *Towards Modern Land Policies*, Padna, n.d., Table 1, p. 174.
12 P. Sylos Labini, 'Precarious Employment in Sicily', *International Labour Review*, 89, 1964, p. 271.
13 P. Strand and C. Zavattini, *Un Paese*, Einaudi, Turin, 1955, and Dolci, op. cit., among many others, provide telling local accounts.
14 For one local example see: D.M. Moss, *Pastoralism in Central Sardinia*, unpublished PhD thesis, University of Kent at Canterbury, 1977, pp. 49–53.
15 S. Somogyi, 'L'Alimentazione nell'Italia Unita', in *Storia d'Italia*, vol. 5, no. 1, Einaudi, Turin, 1973, Table 1, p. 844. This essay summarises all the studies of nutrition carried out in Italy over the last century.
16 *Annuario Statistico Italiano*, 1976, Table 340, p. 374.
17 Banca d'Italia, *Reddito, Risparmio e Struttura della Ricchezza nelle Famiglie Italiane in 1977*, Bollettino XXXII.I, 1977, Table 5.1, p. 211; Table 6.1, p. 216. The data for 1955 are taken from Dewhurst, Coppock and Yates et al., *Europe's Needs and Resources*, Macmillan, London, 1961, Appendix 8–1, Table B, p. 1002.
18 The data for 1948 and 1958 are derived from DOXA surveys of 10,700 and 3,500 households respectively. Both surveys were taken over periods of several months, in 1948 recording the household income in the previous month, and in 1958 taking each household's self-assessment of its monthly income class. The analyst himself comments on the unreliability of such drawn-out surveys in times of inflation and on the certain underestimation of total annual income through the use of self-assessment methods (P. Luzzatto Fegiz, *Il Volto Sconosciuto dell'Italia*, Giuffre, Milan, 1956, pp. 1133–62). The figures for 1966, 1972 and 1975 were compiled by the Central Bank, the Banca d'Italia, on the basis of a sample of *circa* 3000 households. The comparability and the coverage of the data for these three years is vitiated in several ways, the net effect of which is to suggest that the apparent reduction in the share of income appropriated by the richest 10 per cent of Italian households between 1958 and 1972 is misleading, due rather to the exclusion of types of income largely confined to the wealthy than to any decisive equalising trend in income distribution.
19 Perhaps a material basis for an ideology of the family can be identified in this necessity for collaboration to maintain all members of the household at a decent level of livelihood.
20 Banca d'Italia, op. cit., Table 1.5, p. 188.
21 R. Fanfani, 'Crisi e Ristrutturazione della Agricoltura Italiana', *Inchiesta*, VII, 26, 1977, Table 5, p. 16.
22 Banca d'Italia, op. cit., Table 1.14, p. 187.
23 Fanfani, op. cit., 1977.
24 G. Podbielski, *Italy: Development and Crisis in the Postwar Economy*, Oxford University Press, 1974, Table 15, p. 151 notes that government grants (requiring parliamentary assent) which constituted

only 7.6 per cent of ENI's finance in 1962 were equivalent to 23 per cent by 1971.

25 N. Colclough, *Manfredonia Research Project*, Mimeo, University of Kent at Canterbury, 1970.

26 J. Davis, *Land and Family in Pisticci*, Athlone, London, 1973, p. 156, makes the point well for Pisticci.

27 This case is described in J.F. Boissevain, 'Poverty and Politics in a Sicilian Agro-Town!' *International Archives of Ethnography*, 50, 1966.

28 F.G. Bailey (ed.), *Gifts and Poison*, Blackwell, Oxford, 1971.

29 Fanfani, op. cit., 1977, Table 7, p. 18.

30 P. Sylos Labini, *Saggio sulle Classi Sociali*, Laterza, Bari, 1974, Table 4.4, p. 179.

31 J.W. Cole and E.R. Wolf, *The Hidden Frontier*, Academic Press, New York, 1974, p. 215.

32 J.S. MacDonald and L.D. MacDonald, *The Invisible Immigrants*, Runnymede Industrial Unit, 1972, shows this for the UK; M. Livi Bacci and M. Hagmann, *Report on the Demographic and Social Pattern of Migrants in Europe*, Council of Europe, Strasbourg, 1971 shows that it is true for Europe generally, p. 31 and *passim*.

33 The figures for each year can be found in the pages concerning Italy in the IMF Balance of Payments Yearbooks.

34 J. Salt, 'The Geographical Pattern of Demand', in J. Salt and H. Clout, *Migration in Postwar Europe*, Oxford University Press, 1976, p. 137.

35 We might note that in one group of central Sicilian villages households with migrants elsewhere in Europe were receiving 30 per cent more in cash per month than households with a migrant in another part of Italy (Formez, *Ricerche sull'Emigrazione Meridionale nelle Zone di Esodo*, Quaderni Formez, 19, 1977, tab.16, p. 171). From a sample of Italian workers in Switzerland it appears that at least some migrants continue to send back remittances even after they have been in Switzerland for more than 9 years, have long been joined by their wives, and do not intend to return to Italy (R. Bohnet and M. Windisch *Les Immigrés Italiens en Suisse*, in M. Livi Bacci and M. Hagmann, op. cit.).

36 J. Lopreato, *Peasants No More*, Chandler, San Francisco, 1967, p. 5.

37 Ibid.

38 S. Silverman, 'Agricultural Organisation, Social Structure and Values in Italy', *American Anthropologist*, 70, 1968, p. 9: 'Peripheral unattached relatives, the aged and small children can all be assets on the farm . . . unrelated orphaned and illegitimate children are readily taken in as extra hands and often adopted.'

39 Cole and Wolf, op. cit., p. 212.

40 Banca d'Italia, op. cit., Table 1.2, p. 172. At village level, the comparative study of two villages by Cole and Wolf shows that the community whose life-style had been more drastically affected by

the wider society also had a larger proportion of locally-defined 'poor'. (Cole and Wolf, op. cit., p. 225).

41 Berlinguer and Della Seta, op. cit., p. 51.

42 Podbielski, op. cit., p. 157.

43 Berlinguer and Della Seta, op. cit., p. 113. R. Fried, *Planning the Eternal City*, Yale University Press, 1973, gives a detailed and critical account of the politics of Roman urban development.

44 Banca d'Italia, op. cit., Table 4.1, p. 203. The proportion of owner-occupied dwellings varies inversely with population size, with a peak of 65 per cent in villages of less than 5000 inhabitants and a national average of 46 per cent.

45 G. Fua, *Il Lavoro Nero: Contraddizioni nell'Economia Italiana*, Consorzio di Pubblica Lettura, Bologna, 1977, Table 1, p. 5. Compare these figures with the corresponding 82 per cent and 43 per cent for England and Wales.

46 The main contributions to the debate on the economics and sociology of the labour market are discussed in S. Vinci, (ed.), *Il Mercato di Lavoro in Italia*, Angeli, Milan, 1974.

47 M. Salvati, *Il Sistema Economico Italiano: Analisi di una Crisi*, Il Mulino, Bologna, 1975, Table 32, p. 150.

48 M. Paci, *Mercato di Lavoro e Classi Sociali in Italia*, Il Mulino, Bologna, 1973, ch. 1. The study by F. Crespi, 'Aspetti del Rapporto tra Strutture Urbanistiche e Relazioni Sociali in una Borgata alla Peroferia di Roma', *Rivista di Sociologia*, V. 13, of a Roman borgata showed that 36 per cent of his sample worked in the building trade (p. 27).

49 G. Fua, op. cit., Table 10, p. 22. Also C. Forte in F. Cavazza and S. Graubard, *Il Caso Italiano*, Garzanti, Milan, 1974, where the article by Suzanne Berger discusses the expansion of tiny retail outlets and the political protection they have enjoyed.

50 These points are made in C. Dell'Aringa, *Egualitarismo e Sindacato*, Vita e Pensiero, Milan, 1976.

51 Quoted in G. Fua, op. cit., Tables 5 and 6, pp. 14–15. One estimate of the 'precariously employed' (reached by subtracting the number of those recorded in the census of industrial plants from the larger number of those who define themselves as industrial workers in the population census) gives 2 million for industry out of a total of 3.7 million precarious workers (Sylos Labini, op. cit., 1974, p. 179).

52 E. Gorrieri, *La Giungla Retributiva*, Il Mulino, Bologna, 1971, Table 23, p. 127.

53 These arguments are presented by A. Graziani, 'Verso l'Economia del Neodualismo' in Vinci op. cit., and by Fua, op. cit.

54 Estimates from F. Cazzola, 'I Pilastri del Regime', *Rassegna Italiana di Sociologia*, 3, 1976, p. 428; F. Terranova, op. cit., p. 137.

55 Cazzola, op. cit., p. 441.

56 Fried, op. cit., note 30, p. 83; F. Vian, 'Carenze Organizzative e Politiche Emarginanti nella Situazione Veneta dell' Assistenze Economica Pubblica', *Ricerche Economiche*, 3–4, 1972, p. 304.

57 P. Littlewood, 'Strings and Kingdoms', *Archives Européennes de Sociologia*, 15, 1974, pp. 40–2.

58 *Annuario Statistico Italiano*, 1976, Table 56, p. 95; K. Allen, 'Italy', in T. Wilson (ed.), *Pensions, Inflation and Growth*, Heinemann, London, 1974, p. 208, who provides some useful detail about Italian pensions.

59 Ibid., p. 218; also A. Florea, 'Isolamento e Solitudine della Donna Anzianna', in *Rivista di Servizio Sociale*, 1975, no. 4.

60 The present value of family allowances for all workers is £7 per month for non-working wife and each child. £1.60 is payable for a dependent parent.

61 Commissione Parlamentare, op. cit., vol. 13, p. 291.

62 ANEA, *Libro Bianco sull'Assistenza in Italia*, Censis, Rome, 1976, p. 118.

63 *Annuario Statistico Italiano*, 1976, Table 53, p. 90.

64 ANEA, op. cit.

65 Vian, op. cit., Table 9, p. 309.

66 S. Ferraguti, 'A New Approach to Social Action in a Traditional Setting', *International Review of Community Development*, 31/32, 1973.

67 One interesting fact emerges from comparing the average cost of each benefit in institutions run directly by ENAOLI (L. 2,536,111) and in private institutions in which ENAOLI places orphans (L. 1,055,555). This vast differential suggests two explanations: either direct management is very wasteful of money, or the treatment given to orphans in private institutions is wholly inadequate.

68 Terranova, op. cit., p. 256.

69 Previdenza Sociale, 5, 1976, p. 1461.

70 There is no space here to consider a further set of institutions closely related to the relief of poverty: the health services. A first approach to their complexity can be made through A. Maynard, *Health Care in the European Community*, Croom Helm, London, 1975.

71 A sketch of some of the organisational issues facing the ULSS can be found in E. Rogers, 'Importanza di un Modello Organizzativo', *Centre Sociale*, pp. 130–2, 1976.

72 See: M. Corsini, *Problems for the Provision of adequate social services in Italy*, COSSIC, Rome, May 1974 (mimeo).

7 Poverty and inequality in West Germany

Roger Lawson

Introduction

This chapter will first look broadly at the development of personal incomes, wealth and social security in the Federal Republic. It will argue that Germany's post-war prosperity has been accompanied by, and to a large extent been based upon, a quite distinctive pattern of inequalities in which the broad mass of workers, while gaining considerable advantages over workers in other countries where improvements in living standards and security of life are concerned, have obtained only a relatively modest share of the country's wealth. Moreover, Germany's workers, including its many immigrant *Gastarbeiter*, would seem not only to have contributed directly to making the rich richer but also the poor somewhat less poor than in many other western countries. The second half of the chapter will focus more on the question of poverty, where there is again evidence of distinctive developments in Germany. Compared with other European countries, Germany's record appears more favourable when poverty is defined purely in terms of money income than when one uses a definition which takes into account access to schools, medical care or housing or, more generally, attitudes towards the poor and their chances of participating in cultural activities and maintaining social contacts. But even with income poverty a number of recent studies have suggested that significantly more people have had incomes below the severely defined minimum standards of the public assistance authorities than has been widely recognised.

During the past decade there have been important developments in the German social sciences, leading to much more systematic research than previously into many aspects of inequality and poverty. They include the emergence since the end of the 1960s of a powerful Marxist and neo-Marxist critique of capitalism, concerned chiefly with the new patterns of inequality and legitimation associated with 'late capitalism'. In Germany this has not only been a debate about theory: it has also led to more empirical research into working-class life and the role and conditions of minorities like the homeless and the *Gastarbeiter*. But

195

there have been other developments in the social sciences which have been more influenced by the Anglo-Saxon traditions of applied social research and may be seen, too, as a response to the growing demands within government for more rational decision-making and planning. An interesting example – referred to frequently in this chapter[1] – is the work of the SPES project run jointly by institutes at the Universities of Frankfurt and Mannheim. This is a wide-ranging programme of social indicators research or 'social reporting' which began with official sponsorship in the early 1970s with the aim of providing policy-makers with 'regular, systematic and independent information on social structures and procedures' and 'a perspective in which growth rates and economic efficiency are no longer the dominating factors. Instead, they will become just two elements among others such as . . . more equitable distribution of resources, improved opportunities and personal satisfaction'.[2] As this implies, while this is in a sense a technocratic development, it also represents a reaction against the dominant values of the 1950s and 1960s. Moreover, the picture of German society emerging from the SPES research and other similar recent studies is very different from that presented during the 'economic miracle', when the Federal Republic was often described as a 'levelled-out middle-class society', and poverty was seen as mainly a problem of *Randgruppen*, peripheral groups or 'special cases' on the margins of society.

The distribution of income

An important feature of the SPES research has been its attempt to correct certain biases and deficiencies in some of the official data collected on personal incomes, and generally to present a new analysis of the material. So far the group has concentrated mainly on the 1960s, where it has the advantage over other researchers of having been given access to the raw returns of the Income and Consumption Surveys carried out by the Federal Statistical Office in 1962–3 and 1969. These are household budget surveys, similar in purpose to the British Family Expenditure Surveys, in which people in a nationwide sample of approximately 50,000 households have been asked to keep diaries of all financial transactions in one month, and of income and larger items of expenditure over several months. Unlike the British surveys, the German enquiries have not included households with high incomes (over DM 10,000 a month), and they have also not covered foreign workers and their families or people in institutional care. The SPES group has attempted to remedy this by using information from a variety of other sources to simulate a model sample of these groups, and has co-ordinated this with the general sample.[3] Thus the SPES

Integrated Micro-Data File for 1969 contains estimates of the incomes of 11,500 German households and people in institutions and 9,500 foreigners and their families in addition to the reported incomes of the 47,000 households that completed the Income and Consumption Survey. This is, of course, an impressive amount of material and it has enabled SPES to produce the most detailed analysis yet made of income inequality and poverty in the Federal Republic. However, even with the additional data, it still seems likely that it understates the extent of inequality and poverty, because of the problems of misreporting of income and property in surveys like the Income and Consumption Survey, and also since the poorest households tend to be under-represented in them. Because of their exclusion from society, some sections of the very poor are largely outside the representative samples used in this kind of investigation.

The other main source of information on the distribution of income is the work of the German Institute for Economic Research (DIW) in Berlin.[4] This, too, is an independent research institute which has co-operated closely with government during the past decade. In its income studies it has 're-worked' official data to produce estimates of the development of household incomes since 1950 which endeavour to cover the whole population and all sources of income. DIW describes these as 'empirical model estimates': the research is not based on any one particular source but on various economic data and survey and census material, which are co-ordinated and adjusted to produce the final distributions. Not surprisingly, the exercise has provoked some controversy in Germany.[5] Most of the criticisms made of the DIW model suggest that it tends to err in the opposite direction from the SPES research, by exaggerating the number of low-income households and the degree of inequality at upper income levels.

Both studies reveal, as one would expect, a very substantial growth in personal incomes during the 1950s and 1960s. Even in the seven-year period covered by the SPES research, which included the brief recession of 1967, the average German household's disposable income rose in real terms by more than 50 per cent; by contrast, in the British Family Expenditure Surveys there is a 16 per cent increase between 1962 and 1969. As Table 7.1 indicates, the studies also show a steady improvement since 1950 in the relative income shares of the poorest households. More generally, however, there is no evidence of any significant change in the pattern of inequality, though DIW and SPES differ in their estimates of the precise trends as well as the extent of inequality. DIW's findings give the impression that there was a growing disparity between the incomes of the rich and the broad mass of the population during the 1960s and early 1970s. The SPES estimates not only show a somewhat less unequal distribution of income than DIW but more

Roger Lawson

stability in the middle of the distribution and a slight fall in the share of the richest households.

TABLE 7.1   *Distribution of personal income in the Federal Republic*

(a) *DIW and SPES estimates of post-tax distribution of household income*

Households	1950 DIW	1960 DIW	1962/3 SPES*	1968 DIW	1969 SPES*	1973 DIW
Top 5%			18.8		17.9	
Top 20%	45.2	43.9		45.1		46.1
21–40%	22.8	23.1		22.5		21.9
41–60%	15.9	16.2		15.7		15.0
61–80%	10.7	10.8		10.5		10.3
Bottom 20%	5.4	6.0	6.1	6.2	6.5	6.5
Total	100	100		100		100
Gini coefficient	39.6	38.0	36.0	38.7	35.2	38.5

(b) *SPES estimates of post-tax household income**

% of households with:	1962/3	1969
more than *twice* average disposable income	6.7	5.7
more than *average* disposable income	35.9	35.5
more than *half* average disposable income	73.1	78.4

* Including foreign workers' households, excluding persons in institutions.
Sources: see page 232.

These are relatively small differences, though, when one considers the general picture that emerges from the studies, particularly from a comparative perspective. Both the DIW and SPES findings suggest that in the late 1960s and early 1970s the proportion of total income held by the rich in Germany was very similar to that found in Italy and France, well above the average for advanced western countries and, as Table 7.2 shows, substantially higher than in Britain and Sweden. But the comparisons reveal, too, a distinctive pattern of inequality in Germany, in which the high shares of the rich have been compensated for in the middle to lower middle ranges of the distribution rather than at lower income levels. In terms of its income distribution the Federal Republic would certainly seem to have been a much less 'levelled-out middle-class society' than either Britain or Sweden, where the shares of income of households in the middle of the distribution appear to have been consistently some 6 to 7 percentage points higher than in Germany. By contrast, low-income households seem to have been relatively better off in Germany than in most other western countries: even the lower DIW estimates suggest that in 1973 the share of the bottom 10 per cent was somewhat higher than in Britain and Sweden and roughly twice the levels in France and the United States.[6]

TABLE 7.2 *Income inequality in the Federal Republic, UK and Sweden*

Pre-tax incomes of households			
Percentage share of:	West Germany SPES 1969	UK FES 1972	Sweden 1972	Western av.* early 1970s
Top 5%	19.7	14.4	13.9	17.0
Bottom 20%	5.8	5.6	6.0	4.9

Post-tax incomes of households						
	West Germany DIW 1960-73	1973	UK FES 1961-73	1973	Sweden 1972	Western av.** early 1970s
Top 10%	29.1	30.3	23.9	23.9	21.3	26.3
Top 20%	45.0	46.1	38.9	39.3	37.0	41.8
21–80%	48.9	47.3	54.4	54.5	56.4	52.3
Bottom 20%	6.1	6.5	6.7	6.3	6.6	5.9
Bottom 10%	2.5	2.8	2.5	2.5	2.2	2.1

Notes:
* 12-country average taken from Roberti (1978). ** 12-country average taken from OECD (1976).

Sources: see page 232.

It is possible, of course, that these comparisons may be distorted by statistical and other shortcomings, but most other available evidence supports the general impression they give.[7] Moreover, international comparisions of the various components of personal income reveal an interesting pattern in Germany which is both consistent with and helps to shed some light on the pattern of income distribution. They show, for instance, that in the period covered by the DIW and SPES research wages and salaries in Germany, while rising more rapidly in real terms than in many other countries, represented only a modest proportion of total personal income. According to a study of nine countries prepared for the British Royal Commission on Income and Wealth, in 1970 wages and salaries accounted for 59 per cent of all personal income in the Federal Republic as compared with 72 per cent in Britain and

70 per cent in Sweden.[8] When adjustments are made to take account of the differing proportions of wage and salary earners in each country Germany shared with France the bottom place among the nine countries. As one would expect from this, the share of entrepreneurial (i.e. self-employment) income has been relatively high in Germany, but this has been true, too, of social security transfer income. In the Royal Commission study entrepreneurial income accounted for 21.5 per cent and social security transfers for 14.1 per cent of total personal income in Germany in 1970, whereas the levels in Britain were 10.7 per cent and 9.5 per cent respectively, and in Sweden 9.6 per cent and 13.9 per cent.

The European Commission's social reports and a recent OECD study of income maintenance expenditures also reveal an interesting distinction between Germany's social welfare expenditures and those in most other European countries, which has an important bearing on the distribution of income.[9] For most of the period since the end of the 1950s the Federal Republic has transferred more of its national income than any other western European country to pensioners and other people permanently or temporarily outside the labour force. By contrast, its expenditures on family allowances and most other kinds of 'supplementary income' for those at work have been below the European average; they have been considerably lower than in France, where transfers to wage earners in the form of family benefits have to some extent offset the modest share of wages in total personal income.

Economic growth, personal incomes and wealth

In exploring this further it is important to look more broadly at the relationship between Germany's economic growth and its pattern of economic inequalities, and in particular at a self-reinforcing cycle of developments which began with the remarkable recovery of the German economy after the currency reform of June 1948 and has only been seriously threatened during the 1970s. One of the factors which made Germany's recovery possible was the comparatively muted and unaggressive reaction of the unions to policies which sought to stimulate industrial investment and expansion by discriminating heavily in favour of entrepreneurs and businessmen and, initially at least, making few concessions to social equity.[10] In the most critical reconstruction phase between 1948 and 1950, for example, many employers and capital businesses were positively encouraged to amass huge profits, while wages moved up slowly and the unemployment rate climbed from 3.2 per cent in June 1948 to a peak of 12.2 per cent in March 1950. At the time the unions were undoubtedly under considerable pressure from within their own ranks to exercise self-restraint, partly because the growing inequalities after the currency reform were of far less significance to many workers than the fact that it brought financial stability and relatively satisfactory living conditions after the chaos and misery of the *Hungerjahre* (hungry years) between 1945 and 1948. But the unions were also in a much weaker position than in many other countries. The currency reform itself had made them virtually penniless, and there were the millions of refugees from eastern Europe who were under severe pressure to make good and hence provided employers with a vital source of willing and cheap labour.

However one interprets the unions' reactions in this period, and as Henry Wallich has shown there were a number of other restraints on an aggressive wages policy,[11] it is clear that by enabling business to earn high profits and to reinvest them on a large scale labour played a key role in Germany's economic recovery. This in turn added to the pressures on the unions not to push for a higher share in national income, since it quickly brought workers the benefits of rapidly rising real earnings and an increasing supply of consumer goods and services. It also brought an ever-growing demand for labour, but until the second half of the 1950s this was more than met by the continuing flow of refugees into the Federal Republic and the steady supply of workers from agriculture. Hence, as table 7.3 shows, there were still more than one and a half million people unemployed in 1954, and more than three-quarters of a million in 1958. The table also shows how labour continued in effect to help entrepreneurs to accumulate an increasing amount of wealth by allowing the discrepancy between earnings and profits to widen throughout the 1950s. Between 1950 and 1960 the share of income from employment in Germany's rapidly growing national income rose by only 3 per cent whereas the proportion of wage and salary earners in the labour force increased by 13 per cent. Significantly, though, this attracted far less public attention at the time than arguments which stressed how German society was becoming less differentiated with the levelling out of consumer habits and living styles, the growing opportunities for white-collar employment, and the decline in the numbers of unskilled workers.[12] More generally, too, after the intense politicisation of the Nazi period and the traumatic events after the War, many Germans clearly preferred the politics of 'no experimentation' and the stress on material values and economic efficiency of the Adenauer era.

These trends were further reinforced by other developments in the 1950s and 1960s. As Andrew Shonfield points out in his study of *Modern Capitalism*, in the Federal Republic (in striking contrast to Britain in the 1950s and 1960s) 'rising prosperity, which produced windfalls for the exchequer in the form of extra revenue, . . . was not

TABLE 7.3   *Earnings and employment in West Germany, 1950–74*

Earnings		1950		1960		1974
1. Gross income from employment as per cent of national income		58.6		60.6		71.6
2. Wage and salary earners as per cent of labour force		68.4		77.2		84.3
		1950–60		1960–74		1950–74
Per cent increase of 1.		3.4		18.2		22.2
Per cent increase of 2.		12.9		9.2		23.3
	1950		1957	1966		1974
Real hourly male industrial wages (index 1970-100)	32.9		48.4	80.3		116.5
Female as per cent of male wages (manual workers)	–		63.8	71.8		72.6
Unskilled male worker's wages as per cent of wages of trained worker*	79.9		79.5	80.4		80.0
Labour force	1950		1957	1966		1974
Per cent of:						
Self-employed (including family helpers)	31.5		24.7	18.8		15.7
Salaried employees and public officials	20.0		24.4	33.3		39.5
Manual workers	48.5		50.9	47.9		44.8
Total	100		100	100		100
Per cent of farmers and agricultural labourers in labour force	24.6		16.8	10.4		7.4
	1950	1954	1958	1962	1966	1970
Unemployed in 1000s	1869	1411	764	155	161	149
Unemployed as per cent of labour force	11.0	7.6	3.7	0.7	0.6	0.7

*Trained worker refers to those classified as 'skilled' in German labour statistics.
Sources: see page 232.

seized upon as a reason for cutting down the share of income claimed by the state from the nation'.[13] On the contrary, by the early 1960s the German government was regularly taking in taxation 'a higher proportion of the nation's output than the government of any other advanced Western country'. The high level of taxation was needed partly to support the expansion of Germany's social programmes, and especially to provide more social security for many workers and pensioners. But it was also used to an ever-increasing extent to help to finance the nation's capital investment. This became particularly important after 1960, when with the growing labour shortage the unions were in a better position to press for more substantial wage rises. Between 1960 and 1974 the share in national income of gross income from employment rose at a much faster rate than in the 1950s (Table 7.3) and at the same time the share of non-distributed profits fell sharply. However, as Jaroslav Krejci shows in a recent study, the increase in the share of employment income was not only recovered in taxation, but the bulk of it 'went into forced savings which whether they accrued to the state or social insurance funds helped to offset the decline in business savings'.[14] In fact, with the rapid growth in taxation of income from employment, the share in national income of net wages and salaries diminished slightly between 1960 and 1974, while that of distributed profits accruing to private households increased, partly because the taxation of profits was allowed to fall in this period.[15]

In other words, labour was called upon to contribute more directly than previously not just to the financing of capital expansion but also to maintaining the high levels of entrepreneurial income, and ensuring that individual owners of productive assets received a growing share of profits. Again, however, in obvious contrast to events in Britain, the resulting growth in productivity allowed most workers to obtain substantial improvements in their living standards and 'security of life'. And, as David Eversley has written of Germany in this period, the increasing taxation was not only used to finance business expansion or personal social security benefits:[16]

> As real incomes rose, so public authorities were enabled (and indeed encouraged) to raise funds, both from taxation and through borrowing, to accelerate the rate of investment and current spending in projects which are partly immediately productive, partly conducive to the creation of the good life, as seen in Germany. . . . Any superficial examination of the German townscape, let alone perusal of the statistics, shows that Germany has spent sums on hospitals, libraries, theatres, schools, parks, railway stations, socially-aided housing, underground railways, airports, museums and so on which are simply not to be compared with British efforts in this direction.

A more detailed study of the development of personal incomes shows how these general improvements in living conditions were accompanied by growing discrepancies between different social groups, in particular between the incomes of employers and the self-employed and of the mass of employees. Both the DIW and SPES estimates suggest that the gap between the average incomes of these groups widened steadily between the early 1950s and the early 1970s, partly because of the declining numbers of small traders but also, it seems, because of the growing incomes of richer entrepreneurs and businessmen. According to the SPES research, the average household income of the self-employed, excluding farmers but including small businessmen and shop-keepers as well as wealthier employers and professional people, was 83 per cent above the average for all private households in 1962 and 126 per cent higher in 1969.[17] Another section of society which has clearly benefited more than others from post-war developments has been the group of leading salaried employees, the top managers and technicians and higher-paid civil servants. Indeed, the slight levelling tendencies in the upper ranges of the income distribution shown in the SPES study and the DIW estimates for the 1950s and 1960s would seem to be explained more by the growth of this managerial class than by any more egalitarian trends in the economy. By contrast, DIW and SPES both show a slight deterioration over the whole post-war period in the relative position of the average wage earners' and salaried employees' households,[18] and this is consistent with the trends in employment income. However, as was mentioned earlier, there is more evidence in the Federal Republic than in most other European countries of a levelling-up at lower income levels, at least in the period up to the recent recession. We shall discuss some of the reasons for this later when we look at the impact of social security policies, the role of immigrant workers and the trends in unemployment.

As one would expect, studies of personal wealth illustrate even more strikingly how disproportionately Germany's post-war prosperity has been distributed. During the 1950s and early 1960s, in particular, there appears to have been a growing concentration of most forms of wealth[19] and a marked shift in the structure of personal wealth to the disadvantage of employees and pensioners. It has been estimated that employers and the self-employed, excluding farmers, obtained almost 65 per cent and employees less than 25 per cent of all personal wealth accumulated in the Federal Republic between 1950 and 1963.[20] To put this in perspective, in this period the self-employed group made up less than one tenth and employees more than three-quarters of the labour force. Since the early 1960s the overall share of the self-employed seems to have fallen and that of most other groups to have increased, partly as a result of government measures aimed at building up wealth amongst workers and ordinary salaried employees. Even so, as Table 7.4 indicates, at the end of the 1960s the self-employed still held well over half the total wealth accumulated since 1950. Moreover, all the available evidence suggests that it is again the leading salaried employees who, in the 1960s and 1970s, have increased their share of total privately held wealth and of income generated from it at a faster rate

TABLE 7.4 *The distribution of personal wealth in West Germany*

(a) *The accumulation of total personal wealth, 1950–1969*

	Percentage of total wealth formation	Wealth formation per income recipient (1950–69 in DM)
Manual workers	12	6,000
Salaried employees	16	13,000
Public officials	6	19,100
All employees	34	9,500
Pensioners and non-employed	9	6,000
Farmers	4	9,900
Employers/self-employed	53	121,500
All groups	100	16,700

(b) *Percentage of total personal wealth held by top 1.7% of private households*

	Ownership of enterprises, stocks and shares	Agricultural property	Housing and land	Savings deposits life insurances, etc.	Total personal wealth
1960	70	11	16	20	35
1966	74	9	14	20	31

source: see page 232.

than other groups.[21] Another more telling indication of the inequalities of wealth is the estimate shown in Table 7.4 suggesting that by the mid-1960s less than 2 per cent of private households owned almost three-quarters of all industrial and commercial property and stocks and shares. It seems, too, from this and other estimates, that while the 1960s and early 1970s saw a somewhat wider dispersal of the forms of wealth which give people a 'right to defer consumption' there was also a growing concentration of 'productive wealth' or the wealth that provides 'power over people and the structure of society'.[22]

Unfortunately it is difficult to obtain information about the trends in inequality during the past few years, when there have clearly been important changes in the situation in the Federal Republic. On the one hand, the coalition governments led by the Social Democrats since 1969 have made a more determined attempt to tackle the problem of a fairer distribution of income and wealth. Their most important reform has been a tax reform planned as a major redistributive device, which came into effect at the beginning of 1975. On the other hand, though, the German governments like the governments of other western states have had to face the rapidly declining growth rates of the 1970s, and in turn the rising levels of unemployment and difficulties in meeting social expenditures. Given the crucial significance of economic growth and security for post-war German society, these are in some respects more formidable and challenging problems for the Federal Republic than for a number of other countries.

Social security, inequality and relative poverty

A closer look at German social security policies suggests some other interesting relationships with the pattern of economic inequalities. As has been implied, the considerable expansion of social security which took place under the Christian Democrats in the 1950s and 1960s was largely financed by increases in the taxation and social insurance contributions of workers and ordinary employees. It was also concerned much less with establishing national minimum standards for all citizens than with 'protecting the capacities and incentives for gainful employment, including the different rewards acquired through economic activity'.[23] In practice, this has meant generous standards of protection, particularly in retirement and against sickness and disability, for many workers with regular and stable employment: the standards have been much closer to those traditionally enjoyed by public officials and white-collar employees than is the case, for example, in Britain. But because of their work orientation the schemes have had a less benevolent expression for many low-paid workers and those with poor employment records. Moreover, a number of studies have linked the good protection given to the majority of workers with demanding and stressful working conditions in factories,[24] leading to higher accident rates than in many other countries and to a surprisingly high proportion of workers leaving the labour force before the official retirement age. A survey conducted in North Rhine-Westphalia in the 1960s put the proportion at 42 per cent of all manual workers, but 54 per cent for the unskilled and semi-skilled.[25] Until the 1970s, too, Germany's social security schemes have given far less support to larger families than has been given in many other countries.[26] And, in keeping with the emphasis on the ordinary worker with normal responsibilities, they have made few concessions to women but particularly women in one-parent families – or, to use the official jargon, 'incomplete families'.[27] Again, though, this has begun to change during the 1970s.

The distinctive priorities in social security are best illustrated by the major social reform of the post-war period, the reform of old-age and disability pensions enacted by the Christian Democrats in 1957. This raised old-age pensions for an average wage earner with an average employment record to approximately 50 per cent of gross and 60 per cent of net earnings before retirement, levels above those in many other countries. It also pioneered the principle, at least in state superannuation schemes, that pensioners should be given a guaranteed share in increasing national prosperity, by linking subsequent pension increases to the general growth of wages and salaries. Unlike state pensions in most other countries, though, the 1957 reform contained no minimum pension nor any formula favouring the low-paid and pensions were very closely related to lifetime work records. Moreover, in line with the traditional rules in German social insurance, there was no supplement in the new scheme for wives, and a widow continued to receive 60 per cent of her husband's pension. In fact, the whole concept underlying the reform was that a person's pension should reflect 'the value of his work, as expressed by the wage he receives';[28] the only concessions made at the time to social equity were allowances for periods of sickness, unemployment and wartime service. Although these priorities have since been modified by the so-called 'second pension reform' passed by the Social Democratic-Liberal coalition in 1972,[29] the pension schemes still provide relatively meagre benefits for the low-paid and irregularly employed. There is now, for example, a minimum pension, but only for workers with at least 25 years' contributions: for a widow of a worker with a normal employment record it amounts to little more than 20 per cent of national average earnings.

Some of the effects of these low minimum pensions will be apparent when we examine estimates of the number of people with incomes at and around the minimum income standards of the Federal Social Assistance Law. More generally, however, the pension reforms and other related developments, such as the growth of occupational benefits supplementing state pensions, clearly have an important bearing on the pattern of income inequalities in Germany. They have involved a substantial transfer of income from active workers to pensioners, which has both considerably improved the living standards of many old people and, as Table 7.5 illustrates, has led to significant changes in the composition of low-income households. The table is taken from an analysis by the SPES group of people living in the poorest 20 per cent of households, and in households with incomes below a 'mild relative poverty' line: the latter was set at 60 per cent of average *per capita* disposable income for a single person and head of household, with supplements of 70 per cent of this amount for each additional household member. The results indicate a marked decline during the 1960s in the representation of pensioners and other non-employed persons in both categories, but particularly in the proportion of old people in 'mild' poverty. In 1962-3 11 per cent of the over sixty-fives were in households with incomes below this level and this was also the average for the whole population; by 1969 the proportion for the over sixty-fives had fallen to 9 per cent, whereas the national average had risen to 12 per cent.

TABLE 7.5   *Low-income households in West Germany: SPES estimates, 1962-63 and 1969*

Occupation of household head	Per cent of persons in 20% of households with lowest incomes per household member		Per cent of persons in 'mild relative poverty'	
	1962-3	1969	1962-3	1969
Farmer	18.5	12.1	8.6	5.2
Other self-employed	10.1	4.7	5.0	2.6
Public official	6.8	8.8	1.6	3.3
Salaried employee	6.4	10.8	2.2	5.1
Manual worker	27.9	33.1	15.1	21.1
Pensioner and other non-employed	23.7	17.0	17.0	12.5
All households	20.0	20.0	11.1	12.4

Per cent of persons in 'mild relative poverty'

Household type	1962-3	1969	Age of household head	1962-3	1969
Single man	1.6	3.0			
Single woman	13.0	9.5	Under 25	6.1	15.7
Couple, no child	4.3	3.6	25-34	13.5	17.2
Couple and one child	2.9	3.3	35-44	13.3	17.7
two children	13.0	12.6	45-54	9.9	8.3
three children	24.0	24.3	55-64	8.7	5.8
four and more children	48.0	39.0	Over 65	11.2	8.7
All households	11.1	12.4		11.1	12.4

Definitions: see text.
Source: see page 232.

Figures like these are, of course, difficult to compare with research findings from other countries because of differences in the standards used. The SPES allowances for variations in family size are, for example, more generous than those adopted in poverty research in Britain and many other countries. However, the evidence of a number of comparative studies suggests that the incidence of what may be seen as 'mild relative poverty' has been lower in the Federal Republic than in many other countries, mainly because of the German pension arrangements.[30] In a recent investigation sponsored by the European Commission 15 per cent of Germans over retirement age as compared with 47 per cent in Britain were living with incomes below two-thirds of the median incomes of all families interviewed, whereas for most other groups the incidence of this relative 'poverty' was higher in Germany than in Britain.[31]

The Gastarbeiter

Another reason for the changes in the composition of low-income households shown in Table 7.5 was the rapid growth in the numbers of immigrant *Gastarbeiter*. Foreign workers accounted for 3 per cent of all employees in the labour force in 1962 and 6.5 per cent in 1969, while the proportion of foreigners in the population rose in this period from just over 1 per cent to 4 per cent (Table 7.6). The *Gastarbeiter*, most of whom have been employed in the least skilled and most undesirable jobs, appear to explain the marked increase between 1962–3 and 1969

TABLE 7.6   *Foreigners in West Germany, 1955–75*

	1955	1961	1966	1968	1970	1973	1975
Foreign workers as per cent of all employees	0.4	2.4	5.8	4.9	8.5	11.5	9.7
Foreigners as per cent of population	–	1.2	–	3.2	4.9	6.4	6.6

Source: see page 232.

in younger households and single men in 'mild relative poverty'. Moreover, if only German households are considered the incidence of 'mild' poverty appears to have fallen during the 1960s. There was still a rise in the proportion of manual workers' and salaried employees' households below this level, but this seems to have been mainly due to the movement of poorer farmers and other self-employed people into low-paid employment. Other calculations made by Frank Klanberg using the SPES data show a significant fall during the 1960s in the percentage of German workers' households below a more severe relative poverty line (set at just over 50 per cent of *per capita* income for a single person) and growing numbers of younger foreign workers below this line.[32]

A number of studies have also emphasised the role played by immigrant workers in helping to sustain Germany's economic growth during the 1960s and in reinforcing the broader structure of inequalities. As Castles and Kosack have shown, one of the remarkable features of foreign migration to the Federal Republic, reflecting its explicit concern with satisfying the country's labour needs, was 'its character as a highly organised labour migration'.[33] Before each of the various phases of migration the Federal Republic has concluded treaties with the different countries of origin, setting up recruitment centres in these countries equipped with teams of German doctors to seek out the healthy and able-bodied and also representatives of firms and transport organisations. In the 1960s this undoubtedly gave Germany's immigrants certain advantages over immigrants in many other countries. They arrived in the Federal Republic assured of a job and were given more help with accommodation than elsewhere. But it also meant that they were more likely to be directed into specific jobs at lower wage rates than German workers and to be used to enhance profits by, for instance, 'enabling productivity changes which involve some deterioration in working conditions as compared with those acceptable to indigenous labour (e.g. unpleasant shift work or speeding up the production line)'.[34] Significantly, too, the proportion of unskilled manual workers in industry has increased since the *Gastarbeiter* arrived in Germany, whereas it fell during the 1950s.[35]

During the 1960s government and employer policies generally discouraged the entry of dependants, and very tight legal restrictions were placed on foreign workers, underlining their transitory role in German society. Once in the Federal Republic they were normally attached to an employer on a one-year contract; and attempts to change jobs, and in some cases even to protest against conditions in factories, could be regarded as a violation of contract and workers could be repatriated. Although they contributed through their tax and social insurance payments to Germany's health and social services, the foreigners made little demand on these services; partly because they were normally single and healthy but also because they could again be sent home 'in the event of serious illness, disability, injury, mental breakdown, alcoholism, drug addiction or of offences against the civil or criminal codes'.[36] The 1967 recession showed, too, that their rights to unemployment insurance were almost impossible to take up because of the pressures on them to return home: between 1966 and 1967 only 28,000 *Gastarbeiter* received unemployment benefits, but their numbers fell by nearly 400,000. Hence, while the foreign workers helped to raise the living standards of many low-paid Germans, and indeed contributed more generally through tax and social security payments to the improvements in German social benefits, any threatening social problems amongst the *Gastarbeiter* were, in effect, exported during the 1960s. This is clearly far less true of the situation in the Federal Republic today, since the *Gastarbeiter* 'system' has changed significantly in the 1970s, partly as a result of pressures from immigrants themselves who have become better organised and better informed about wages and working conditions. Basically, though, there is now more recognition of social responsibilities towards the immigrant community and its presence is much more widely seen as not a transitory phenomenon but a long-term feature of German society. This change began in the late 1960s with the increasing acceptance of the entry of dependants into Germany, and since then there has been a distinct relaxation of legal restrictions on foreigners and other important changes in employment and social policies. For instance, the Federal Social Assistance Law now states explicitly, as was not the case in the 1960s, that foreigners have a right to public assistance. As this implies, of course, with these changes the Federal Republic is now faced with the formidable and costly problems of integrating immigrants and their families into the community. An estimate made in 1973, and quoted in a recent study by Suzanne Paine,[37] reckoned that infrastructural investment to the tune of DM 150,000–200,000 per family would be needed if the quality and quantity of services for immigrants were to be raised to the average for German families, and this is now accepted as having been a conservative estimate.

More generally, the poverty and inferior status of *Gastarbeiter* have become increasingly visible in the 1970s, as have the social tensions arising from immigrant ghettos in most German towns and from the growing demands made by immigrants on social and educational services.[38] Not surprisingly, too, the more liberal policies of the 1970s have been severely tested by the economic recession. Since 1973 the proportion of the foreign workers in the labour force has again fallen; and, as Paine shows, there is evidence of similar pressures being applied to immigrants as in 1967, even though they now have more formal protection. It seems, too, that in some areas of high unemployment local controls have been introduced denying work permits to foreigners' wives and children, and hence denying them also the right to be 'unemployed' or to receive certain social benefits.[39]

Unemployment and poverty

As was mentioned earlier, the coalition governments led by the Social Democrats since 1969 have placed more emphasis on redistributive

TABLE 7.7   *Unemployment in West Germany, 1973–77*

(a) *Numbers unemployed and working short-time, in thousands*

	Registered unemployed	Short-time workers	Hidden unemployment
1973	274	44	151
1974	582	292	206
1975	1074	773	453
1977	1030	–	–

(b) *Long-term unemployed in May of each year*

	Between 1 and 2 years unemployed		More than 2 years unemployed
1975	59,883	10,957	10,957
1976	129,996	30,375	30,395
1977	112,653		56,676
Per cent increase 1975–77	88%		436%

(c) *Unemployment rates for selected groups*

	Total	Men	Women	Manual workers	Under 20s	55–65 olds	Foreign workers
1975	4.7	4.3	5.4	5.4	5.8	5.0	5.6
1976	3.9	3.0	5.4	4.3	4.6	–	3.8

(d) *Recipients of unemployment benefits in 1975: % of all unemployed*

Unemployment insurance	Unemployment assistance	No unemployment insurance or assistance
64.7%	10.3%	25.0%

Sources: see page 232.

policies favouring the lower-paid, larger families and single parents, and there have been further improvements in social benefits for pensioners and the disabled. For many poorer German households, however, the recession of the 1970s has clearly dramatically reversed the trends of the previous two decades. Including estimates of the hidden or un-registered unemployed, the numbers out of work have increased from 300,000 in 1969 to just under one and a half million in the second half of the 1970s, while those on short-time work rose from 1,000 in 1969 to a peak of 770,000 in 1975. While the general level of unemployment has dropped slightly since 1975, as Table 7.7 shows, the numbers out of work for longer than a year rose from 70,000 in 1965 to 170,000 in 1977 (and are now estimated as over 200,000). Amongst the many disturbing social implications of this trend is its effect on the incomes of those concerned. After one year the unemployed lose any rights they may have to unemployment insurance benefits and become eligible for means-tested unemployment assistance, the levels of which are often below the general public assistance levels and hence need to be supplemented by public assistance to reach the 'official' and, as we shall see in the next section, severely defined poverty line.[40] After two years the unemployed are expected to rely entirely on public assistance. With both these assistance schemes many of the unemployed find themselves in a 'poverty trap', since their means tests apply to the whole household and thus create considerable difficulties when wives and children are working. Moreover, it is generally accepted that unemployed workers are likely to be more reluctant than others to apply for public assistance because of the sense of shame: 'workers' have normally kept well clear of dependence on this kind of state relief.[41]

Several recent studies have shown, too, how Germany's unemployment insurance schemes have given much less support to the majority of the unemployed than many people have assumed is given, mainly because most of the unemployed are the lower-paid unskilled workers least favoured by the work-oriented and earnings-related social insurance arrangements. According to a report on unemployment and poverty by the Rhineland-Palatinate Department of Social Affairs, at the beginning of 1977 the incomes of between 300,000 and 700,000 households or between one and two million people affected by unemployment in the Federal Republic had fallen to or below the public assistance level of living.[42] The figures have been challenged by the Federal Government and a closer study of the report suggests that its interpretation of the public assistance standards was too generous and exaggerated the numbers in 'official' poverty. Even so, its poverty line was set at roughly 80 per cent of the SPES 'mild' poverty line, and for a four-person household it fell some 10 per cent below the amount which German respondents in a Common Market opinion poll felt was 'the real minimum income on which a family of four persons . . . can make ends meet'.[43] The report listed the unemployed falling below its poverty line as follows:[44]

Between 100,000 and 130,000 households out of the 160,000 receiving unemployment assistance.

Of the recipients of unemployment insurance:
the vast majority of the unemployed with children,
virtually all single women with children,
virtually all married manual workers without children but with only one 'earner',

the majority of married salaried employees without children
but with only one 'earner',
the majority of single women.

This left only two groups of the unemployed who were not normally seriously threatened by poverty: single men and 'small' families with two earners.

There are other ways, too, in which unemployment has brought the threat of poverty closer to many households. Amongst the reasons for the levelling-up at lower income levels in the late 1950s and 1960s were the abundant opportunities for women and young people to work and supplement the incomes of poorer families and the improvement in conditions in some of the poorer rural areas. The latter was due both to new industries being attracted to these areas and to structural reforms in agriculture which had the effect of forcing out some of the more inefficient farmers and their workers and provided them with inducements to leave for the larger industrial centres.[45] These are all trends which have been reversed since 1973. Regionally, unemployment has been highest in the poorest rural areas, in particular in areas around the North Sea coast and in the *Bayerische Wald*, the region of Bavaria close to the Czech border, where there have been local unemployment rates of up to 30 per cent.[46] As Table 7.7 shows, in Germany as elsewhere women and young people have been hard hit by unemployment, and this in turn helps to explain the surprisingly high proportion of the unemployed (25 per cent of all the registered unemployed) apparently not receiving any form of unemployment benefit. The financial effects of youth unemployment, in particular, have been more severe in Germany than in Britain, since young people not only do not qualify for unemployment pay if they have not worked but also have no rights by themselves to public assistance if they are living with their parents.

As with the situation of the *Gastarbeiter*, unemployment is likely to pose considerable problems during the 1980s. There seems little doubt that because of Germany's demographic structure the problems of youth unemployment will increase. It has been estimated that around one million new work places will be needed in the period up to 1985 just to cater for the numbers of young people entering the labour market.[47] It remains to be seen, too, whether the financial situation of those unemployed will improve. The recent studies have led to pressures for changes in benefits and conditions, but, as in Britain, public attitudes remain ambivalent towards the unemployed – still often assumed to be work-shy and 'on to a good thing'.[48]

The poorest Germans and the 'official' poverty line

While the 1970s have seen the emergence of new problems of poverty facing the unemployed and foreign workers, recent research has also focused attention on a hitherto neglected minority of Germans, mainly the poorest pensioners and others outside the labour force, whose living standards have always fallen well below those of the broad mass of the population; more, so it seems, than with the minority at the bottom of the social pyramid in Britain and much more so than in the Scandinavian welfare states. To measure the size and composition of this poorest section of German society a number of studies have adopted as their main yardstick the standard of living associated with public assistance. Under the Federal Social Assistance Law local social welfare authorities are required to provide this last-resort assistance, known as *Hilfe zum Lebensunterhalt*, to cover the minimum requirements of those with inadequate incomes and to enable them, in the words of the opening paragraph of the Law, 'to lead a life that corresponds to the dignity of man'.[49] Like the British supplementary benefit levels, this assistance can be said to represent the state's poverty line or 'an official view of the minimum standard of living at a certain date – it is the floor set by the government to the social security system'.[50] In principle, at least, the German minimum is a floor set for all households, since full-time work has never been a bar to the receipt of benefit. There are also regional and local variations in the minimum rates, but these are now very small and mainly reflect cost of living differences between areas.

Unlike its social security provisions for the average worker, Germany's public assistance payments have been generally more meagre than those in Britain – and more explicitly so. One of the main guidelines used by the authorities in setting assistance scales is an official 'basket of wares' (*Warenkorb*), which sets out in great detail and on the basis of expert advice the official definition of 'a life that corresponds to the dignity of man'. It appears from this that the monthly 'needs' of a grown-up person who is not a head of household include 1 bottle of beer, 4 bus tickets, half a cinema ticket, 100 grammes of coffee and 50 grammes of tobacco.[51] In practice, many claimants – amongst them disabled people, those over sixty-five and single parents – also receive supplements to their 'scale-rates' to take account of special needs and housing, and certain other costs are normally met in full. But even when these are taken into account the assistance given in many areas seems hardly designed to provide the resources needed to participate in cultural activities and maintain social contacts. In 1976, for example, the Federal average levels of assistance for a couple and two children, including a generous allowance for additional payments and housing costs, was just over three-quarters of the amount that respondents in the Common Market opinion poll felt was necessary to make ends meet.[52] Table 7.8 gives an indication of the differences between the German and British rates, expressed as a percentage of average industrial wages. The differences would appear more marked if the assistance rates were compared with average disposable income in the two countries, since, as we have seen, wages represent a lower proportion of total income in Germany.

TABLE 7.8   *Selected social assistance rates (excluding rent) in West Germany and the UK*

Rates as percentage of average gross earnings of men in manufacturing industries

| | | | Unemployed man, wife and: | |
	Single person over 65	Couple over 65	two children (aged 5, 8)	four children (aged 5,8,10,12)
West Germany*				
June 1969 a	16.0	25.6	36.7	51.6
b	17.7	28.1	40.5	56.7
Oct. 1977 a	17.4	28.0	38.7	53.3
b	19.1	30.1	42.6	58.7
UK				
June 1969	20.5	33.2	44.7	56.7
Jan. 1978	22.7	35.9	43.8	55.3

* In the German columns a. refers to the Federal average rates of assistance and b. to the levels used by the SPES researchers in estimating the numbers with incomes below the 'official' minimum. The SPES group allowed an additional amount for certain items normally paid for by the authorities.
Source: own calculations.

The poor in Germany would also seem to have been under more pressure than in Britain and a number of other countries to keep silent about their poverty and not claim assistance, partly because less has been done to publicise rights and persuade people to exercise them. It is only very recently that 'welfare rights' movements have begun to develop in Germany, and there are still no national pressure groups campaigning explicitly on behalf of the poor. A number of studies suggest that old people in particular have been affected by this lack of effective publicity and pressure. In a survey in Berlin many elderly people felt that if they claimed assistance their children or grandchildren would be asked to contribute towards supporting them or to refund any grants which they might have drawn from the authorities; such practices were still quite prevalent in the 1950s, but subsequent changes in the law have considerably restricted their possible use and they are in any case hardly ever enforced now.[53] There are, though, some aspects of the German code of relief, especially in the means test itself, which are more stringent than in Britain; suggesting, perhaps, that even more than in Britain 'the old spectre of a minority who might abuse any support given is still a haunting presence'.[54] More generally,

TABLE 7.9   *SPES estimates of the number of persons below the 'official' poverty line and persons receiving social assistance*

	SPES estimates		Social assistance recipients
	(1) Persons in households where total household income below official minimum	(2) Persons in social assistance groups with income below official mimimum	(3) Persons receiving assistance at end of year
Number in thousands			
1962–3	573	–	–
1969	365	669	510
1974	496	1063	768
Percentage of population			
1962–3	1.0	–	–
1969	0.6	1.1	0.8
1974	0.8	1.7	1.2

Notes: Column 1 gives the estimates for all persons sharing a dwelling and constituting a household as conventionally defined. Column 2 follows the categories used by the social assistance authorities in defining maintenance responsibilities, and hence includes persons living with relatives and friends who may have no legal obligation to support them. The estimates in columns 1 and 2 are for all persons in the Federal Republic, Germans and foreigners, except those in institutions. Column 3 contains the number of persons living in households receiving assistance, except those in institutions.

Sources: see page 232.

too, the shame felt by many people in publicly declaring their poverty would seem to have been intensified in Germany both by the *Konsumterror*, the preoccupation of the majority with consumption and material achievement, and by a tendency, much less evident now than in the 1950s and 1960s, for society in general to keep quiet about 'a minority that makes the majority uncomfortable'.[55] Even though the climate of opinion has undoubtedly changed during the past decade, it is interesting that in the Common Market opinion survey in 1976 Germans appeared less inclined than respondents from any other country to give time and money to combat poverty, whereas a surprisingly large number (48 per cent in Germany as compared with 16 per cent in Denmark, 22 per cent in the Netherlands, 36 per cent in the UK and 47 per cent in France) said they had perceived people in poverty in the area where they lived.[56]

Some of the effects of this are illustrated in Table 7.9, where comparisons are made between the SPES estimates of 'official' poverty, including estimates for 1974 as well as for 1962–3 and 1969, and the number of people in households actually receiving assistance. According to SPES, in 1974 approximately 500,000 people were living in households where the total household income was below public assistance standards and a further 500,000, many of them clearly old people, were being supported by relatives or friends although they would appear to have been eligible for assistance. In both cases there is an increase over the 1969 levels: this seems to have been due mainly to an improvement in assistance rates, but the research also reveals an above-average rise in the numbers of foreign workers and their families in poverty. Apart from this, there is no reason to believe that the characteristics of households below the 'official' poverty line were much different in 1974 (before the full impact of the recession was felt) than in 1969, for which detailed estimates are given in Table 7.10.

Table 7.10 shows that the risk of this severe poverty has been greatest amongst the elderly and households headed by women. The latter include elderly widows, who have constituted one of the largest single groups in poverty, and also single, separated and divorced women over sixty-five. Like the widows of the lower-paid and irregularly employed, separated and divorced women have been particularly harshly treated by German pension provisions. Indeed, until recently when some improvements have been made in their position, the pension regulations made no provision for divorced women to share in their former husbands' pensions as long as the husbands were living, and when they died benefits based on the length of marriage and with no minimum pension were paid only if the women had been receiving alimony.[57] Amongst younger households those headed by single, separated and divorced mothers appear also to have been most at risk, again because of discriminatory legal and social provisions. Studies of single-parent families show that non-payment and irregular payment of maintenance has been a big problem, but one made worse by a widespread public expectation that they should be 'independent of the state' and not rely on public assistance, even though single mothers can often only find low-paid work or can only afford to do part-time work.[58] The SPES research also reveals, as one would expect, that the risk of poverty has been generally higher amongst larger families, and it shows too that at the end of the 1960s farmers as well as *Gastarbeiter* were three times as much at risk than others in the labour force.

TABLE 7.10 *Characteristics of households with incomes below social assistance levels (official minimum) in 1969*

Head of household	Risk of poverty %	Percentage distribution	Household size	Risk of poverty %	Percentage distribution
Farmer	0.5	2.5	1 person	1.7	58.9
Other self-employed	0.2	1.9	2 persons	0.7	24.0
Public official	0.0	0.2	3 persons	0.2	4.6
Salaried employee	0.1	1.2	4 persons	0.2	3.5
Manual worker	0.2	7.5	5 persons	0.3	2.8
Non-employed	2.0	86.7	6 persons	0.7	2.9
All households	0.7	100.0	7 and more	1.1	3.3
			All households	0.7	100.0
Age					
Under 21	0.9	0.2	**Household type**		
21–24	0.1	0.4	Single man	0.8	9.3
25–49	0.3	17.2	Single woman	2.1	49.5
50–59	0.3	6.2	Couple, no children	0.6	18.3
60–64	0.5	6.6	one child	0.1	0.8
Over 65	2.3	69.3	2 children	0.1	2.3
All households	0.7	100.0	3 children	0.2	1.8
Male head			4 and more children	1.2	7.1
unmarried	0.5	3.8	Others	0.9	10.8
married	0.3	30.6	*All households*	0.7	100.0
widowed	1.5	4.1			
divorced	0.7	1.4	**Population of area where household lives**		
Female head			Under 20,000	1.0	59.9
unmarried	1.9	15.1	20,000–100,000	0.6	16.1
married	4.2	1.1	Over 100,000	0.4	27.6
widowed	1.7	29.7	No answer	1.3	6.3
divorced	3.7	14.3	*All households*	0.7	100.0
All households	0.7	100.0			

Source: Information supplied by Klaus Kortmann of SPES Project.

In assessing the results of the SPES research it is important to remember that the severest effects of unemployment have only been felt since 1974, and also that the very poor were probably under-represented in the SPES sample. For example, it is highly unlikely that the sample would have included homeless persons or those with no fixed residence; between 500,000 and one million persons are officially classed as *Obdachlose* or homeless, and there are approximately 100,000 *Nichtsesshafte* or persons of no fixed abode.[59] Because of their official status many homeless people would probably receive public assistance or have incomes above the poverty line. However, according to one of the SPES reports, when they are taken into account and other biases in the sample allowed for, it would seem that at least a further 500,000 would be added to the numbers in poverty.[60] In other words, the SPES study suggests that in 1974 between one and one-and-a-half million people were living below the state's poverty line. This was rather more than 2 per cent of the German population, and almost twice the number of people actually receiving regular public assistance payments. Given the increase in unemployment since 1974, it seems likely that the proportion would now be nearer or even above 3 per cent of the population. While it is clearly impossible to make any precise comparisons with the findings of British research, it is interesting that the British surveys also show a similar proportion of the population living below the supplementary benefit standard, but when compared with the average standard of living this seems a higher 'poverty line' than the German minimum. As has been implied before, however, the German record looks much more favourable, at least according to the SPES research, if one moves from this severe form of poverty to a measure of mild poverty; mainly because there is not the dependence on public assistance nor the significant grouping of households just above the minimum found in Britain.

There are a number of indications from other research that the SPES study still understates the incidence of 'official' poverty, even with the allowances made for biases in its sample. How far this is the case is, though, difficult to evaluate since most other evidence is either based on local surveys[61] or would appear to err much more than the SPES estimates. An example of the latter, which illustrates also some interesting aspects of the politics of poverty in the Federal Republic, is the report on *Armut im Wohlfahrtsstaat* (Poverty in the Welfare State) published in 1975 by Heiner Geissler, a close colleague of the leader of the Christian Democratic opposition in the *Bundestag*, Helmut Kohl, and at the time Minister for Social Affairs in the state government of the Rhineland-Palatinate.[62] The Geissler report applies its own calculations of the public assistance level of living to the DIW data on incomes to produce estimates of the extent of 'official' poverty which are widely at variance with the SPES findings. They suggest that in 1974, when just over three-quarters of a million people were receiving public assistance, 'the monthly net incomes of around two million households – about 9 per cent of all households – containing 5.8 million people fell below the public assistance levels'. Or, as the opening sentence of the report puts it, 'Poverty, a theme long since thought dead, is an oppressive reality for millions of people.' In contrast to the SPES estimates, too, the Geissler report suggests that workers' and employees' households constitute more than 40 per cent of poor households.

These calculations are in turn used as evidence of the emergence of a 'New Social Question' (*Neue Soziale Frage*) affecting those sections of society not protected by the powerful groups and associations of the modern welfare state. This is a theme which the Christian Democrats, in common with conservative parties in a number of countries, have developed increasingly in the 1970s as part of a much more wide-ranging argument for counterbalancing and containing union power. The theory underlying the 'New Social Question' still stresses the levelling tendencies at work in modern German society; but, in contrast to the 'levelled-out middle-class society' theory of the 1950s and 1960s, these are now seen to have applied mainly to the organised majority of workers represented by strong trade unions. Indeed, according to Geissler, organised labour has now become so strong that it not only effectively shares power with those representing the interests of capital but also adversely affects the minorities in the labour force and many people outside it:[63]

> We can see that in the tug of war between unions and employers over the redistribution of rewards in an inflationary society it is not possible for either side to wrest permanent advantages at the expense of the other. It is the non-organised people at whose expense such advantages are gained, namely large families, single mothers and their children, senior citizens and people no longer capable of working, and the handicapped.

In policy terms the 'New Social Question' has led the Christian Democrats to advocate greater selectivity and discrimination in social policy, not just to provide more protection for these unorganised sections of society, but also as a way of reducing the support given by the state to the organised majority.

Not surprisingly, these arguments have provoked a lot of controversy, particularly since neither the development of personal incomes nor the distribution of wealth would seem to justify the conclusions about the balance of power between capital and labour. Moreover, while there is clearly a sense in which the poorest sections in Germany, as elsewhere, have lacked organisation and have not been well represented by trade unions, their poverty – in particular, that of the poorest pensioners and wage earners – is, as we have seen, for the most part rooted in the broader pattern of inequalities, which itself reflects the imbalance between capital and labour. But the arguments have been seriously weakened also by some detailed criticisms of Geissler's

methods in measuring poverty. These leave little doubt that the DIW
model errs more than the SPES research by exaggerating the numbers
in poverty and, more important, that Geissler's poverty line was set
significantly higher than the public assistance received by most claimants or the SPES version of the 'official' minimum.[64] To give an
example, the poverty line for single pensioners included an allowance
for housing costs that was almost twice the amount used in the SPES
research, which had the advantage of knowing the actual housing costs
of people in the sample, and a 25 per cent increase in the assistance
rates for additional payments by the authorities (compared with a 10
per cent supplement in the SPES study). In effect, the Geissler standard
appears to have been closer for all except large families to the SPES
'mild' poverty line and, in relative terms, to have been above the British
supplementary benefit levels. Nevertheless, it was still a far from
generous standard. It was more than 10 per cent below the 'subjective
minimum' in the Common Market survey and not dissimilar to levels
which some researchers have argued would represent a minimum 'citizenship standard', allowing participation in the community's normal
style of living.[65]

Other aspects of poverty and inequality

Despite these recent revelations and the trends in unemployment, the
Germans interviewed in the EEC opinion poll in 1976 left little doubt
that they felt themselves in a more favourable position than most
others in the Community where personal incomes and social security
benefits were concerned. However, a more detailed analysis of attitudes to living and working conditions, including answers to questions
about health, housing, work, spare-time and relations with other
people as well as incomes and social benefits, revealed a different
picture in which a significant minority of Germans (19 per cent as
compared with 18 per cent in the whole Community) were classed by
the researchers as 'discontented'.[66] These were in turn divided into
two types. The first was 'a small sub-group (4.5 per cent of the European population) whose answers all tend to give an impression of profound and lasting poverty': this contained 4 per cent of both German
and British respondents, but barely 1 per cent of the Danes and Dutch.
The second group, with 15 per cent of Germans compared with an EEC
average of 13 per cent and 11 per cent in Britain, was seen as sharing
'many of the same characteristics as the first, although to a lesser extent. We feel they are more embittered than really poor'.
    Many problems arise, of course, in attempts to measure and inter-
pret feelings of contentment and discontent, and particularly to make

cross-national comparisons like these. The researchers point out that answers often appeared to depend less 'on the actual situations experienced by respondents than on . . . subjective, psychosocial and probably cultural characteristics'. In the German case, though, there is more objective evidence suggesting that a broadening of the definition of poverty to take account of other aspects of deprivation than lack of income or the possession of certain consumer durables leads to a more marked increase in 'poverty' than in a number of other countries. This is certainly the impression gained from comparing some of the other findings of the SPES study with the results of British research, and also from comparative studies of poverty carried out in different parts of Germany and Britain.[67] These reveal, for instance, more of a discrepancy between the housing standards of the poor and the average family in Germany than in Britain, mainly, it seems, because the Federal Republic's much vaunted social housing programme has conspicuously failed to reach the poor. According to the SPES study, only a very small minority of those with incomes around the 'official' poverty line were living in social housing in 1969, whereas in Britain almost half the households with incomes below supplementary benefit levels have been living in local authority housing.

A study by Frank Klanberg of the SPES team gives an indication of the very poor quality housing of the families below the 'official' poverty line in 1969.[68] More than three-quarters had no bathroom or shower or central heating, and the majority of the elderly had no personal flush-toilet. Klanberg shows also that if the poverty line is redefined to include an allowance for housing costs based on officially recommended minimum standards of housing space and the average rent in socially-aided housing the proportion of households below the minimum in 1969 would have risen from 1 per cent to 3 per cent and those below 150 per cent of the minimum from 10 per cent to 16 per cent. Since 1969 the situation has undoubtedly improved as the Social Democrat-Liberal governments have given more priority to raising minimum housing standards. However, in common with other countries, Germany's land and building prices have risen dramatically in the 1970s, and there are many examples of housing projects directed at low-income groups and large families having to be postponed or abandoned because the costs necessitated rents that were too high, even when housing allowances were taken into account.[69] There still remains, too, a serious take-up problem with Germany's means-tested housing allowance scheme, which aims in principle both to stimulate house-building for the poor and to keep essential expenditures on housing below about 10 per cent of net income in the case of families with very low incomes. Statistics are not readily available; but, for example, one study quotes an estimate from the head of Munich's housing department that the take-up rate there in 1973 was less than 50 per cent.[70]

The efforts of the Social Democrats have also done little to reduce the surprisingly large numbers of people who, because they are classed as 'problem families' or for some other reason have been evicted or failed to obtain ordinary housing, are housed in local authority accommodation for the *Obdachlose* or homeless. The 500,000 to one million homeless provide a striking example of a group which may well contain people with incomes above the 'official' minimum, but which in every other respect constitutes a distinctive 'pauper' group, socially despised and often segregated from the rest of the community. The conditions of the homeless again illustrate the distinction which persists in many parts of Germany between the relatively generous social provisions made for the 'good' worker and the average family and the much harsher treatment of certain marginal groups whose problems are still commonly attributed to their 'asocial' behaviour and who are hence seen as needing regulation and control.[71] Under pressure from the Federal Government the treatment of the homeless has clearly improved since the early 1960s, when in many areas the grim barrack-like *Obdachlosenlager* were still run in the old Prussian tradition by the police authorities. But this is how a recent report of one of the Federal Ministries described the present predicament of the homeless:[72]

> The accommodation in which the homeless are placed frequently does not correspond to the housing standards which human dignity demands. It is often isolated from other residential areas and is not sufficiently connected to public transport systems, so that problems arise as regards children going to school or receiving medical treatment or people shopping for daily needs. Often these settlements lack adequate social and socio-pedagogical amenities. . . . The problems are aggravated by discrimination and stigma which in turn lead to more social isolation. This adversely affects the intellectual, vocational and social development of children and young people. Hence in times of economic recession the financial security of these families is especially endangered. Because so many people live together in a restricted space, and because of the lack of hygienic facilities, there is an increased danger of infectious diseases spreading.

Medical care provides some further illustrations of more marked differences between policies and standards of provision for the poor and for average families, and more generally of wider inequalities than are found in a number of other countries, including Britain. The evidence of recent research suggests that, while Germany's health insurance and assistance schemes provide vitually free access to medical care, the poor are disadvantaged both by the unequal distribution of resources and because of the mismatch between the organisation of medical services and the life-styles of lower-income families.[73] To give one example, a study in Cologne showed that whereas 95 per cent of all children in the city were born in a clinic, in some of the poorest areas up to 60 per cent were not, but were often brought into the world under extremely unfavourable circumstances.[74] The study concluded that there were three main reasons why mothers from poor families resisted going into a clinic: their fear of being regarded as outsiders; the difficulties they had in leaving their husbands and children to fend for themselves; and that they were often frightened by the difficult bureaucratic procedures which had to be contended with to enter a clinic. While this is perhaps an extreme example from a local study, such differences would seem partly to explain Germany's poor ranking by a number of health indicators, but particularly in infant and maternal mortality rates. At the end of the 1960s its infant mortality rate of 23 per 1000 live births put the Federal Republic in twelfth place amongst European countries. More recent figures for the mid-1970s show that the rate is still 30 per cent higher than in Britain, while the German maternal mortality rate is five times the British level.[75]

German studies of poverty and inequality have also placed a lot of emphasis on the health problems of workers arising both from the pressures of the *Konsumterror* and from demanding and stressful working conditions.[76] On the latter there is evidence, for instance, that at least until the early 1970s an increasing number of workers were doing difficult shift work and night work: between 1965 and 1972 the proportion on night work rose from 11 per cent to 13 per cent of the labour force, the latter representing more than three million workers.[77] In the most intensive phase of economic growth during the 1950s and early 1960s industrial accident rates also rose dramatically, and although they have since been steadily reduced they still appear high by comparison with other countries. According to an EEC report on accidents in the iron and steel industry, in the early 1970s only Italy had a worse record than the Federal Republic: the German rate of 105 accidents per one million working hours compared with 70 in France and 45 in the Netherlands.[78] Earlier we referred briefly to research suggesting a link between stressful working conditions and the high accident rates and the high standards of social security and accident compensation.

Another feature of post-war German society which has often been commented on has been the persistence of considerable inequalities of educational opportunity and constraints on social mobility, more so than in many other comparable countries. This again was particularly evident in the 1950s and 1960s and was also linked at the time by critics of German society with the high standards of social security. In *Society and Democracy in Germany*, which was written in the mid-1960s, Ralf Dahrendorf argued that social and educational policies in Germany often appeared to have less to do with laying an effective basis for citizenship rights than with 'preventing people from a modern rationality of choice by securing them forever at the place they happen to be'.[79] In Dahrendorf's analysis, too, the reversion to traditional educational policies after the War, or rather after the end of the Allied Occupation, was mainly responsible for an almost insurmountable barrier in German society, which he saw as dividing 'approximately the upper third of the edifice of stratification from the lower two thirds' and powerfully reinforcing the broader structure of inequalities. 'Whether an individual stands on one side of the barrier or the other is a position falling to him without his doing, and one he can escape only in the exceptional case. In this sense, German society continues to be a divided society: divided into an Above that knows little of the Below, and a Below that knows equally little of the Above'.[80]

TABLE 7.11   *Working-class students in higher education*

a. *OECD estimates of students from lower socio-economic groups as a percentage of all students in 1965*

West Germany	5.3	Italy	15.4
Belgium	22.8	Norway	23.9
France	9.0	UK	26.6

b. *The proportion of German students in higher education whose father is/was a manual worker (Arbeiter)*

	All students %	Males %	Females %
1928–9	2.1	2.3	0.7
1952–3	4.4	4.9	1.4
1958–9	5.2	6.0	2.1
1967–8	6.7	7.5	4.1
1973	11.5	12.7	8.3

Sources: see page 232.

As Table 7.11 shows, since this was written the proportion of working-class students in higher education appears to have doubled, and in most other respects too the past decade has seen a much more determined attempt to promote more educational opportunity. As elsewhere, there are still formidable obstacles to change, which have led to some reform initiatives having to be postponed or modified; but the main impression one gains is that a gradual but profound transformation is taking place in German education. Similarly, and as part of the wider debate on the quality of life in the Federal Republic, there has been far more public discussion of working conditions during the 1970s, and this has led to the widespread adoption of more flexible working hours and more efforts to reduce accident rates. Significantly, too, recent studies have shown how younger workers appear far less inclined than their fathers to accept their existence 'below'.[81] Hence, in these as in other respects, the pattern and structure of inequalities in the Federal Republic appears to be in an interesting state of transition.

References

1 I am extremely grateful to Klaus Kortmann, Wolfgang Glatzer, Frank Klanberg and other members of the SPES team for discussing their work with me and providing me with much of the empirical data on income inequality and poverty referred to in the chapter.

2 W. Zapf (ed.), *Lebensbedingungen in der Bundesrepublik,* Campus Verlag, Frankfurt / New York, 1977, pp. 11ff. A number of other SPES studies are referred to below.

3 K. Kortmann and G. Schmaus, *Generierung des Mikrodatenfiles 1969 für die Bundesrepublik Deutschland,* SPES Arbeitspapier no. 39, 1975.

4 The main income studies by DIW are: Deutsches Institut für Wirtschaftsforschung, *Einkommensverteilung der privaten Haushalte in der Bundesrepublik Deutschland 1950–1975,* Berlin, 1972; 'Einkommensverteilung und -schichtung der privaten Haushalte in der Bundesrepublik Deutschland 1950–1970', in *Wochenbericht,* 25, 1973; 'Das Einkommen sozialen Gruppen in der Bundesrepublik Deutschland im Jahre 1973', in *Wochenbericht,* 35, 1975.

5 For criticisms of the available information on personal incomes see H-J. Krupp, *Möglichkeiten der Verbesserung der Einkommens und Vermögensstatistik,* Otto Schwarz, Göttingen, 1975; and K-D. Bedau, 'Einige Bemerkungen zur Statistik der Einkommensverteilung', in *WSI-Mitteilung,* 4, 1975.

6 According to an OECD survey, the share of income of the bottom 10% was Germany (1973) 2.8%, France (1970) 1.4%, Sweden (1972) 2.2%, UK (1973) 2.5%, United States (1972) 1.5%. That of the top 10% was Germany 30.3%, France 30.4%, Sweden 21.3%, UK 23.5%, and the USA 26.6%. The survey also made estimates of the incidence of relative poverty which are discussed in the final chapter. OECD, *Public Expenditure on Income Maintenance Programmes,* Paris, 1976.

7 See, for example, P. Roberti, 'Income Inequality in some Western Countries', *International Journal of Social Economics,* 5 January,

1978; and Economic Commission for Europe, *Incomes in Postwar Europe*, United Nations, Geneva, 1967.

8 Royal Commission on the Distribution of Income and Wealth, *5th Report of the Standing Committee*, HMSO, London, 1977, pp. 115–18.

9 OECD, op. cit., chs 2 and 3; and European Commission, Annual Reports on the Development of the Social Situation in the Community. According to the OECD study, the Federal Republic's total expenditures on public income maintenance programmes amounted to 11.9% of 'trend' GDP in 1962 and 12.4% in 1973. The average for OECD countries was 6.8% in 1962 and 8.6% in 1972/3.

10 See, for example, H. Wallich, *Mainsprings of the German Revival*, Yale University Press, New Haven, 1955.

11 Ibid., ch. 10.

12 For an interesting critical discussion of the attitudes towards inequality in the 1950s and early 1960s, see D. Claessens, A. Klönne and A. Tschoepe, *Sozialkunde der Bundesrepublik Deutschland*, Eugen Diederichs Verlag, Düsseldorf/Cologne, 1974, p. 320ff.

13 A. Shonfield, *Modern Capitalism*, Oxford University Press, London, 1969, p. 266.

14 J. Krejci, *Social Structure in Divided Germany*, Croom Helm, London, 1976, p. 60.

15 Krejci's study shows the following changes in national income by distributive shares between 1960 and 1974:

	1960	1970	1974
Total gross income from employment	60.6	66.7	71.6
of which			
net wages and salaries	44.5	44.8	43.9
income from social insurance, etc.	16.0	16.4	18.6
balance	0.1	5.5	9.1
Total gross income from enterprise and property	39.4	33.3	28.4
of which			
tax and other obligatory payments	8.9	6.6	6.7
distributed profits accruing to private households	19.8	21.1	21.3
distributed profits accruing to the government	1.2	0.8	0.3
Non-distributed profits	9.5	4.8	0.1

16 D. Eversley, 'Britain and Germany: Local Government in Perspective', in R. Rose (ed.), *The Management of Urban Change in Britain and Germany*, Sage Publications, London, 1974, p. 264.

17 Quoted in Deutscher Bundestag — 7 Wahlperiode, *Drucksache 7/2423*, p. 437.

18 The DIW estimates show the following differences between social groups:

		Households	Average household income
		1000s	DM
Self-employed	1950	2820	567
	1970	2500	3267
Salaried employees/ Public officials	1950	2885	425
	1970	5285	1842
Manual workers	1950	5285	331
	1970	6895	1519
Pensioners and non-employed	1950	4260	203
	1970	7720	911
All households	1950	15250	357
	1970	22400	1581

19 E. Helmstädter, J. Heubes, R. Krupp and B. Meyer, *Wirtschafts-kunde der Bundesrepublik Deutschland*, Eugen Diederichs Verlag, Düsseldorf/Cologne, 1975, pp. 213ff.
20 J. Siebke, *Die Vermögensbildung der privaten Haushalte in der BRD*, Bonn, 1971, quoted in Claessens *et al.*, op. cit., p. 230.
21 Krejci, op. cit., pp. 52–9.
22 Claessens, *et al.*, op. cit., p. 233.
23 A. Heidenheimer, H. Heclo and C. Teich Adams, *Comparative Public Policy*, Macmillan, London, 1976, p. 200.
24 See, for example, F. Böhle and D. Sauer, 'Intensivierung der Arbeit und staatliche Sozialpolitik', in *Leviathan*, 3, 1975, pp. 49–78; and F. Nohle, 'Humanisierung der Arbeit und Sozialpolitik', in C. von Ferber and F-X. Kaufmann (eds), *Soziologie und Sozialpolitik*, West Deutscher Verlag, Cologne, 1977.
25 Quoted in J. Roth, *Armut in der Bundesrepublik*, Fischer Taschenbuch, Frankfurt, 1974, p. 29.
26 R. Lawson and M. Young, 'Poverty and Social Security in Britain and Germany', in M. Young (ed.), *Poverty Report, 1975*, Temple Smith, London, 1975.
27 The development of policies for single-parent families in Germany, with comparisons with France, Belgium, Denmark and the UK, is discussed in R. Lawson, 'Social Security, Employment and the Single-Parent Family' in A. Samuels (ed.), *Social Security and Family Law*, Oceana Publications, London, 1980.
28 K. Jantz, 'Pension Reform in the Federal Republic of Germany', in *International Labour Review*, 83, 1961.
29 Young, op. cit., p. 166.
30 Recent comparative studies of poverty in the Federal Republic and other countries include OECD, op. cit., part II; Peter Willmott, Phyllis Willmott and Linda McDowell, *Poverty and Social Policy in Europe – A Pilot Study in the United Kingdom, Germany and France*, Institute of Community Studies, London, 1978; Young, op. cit., part 3.

230   Roger Lawson

31 P. Willmott *et al., op. cit.*, p. 170.
32 F. Klanberg, *Armut und Ökonomische Ungleichheit in der Bundes-republik*, doctoral dissertation, University of Frankfurt, 1977. According to Klanberg's estimates, in 1969 7.6 per cent of all manual workers' households with a head of household under 25 had incomes below a poverty line set at just over 50 per cent of average *per capita* income for a single person. But when guest-workers were excluded the proportion fell to 1.6 per cent.
33 S. Castles and G. Kosack, *Immigrant Workers and the Class Structure in Western Europe*, Oxford University Press, 1973, pp. 39f.
34 S.H. Paine, 'The Changing Role of Migrant Workers in the Advanced Capitalist Economies of Western Europe', in R.T. Griffiths (ed.), *Government Business and Labour in European Capitalism*, Euro-potentials Press, London, 1978, p. 205.
35 Zapf, op. cit., p. 295. The proportion of unskilled manual workers in industry has developed as follows:

	Male %	Female %
1950	20.4	37.8
1960	14.1	48.5
1964	11.9	47.2
1968	12.0	47.6
1974	12.4	49.5

36 R. Titmuss, *Social Policy: an Introduction*, Allen & Unwin, London, 1974, p. 18.
37 Paine, op. cit., p. 214.
38 See, for example, Der Spiegel-Redaktion, *Unterprivilegiert – Eine Studie über sozialbenachteiligte Gruppen in der BRD*, Luchterhand, Neuwied/Darmstadt, 1973, pp. 39–89.
39 *Der Spiegel*, no. 4, 22 January 1979, pp. 85–6; *Der Spiegel*, 'Gastarbeiter – ab nach Hause?', no. 9, i.3, 1976.
40 For a description of German unemployment insurance and assistance benefits, see the Federal Ministry for Labour and Social Affairs, *Survey of Social Security in the Federal Republic of Germany*, Bonn, 1972. An unusual feature of the means-tested unemployment rates is that its benefits are earnings-related.
41 H. Geissler, *Die Neue Soziale Frage*, Herder, Freiburg, 1976, pp. 47–8.
42 Rheinland-Pfalz Ministerium für Soziales, Gesundheit und Sport, *Begleiter der Arbeitslosigkeit: Abstieg und Armut*, 1978.
43 Commission of the European Communities, *The Perception of Poverty in Europe*, Brussels, 1977, p. 19.
44 Rheinland-Pfalz Ministerium, op. cit., p. 51.
45 For a discussion of the changes in agriculture, see Krejci, op. cit., pp. 90–3; and G. Hallett, *The Social Economy of West Germany*, Macmillan, London, 1973, ch. 4.

46 *Der Spiegel*, 'Arbeitslosigkeit: Viele Pläne, kein Rezept', no. 21, 16 May 1977, pp. 21ff.
47 Quoted in Rheinland-Pfalz Ministerium, op. cit., p. 1.
48 *Der Spiegel*, 'Arbeitslos – feines Leben auf fremde Kosten', no. 21, 16 May 1977, pp. 24ff.
49 W. Heimann, *Bundessozialhilfegesetz*, Reckinger, Siegburg, 1969, p. 25.
50 A. Atkinson, *The Economics of Inequality*, Clarendon Press, Oxford; 1975, p. 190.
51 K. Peterson, *Die Regelsätze nach dem BSHG*, Deutsche Verein für öffentliche und private Fürsorge, 43, Frankfurt, 1972, pp. 68f.
52 Commission of the European Communities, op. cit., p. 19.
53 O. Blume, *Die Lebenssituation über 65 jähriger Bürger in Berlin*, Institut für Sozialforschung und Gessellschaftspolitik EV, Cologne, 1974.
54 Lawson and Young, op. cit., p. 158.
55 Ibid., p. 156. See also R. Dahrendorf, *Society and Democracy in Germany*, Weidenfeld & Nicolson, London, 1968, ch. 22. Dahrendorf writes of a 'great quiet' that ruled amongst the citizens of the Federal Republic in the 1950s and 1960s. 'It is not done to get worked up, and definitely not about the inhumanities in one's own world' (p. 363).
56 Commission of the European Communities, op. cit., part 3.
57 D. Hoskins and L. Boxby, *Women and Social Security*, US Social Security Administration, New York, 1973, p. 28.
58 Lawson, op. cit.
59 Bundesministerium für Jugend, Familie und Gesundheit, *Bericht über die Eingliederung von Personen mit besonderen sozialen Schwierigkeiten*, Bonn, 1976, p. 4f.
60 K. Kortmann, *Zur Armutsdiscussion in der Bundesrepublik Deutschland*, SPES Arbeitspapier, Frankfurt, no. 50, 1976.
61 See, for example, M. Young, op. cit., ch. 9, and Institut für angewandte Sozialwissenschafte, *Soziale Sicherung und Armutspotential*, Bad Godesberg, 1975.
62 Geissler, op. cit., pp. 45–56.
63 Ibid., p. 15.
64 Kortmann, op. cit., contains a detailed criticism of the methods of the Geissler Report.
65 For a discussion of the notion of the citizenship minimum see, for example, U. Christiansen, *Obdachlos weil arm*, Edition 2000, Giessen, 1973, ch. 1.
66 Commission of the European Communities, op. cit., part 3.
67 Lawson and Young, op. cit., ch. 10; Wilmott et al., op. cit.
68 Klanberg, op. cit., pp. 153f.
69 R. Lawson and C. Stevens, 'Housing Allowances in West Germany and France', *Journal of Social Policy*, vol. 3, no. 3, 1974; and R. Lawson, 'Housing Allowances in Germany', *Roof*, vol. 1, no. 1, 1976.

70 Quoted in W. Zollner, *Obdachlos durch Wohnungsnot*, Rowohlt, Hamburg, 1973.
71 Studies of the conditions of the homeless include: Christiansen, op. cit.; Zollner, op. cit.; and Der Spiegel Redaktion, op. cit., pp. 1–39.
72 Bundesministerium für Jugend, Familie und Gesundheit, op. cit., pp. 5–6.
73 See, for example, H. Reiners and V. Volkholz (eds), *Das Gesundheitssystem in der BRD*, VSA, Hamburg, 1977.
74 Quoted in Roth, op. cit., p. 56.
75 In 1974 the British infant mortality rate was 16.7 per 1000 live births and the German rate 21.7; maternal mortality rates per 1000 live births were 0.1 in Britain and 0.5 in Germany. For a further discussion of the problems in Germany, see Reiners and Volkholz, op. cit.
76 See, for example, Roth, op. cit.; and Zapf, op. cit., pp. 677–743.
77 Zapf, op. cit., p. 263.
78 Ibid., p. 276.
79 Dahrendorf, op. cit., p. 437 and ch. 5.
80 Ibid., p. 109.
81 See, for example, Zapf, op. cit., pp. 209f.

Source of Tables
7.1 Deutsches Institut für Wirtschaftsforschung, op. cit. (1972); OECD, op. cit., p. 351.
7.2 Zapf, op. cit., p. 351; OECD, op. cit.; Roberti, op. cit.
7.3 Zapf, op. cit., p. 209 f.
7.4 Claessens, *et al.*, op. cit., p. 231; Siebke, op. cit.
7.5 Zapf, op. cit., pp. 353 and 359.
7.6 Ibid., p. 209 f.
7.7 For (a), (c) and (d) — Zapf, op. cit., p. 209 f. For (b) — Rheinland-Pfalz Ministerium, op. cit., p. 5.
7. 9 Zapf, op. cit., p. 359; Kortmann, op. cit.
7.11 Zapf, op. cit., p. 794; OECD Observer, August 1970.

8 An assessment

Roger Lawson and Vic George

We have so far documented in detail the extent of poverty and inequality in six of the Common Market countries. In this chapter we wish to bring together the main conclusions emerging from this detailed discussion and to discuss more specifically the relationship between social security and poverty.

Trends in income inequality and poverty

The period under discussion includes two decades in which the levels of economic growth in Europe as a whole well exceeded those of any earlier period for which records are available. According to recent calculations by Bairoch, European *per capita* income growth barely reached 1 per cent per annum from 1800 to 1950, as against 4.5 per cent

TABLE 8.1 *Economic growth in the EEC countries*

GDP at constant prices: annual percentage rates of growth

	1950–2 to 1958–60	1958–60 to 1967–69	1970 to 1975
Belgium	2.5	4.5	3.4
Denmark	3.2	4.7	2.1
West Germany	7.5	5.1	1.9
France	4.3	5.5	4.6
Ireland	9.8	4.0	2.7
Netherlands	4.5	5.5	3.1
UK	2.4	2.9	2.0
EEC average	3.8	4.7	2.8

Sources: D. Aldcroft, *The European Economy 1914–1970*, Croom Helm, London, 1978; European Commission, *Social Indicators for the European Community 1960–1975*, Brussels, 1977.

between 1950 and 1970.[1] As Table 8.1 shows, all the present EEC
states, with the exception of the UK, experienced similarly high levels
of growth in the late 1950s and 1960s. Even Britain's relatively poor
economic performance produced average annual growth rates of 2.7
per cent between 1950 and 1970 as compared with 1.7 per cent between 1913 and 1950 and 2.2 per cent between 1870 and 1913.[2] The
table also shows that most countries' growth rates in the 1970s have
remained at respectable levels by historical standards, in spite of the
recession and the problems of inflation. Western Europe's other post-
war achievements include, of course, more formal political and civil
equality than at any previous stage in its history, and an enormous
expansion of the social services. Like economic growth and the general
improvement in living standards, these are developments which have
often been equated with a reduction of relative inequalities.

TABLE 8.2   *Trends in social welfare expenditures in the EEC countries*

	OECD		European Commission		
	Public income maintenance expenditures in per cent of 'trend' GDP at current prices		Social security, health and welfare expenditures in per cent of GDP at current prices		
	1962*	1972*	1962	1970	1975
Belgium	11.7	14.1	15.8	18.5	24.4
Denmark	6.5	9.9		19.9	27.6
France	11.8	12.4		18.9	22.7
Germany	11.9	12.4	19.6	21.4	27.9
Ireland	5.3	6.4		13.2	20.4
Italy	7.5	10.4	14.4	18.8	23.7
Netherlands	8.6	14.1	14.1	20.7	28.4
UK	5.7	7.7		16.3	19.2
EEC average	8.2	10.6		18	24

Notes: *OECD figures for Ireland are for 1961-71, and the second column for
Germany and the Netherlands refers to 1973.
Sources: OECD, *Public Expenditures on Income Maintenance Programmes,*
Paris, 1976. European Commission, *Social Indicators for the European
Community 1960-1975,* Brussels, 1977.

The reasons for the growth of public expenditure in the social
services are many and in dispute, but they do not concern us here. We
merely want to note the important fact that the trends in income inequality and poverty which we are discussing took place during a
period of unprecedented high rates of growth both in the economy and
in government expenditure. In other words, there was abundant national

wealth and government activity to deal with the problems of excessive income inequality and poverty.

As the previous chapters have stressed, the reliability of data collected on income distribution must always be in question and hence, too, the conclusions drawn from the data. However, all the evidence in the chapters points to the persistence of considerable inequalities of income both before and after the payment of taxes. In most countries there appears to have been a slight redistribution of income away from the very rich, but this seems to have been mainly in favour of the relatively well-off. Moreover, in all the countries studied the richest 5 per cent and 10 per cent have retained between two-and-a-half and three times their 'parity shares', the shares they would have had if incomes had been equally distributed. Looking at incomes after taxes were paid in the UK, Italy and West Germany, the three countries for which we have detailed estimates covering the whole post-war period, the income shares of those with average and below average incomes have remained remarkably stable. In these countries, the shares of the bottom 60 per cent were as follows: UK (1949) 36 per cent and (1972) 36.3 per cent; Italy (1948) 31.4 per cent and (1973) 31.8 per cent; West Germany (1950) 32 per cent and (1973) 31.8 per cent. As regards the poorest groups, only the German data show a slight and sustained improvement over the whole post-war period; but, even so, the bottom 20 per cent and 30 per cent received a mere one percentage point more of total income in 1973 than in 1950.

While the main impression conveyed by the data is of underlying similarities between the countries, there are also some interesting differences in their patterns of income distribution and the extent of inequalities. Table 8.3 suggests that France and Italy are the most unequal countries judged by the shares going to the top and bottom deciles: they give most to the richest and least to the poorest 10 per cent of the population. By other measures, too, and according to other surveys, there appears to be more widespread inequality of incomes in France and Italy than in most other advanced western countries.[3] The UK, on the other hand, has a less unequal distribution than most other countries and a pattern of inequality which is broadly similar to that found in Sweden and Norway: in this there is relatively less inequality at the top and comparatively greater equality at the lower levels of distribution. By most measures, income differentials in Belgium and West Germany would seem to lie somewhere between those in Britain on one hand and France and Italy on the other, though, as the German chapter has emphasised, the Federal Republic has had a quite distinctive pattern of inequality. The rich in Germany appear to have been relatively as well-off as the rich in France and Italy, but the poor seem to have been somewhat less poor than in most other countries.

TABLE 8.3   *Comparison of the income shares of rich and poor households**

Pre-tax income: percentage shares

	UK				Italy			
	1957–60	1961–5	1966–70	1971–4	1948	1958	1966-70	1971–2
Top 10%	25.8	24.6	23.7	24.2	34.8	30.8	29.3	28.8
Top 20%	41.1	40.1	39.4	39.9	49.6	46.4	45.4	45.4
Bottom 20%	5.8	6.1	6.2	5.6	5.5	4.4	4.9	4.5

	France		Ireland			Belgium	West Germany
	1965	1970	1966-7	1973	1973	1968	1973
Top 10%		31				32.6	31.1
Top 20%	50.5	47	42.3	42.5	44.5	46.8	46.8
Bottom 20%	3.6	4.3	5.4	4.7	4.1	5.7	5.9

	Denmark		Netherlands	
	1949	1966	1951-55	1967
Top 10%	29	26	31.8	30.5
Top 20%	45	42	46.9	46.4
Bottom 30%	9	9	8.8	8.9
Bottom 20%	4	4	4.2	4.3
Bottom 10%	1	1	1.3	1.2

Post-tax incomes: percentage shares

	UK			Italy		
	1961-5	1966-70	1971-3	1948	1966	1973
Top 10%	23.7	24.2	23.5	33.9	28.4	30.9
Top 20%	38.7	39	39	48.3	43.7	46.5
Bottom 30%	12.7	12.7	12.1	11	10.7	9.8
Bottom 20%	6.6	6.8	6.5			5.1
Bottom 10%	2.4	2.6	2.6			1.7

	West Germany				France	Belgium
	1950	1960	1968	1973	1970	1968
Top 10%	29.4	28.1	29.2	30.3	30.4	28.6
Top 20%	45.2	43.9	45.1	46.1	56.9	42.9
Bottom 30%	10.1	10.7	10.9	11.1	8.5	
Bottom 20%	5.4	6	6.2	6.5	4.3	6.6

Table 8.3 (continued)

Bottom 10%	2	2.4	2.6	2.8	1.4	2.2

Notes:
* the income units are households, except for France and Belgium where they are tax units.
** the first two columns for Ireland refer to urban households only. The third refers to all households.
Sources: See previous chapters.

Compared with Britain, those in the lower middle ranges of the distribution in Germany, the area where the mass of wage earners and lower-paid salaried employees are found, have had a relatively modest share of total personal income, though their real incomes and standards of living have obviously improved at a much faster rate than those of their British counterparts.

A person's income can be derived from various sources: employment, wealth, social security and other minor sources. As shown in the chapter on Britain, different sources of income relate to different income groups, with the result that the richest population group relies more on income from wealth than any other source, whilst the poorest group relies more on income from social security and employment than other sources. The importance of these sources varies from one country to another. The report of the Royal Commission on the distribution of income and wealth showed how the relatively higher levels of income inequality in France, West Germany and Ireland than in the UK accorded with the comparatively lower proportion of total income accounted for by earnings from employment and the higher share of entrepreneurial income in these countries.[4]

Our evidence on poverty, and particularly on changes in poverty over time, is much more difficult to summarise than that on income inequality. Of the countries studied, only the UK has a long-established tradition of poverty research, but much of the available evidence of poverty in Britain relies heavily on the 'official' definition of poverty associated with eligibility for supplementary benefits. While this is in many ways a useful yardstick for researchers and for pressure groups wishing to attract attention to the persistence of poverty, it is an inadequate measure of trends, and poses other serious conceptual problems. As Atkinson points out,[5]

> While the Supplementary Benefit scale has been approved by the British Parliament as a minimum income level, it does not necessarily enjoy widespread social approval as a national minimum and may well not provide the resources required to participate in the customary activities of the society in which people live. . . . An important objection to the use of the official poverty standards is

that they are based purely on money income and ignore other aspects of deprivation.

In recent years, West German researchers have faced similar criticisms as they have used the minimum standards of the Federal Social Assistance Law to measure poverty, and there has also been more dispute in Germany than in Britain about the precise levels of social assistance, partly because there is more scope for regional and local variations in assistance. Hence, estimates of the proportion of German households below the 'official' poverty line have ranged from just under 1 per cent to nearly 10 per cent. More generally, the previous chapters have revealed considerable differences in the poverty lines adopted by European researchers; not only in the basic standards used but also in the allowances made for differences in family size. Belgian researchers have, for instance, adopted poverty standards for pensioners not dissimilar, when related to average earnings, to the British supplementary benefit levels, but the Belgian poverty lines for families with children have been considerably higher than the British standards. Differences like these are themselves an interesting subject for research; and it may be argued, too, that the investigation of poverty would benefit if more attention were paid to work done in other countries. At present, though, it is clearly extremely difficult to evaluate comparatively evidence collected in different countries.

An OECD report contains an interesting attempt to obtain a general impression of the extent of poverty in a number of countries by applying a 'standardised relative poverty line' to income distribution data.[6] In the enquiry, it was arbitrarily assumed that a person would be poor if his income was below two-thirds of the average *per capita* disposable income in his country, and standard supplements to this figure were made for family size. The findings suggested that the extent of relative poverty in the early 1970s was 3 per cent of the population in West Germany, 7.5 per cent in the UK, and 16 per cent in France, while the average for the countries studied was 10 per cent (other national estimates were: Australia 8 per cent, Canada 11 per cent, Norway 5 per cent, Sweden 3.5 per cent, USA 13 per cent). Using the standardised poverty line and another cruder measure of relative poverty, the study also concluded that relative poverty had declined in West Germany and France during the 1960s and early 1970s but had 'possibly' risen in Britain. Our figures would seem to be broadly consistent with these findings on the extent of poverty, though there is reason to believe that the income data for West Germany used by OECD would have understated the extent of poverty. Rough comparisons between British and German research findings suggest that if a somewhat more severe measure of relative poverty than the OECD standard is used the proportions in poverty in the two countries are broadly similar, and possibly higher in West Germany. By a 'milder' definition of poverty, though, the extent of poverty in Germany would seem to be below that in Britain.

Our other figures are too disparate to be summarised easily. They show, however, that poverty persists on a substantial scale in Ireland and Italy. In Ireland at least 20 per cent of the population were esti-mated to be in poverty in 1970; by 1975 the proportion was estimated at 20–30 per cent on a more generous poverty line. In Italy, the picture is too complex, diverse and uncertain for meaningful estimates to be made, but in relative terms the proportion of people in poverty may not be all that lower than the 24 per cent of the population estimated in 1952. In Belgium, 5 per cent of all households were estimated as living below a severely defined official poverty line in 1976; using the more generous poverty line of the Centre for Social Policy the propor-tion was put at 24 per cent. A comparative study of old people in Denmark, Britain and the USA in the mid-1960s, using standardised poverty lines, found that poverty among this population group was less prevalent in Denmark than in Britain. In Britain 'nearly 23 per cent of the couples, 29 per cent of the men and about 50 per cent of the women . . . had incomes below this poverty line'. The corresponding proportions for Denmark were 20 per cent, 16 per cent and 12 per cent respectively.[7] This finding highlights the often forgotten fact that poverty among the elderly is predominantly a problem for women. When it is borne in mind that one-parent families are headed mostly by women and that it is women who are most likely not to qualify for insurance benefits, then it becomes clear that poverty affects women more than men. This, however, does not alter the basic fact that poverty is rooted in social class.

Income inequality and poverty are obviously related. Evidence from all countries shows that the low-paid worker of today is the pensioner in poverty of tomorrow; low-paid workers are more likely to be the unskilled workers who suffer from both repeated bouts of unemploy-ment and from long-term unemployment; and so on. Our evidence also shows that income inequality and poverty are related to other forms of deprivation in society: illness, inadequate housing and low educa-tional achievement. In all countries, too, there is evidence that newly arrived immigrants are over-represented among the low-paid and the deprived.

Social security and poverty

Several studies have shown that, among advanced industrial societies, the level of public expenditure on social security bears no relationship to the level of relative poverty. Among our countries, West Germany and France have high levels of social security expenditure; but the first has a low level of relative poverty while the second has a high level. As we pointed out earlier in this chapter, the poverty levels of Britain and West Germany are similar; so are those of France and Italy. These findings are in agreement with those of the OECD study which concluded that 'the relative level and changes in income maintenance expenditures do not bear much relationship to the extent or change in relative poverty'.[8]

This would seem to be partly because there are other more powerful structural and economic determinants of inequality and poverty, but also because, in most countries, the bulk of the post-war expansion of social welfare has not been aimed at low-income groups. It has been much more concerned with maintaining acquired social status and protecting the capacities and incentives of ordinary workers for gainful employment. On the Continent, in particular, it is the average employees and their families who have benefited most from improvements in 'security of life' and who have also through their tax and social insurance contributions played a prominent role in the financing of provisions. Hence, the impressive French and Belgian expenditures on family benefits have, to a large extent, redistributed income horizontally within similar income groups and, until recently at least, have done little to relieve poverty amongst the low-paid or single-parent families. In France, Belgium and Italy, too, most of the changes made in old age and disability pensions during the 1950s and 1960s were designed to benefit those in the broad middle stratum, but left significant numbers of the elderly, those who were previously lower-paid workers or intermittently employed, in poverty. Even in Germany, which has gone further than other countries in developing generous 'dynamic' pensions, there is still a significant minority of elderly and disabled people in poverty, mainly widows of unskilled or semi-skilled workers and others with very low pensions because of their failure to fulfil the necessary insurance contributions.

As the German chapter points out, too, the Federal Republic's social welfare programmes, which have involved larger expenditures than in most other western countries, have been far from egalitarian in their conception. Moreover, they have been financed in part by a 'guest-worker' population which, until recently, has rarely used social services and in a more general sense has acted as a buffer against poverty for many German workers. By comparison with these countries, Britain's social security policies have placed more emphasis on comprehensive minimum standards of benefit. Even though its levels of assistance are often considered inadequate, the OECD study shows that the supplementary benefit scheme in Britain provided a minimum pension in

1972 equal to 108 per cent of the OECD poverty line (for a single person) compared with 70 per cent in Germany and 45 per cent in France. In contrast to Germany, however, Britain has conspicuously failed to develop policies preventing large numbers of old people having to depend on social assistance or having incomes just above the 'official' minimum.

The persistence of income and other material inequalities over the years is natural to welfare capitalism, if one accepts the theoretical framework suggested in the first chapter. Without substantial inequalities and without the inheritance of wealth, capitalism loses both its driving force and its *raison d'être* as an economic system. The persistence of poverty, in terms of a minimum income for survival in an affluent society, is not, however, a necessary precondition to the survival of welfare capitalism. This type of poverty can be abolished within welfare capitalism. The fact that it has not so far been abolished does not mean that it cannot. In terms of direct costs, a social security scheme that ensures that everyone has an income adequate for a minimum standard of living is not likely to be that much more expensive than the existing schemes of most of the countries in our study. It is the fear of indirect costs to welfare capitalism that is more real: the fear that such a scheme will undermine work incentives and that it will act as a springboard for demands for further improvements in the guaranteed minimum living standards. In other words, abolition of poverty will lead to increased demands for reductions in income and wealth inequalities. Whether these fears – or hopes – are justified is impossible to say from the existing evidence. Much, of course, will depend on the level at which the guaranteed minimum income is set.

In spite of the failure of all our countries to reduce or to eradicate poverty, a slight change of emphasis in social security policies can be detected during the past decade, with more attention being given to the low-paid and disadvantaged workers: the introduction of the family income supplement and child benefit schemes in Britain; the new 'social minimum' benefits in Belgium and in France; and the liberalisation of social assistance and important changes in family allowances in Germany. These and other changes may be the beginning of a new awareness that some of the vast sums spent by social security systems should be re-directed to ensure that no one lives in poverty.

Whether these unco-ordinated measures will develop into a coherent policy for the low-paid will depend on the strength of the political forces demanding such a change. The population groups in poverty are directly related to the working class but they are not seen as such, nor do they form a unified social group wielding substantial political power. So far, the trade unions have not treated such groups as part of the working class meriting their support in the political and industrial

242   Roger Lawson and Vic George

arena. Each group has had to fight its own battles, often in open conflict with the demands of other groups. If and when such groups act
in unison and with the support of the trade unions, the battle for a
guaranteed minimum income for all will be won, and easily at that.
The prospects of this happening in the immediate future, however,
appear negligible.

References

1 D.H. Aldcroft, *The European Economy 1914–1970*, London,
   Croom Helm, 1978, p. 161.
2 A. Shonfield, *Modern Capitalism*, Oxford University Press, 1969,
   p. 4.
3 P. Roberts, 'Income Inequality in some Western Countries: Patterns
   and Trends', *International Journal of Social Economics*, vol. 5, no.
   1, 1978.
4 Royal Commission on the Distribution of Income and Wealth, *5th
   Report of the Standing Committee*, HMSO, London, 1977, Table
   53, p. 116.
5 A. Atkinson, *The Economics of Inequality*, Clarendon Press, Oxford,
   1975, p. 191.
6 OECD, *Public Expenditure on Income Maintenance Programmes*,
   Paris, 1976.
7 E. Shanas *et al.*, *Old People in Three Industrial Societies*, Routledge
   & Kegan Paul, 1968, p. 373.
8 OECD, *Public Expenditure on Income Maintenance Programmes*,
   op. cit., p. 71.

Index

Symbols used to distinguish countries are as follows: B Belgium, F France; G West Germany; Ir Ireland; It Italy; UK United Kingdom.

A. à T.D., *see* Bureau de Recherches Sociales of Aide à Toute Détresse
Abel-Smith, B., 37, 38, 39, 54
accident rate, G, 206
Accords de Grenelle, to help lowest paid, 117
'Agenda for Poverty Research, An', 128
Agricultural Institute, Ir, *see* An Foras Taluntais
agriculture, *see* farmers and farming
Aiach, Pierre, 109, 110, 111
Alps, 166
Anderson, Ch. H., 18
An Foras Taluntais (Agricultural Institute), incomes of farmers, 150
Antwerp, generous assistance in, 67
Antwerp University, Centre for Social Policy, 67, 68, 71, 73, 74, 76, 77
Apennines, 166
Armut im Wohlfahrtsstaat (Poverty in the Welfare State) (Geissler), 220
ASSEDIC (supplement to unemployment assistance scheme), F, 108–9
assistenza, 185
Association of Belgian Towns and Communes, 69
Atkinson, A., 18, 38, 237
Atwater, 33

AVTS (retired manual workers), F, 106

Bachrach, P., 7–8
Bagnoli, 173
Bairoch, P., 233
Baratz, M.S., 7–8
Bari, 177
bariada, 14
Bayerische Wald, unemployment in, 214
Becker, G., 11
Belfast, 39
Belgium, poverty in: development of, 61; difficulties in interpreting information, 72; a fundamental issue, 68; numbers involved, 64, 72, 77
beneficenza (relief), 185
Berthoud, R., 20
Bethnal Green, 39
Beveridge Report, 34, 43, 61, 105
'bidonvilles', 110
Birmingham, 114
Blaug, M., 11
Bohning, W., 19
Bonilla, F., 14
Borel, Nicole, 98
borgate, 177
Boston, 113
Bowles, S., 11
Brittany, 113
Brussels, 64
Buckley, W., 6
Bureau de Recherches Sociales of Aide à Toute Détresse (A. à

incentives, *see* motivation
income: net, in EEC countries,
235; sources of, 236; B, distribution of, 79–80, guaranteed,
for the elderly (GIE), 68, 73,
75, 76, needs, 71, redistribution of, 80, replacement, 85;
F, distribution, 115, inequality,
114–17, little material on, 95,
Le Monde on distribution of,
92, suggested figures for the
poor, 98–9; G, 196–206, comparison with other countries,
199, distribution, 204–6,
large proportion to pensioners,
200, small proportion on
supplementary income, 200,
SPES and DIW, 196–206,
statistics, 202; Ir, basic income
units, 137–9, distribution data
inadequate, 137, earlier data,
144–5, income maintenance,
139, 140, 141, 142, 145–6,
147, 151, number eligible for
medical care, 144, on farms,
139–40, rates, 134, sources,
137, 144; It, 166–71, benefits
to home communities not
known, 175, from emigrants,
172, 174–5, how used, 175,
from wages, 178–9; UK, definition, 24, distribution, 24–6,
from employment, 26–8, inequality has changed little,
56, items omitted, 25, records
unreliable, 24, source of information, 24–5, unreal reflection
of value of income, 26; *see also*
earnings; poverty line
Income and Consumption Surveys
(Federal Statistical Office),
196–206
'incomplete families', *see* one-
parent families
industrial accident rate, G, 225
industrial workers, It, payment of
benefits, 184
industry, It: political involvement
in, 172; characteristics of, 179
inequality: accentuates strife, 6;
compared with poverty, 3; defined, 1–2; harmful to society,
6; a universal phenomenon, 4;

F, due to area, 111–12; Ir, compared with other countries,
151; It, opposed to poverty,
164; *see also* poor; poverty
infant mortality, G, 225
Inland Revenue: basis of estimates
of poverty, 38; and distribution
of wealth, 28, 29, 30
INPS, It, 183
INSEE, *see* National Statistical
and Economic Studies Institute
Integrated Micro-Data File, G, 197
intelligence, 10–11; definition of,
10; and income, 10; little
effect on earnings, 12; measurement of, 10–11
IQ tests, 10–11
Ireland, poverty in: among
women, 239; attitudes to
causes, 156; better than
formerly, 156; British parliamentary enquiries on, 126;
compared with other EEC
countries, 124, 239; decrease
1966–75, 151; EEC survey,
133; high incidence of, 156;
public opinion surveys on, 133;
relative interpretation of, 136;
very little information, 124,
126; ways of estimating, 137
IRI, 173
Irish Congress of Trade Unions,
149
Italy, poverty in: causes, 165–6;
Christian views on, 162;
defined, 162; part of larger
examination of inequality, 164;
and politics, 172–4; statistics,
165; very widespread, 164

Jacini Inquiry into Agriculture
(1885), It, 161
Jencks, 11
Johnson, L.B., 94
Joseph, Sir Keith, 12

Kaim-Caudle, P., 127
Keating, 125
Kennedy, J.F., 94
Kilkenny Conference on Poverty,
128–9, 130, 134–5, 156
Klanberg, Frank, 209, 223
Klanfer, Jules, 96, 99

self-employed: B, 63, higher
incidence of poverty than
among employed, 74, numbers
likely to fall, 74; F, statistics
limited, 99
VII plan, F, 108
Schonfield, Andrew, 201
short-time working, *see cassa
integrazione*; underemployment
Sicily, 113, 166; and paradox of
state finance, 173
Silburn, R., 39
Sinfield, A., 50
single-parent families, *see* one-
parent families
situation of poverty, compared
with culture of poverty, 15–
16
Sixth Quinquennial National Plan,
1971–5, F, 95
slums, of Dublin, 126
smallholders' assistance, 141
SMIC (Salaire minimum interprofessionel de croissance),
97–100
SMIG (Salaire minimum interprofessionel garanti), 97, 115,
117
Smith, Adam, on necessities of
life, 2
Smith, R.T., 15
Social Action Programme of the
European Communities, 129–
30
social assistance: G, compared
with UK, 216; Ir, 130, 132;
benefits, 145, 147; It, benefits
from ECA, 186–7
social assistance committees, B,
62–3; Antwerp, 69–70;
Brussels, 64; reluctance to
apply to, 64; replaced by public
centres for social welfare, 67
'social decomposition' (poverty),
It, 163
Social Democratic-Liberal coalition, G, 207, 223
Social Democrats, G, 211–12,
224
social differentiation, 6
social insurance: B, characteristics
of, 62, complicated and not

helpful to non-trade unionists,
62; Ir, 127–30, 132, benefits,
145, 147; It, 182–4, Fascist
schemes, 182, low benefits,
184, payments, 147, pensions,
183–4, various forms, 182
social security: in EEC countries,
239–42; indirect cost of, 241;
F, 93–6; G, 206–9, expansion,
206, standards, 206; Ir, 127–36,
rates paid, 131
social stratification, 4; dysfunctional, 6; an inevitable state, 4
social welfare: in EEC countries,
general trends, 234; It, 181–90,
beneficenza and *assistenza*,
185, ECAs, 186–7, complex
structure of, 181, fragmented
organisation, 185, the future,
189–90, institutions, 187–8,
number of agencies, 181,
reasons for development, 181,
Regional intervention, 189–90,
welfare system, 185–90
socialist society, conflict in, 17
socially disadvantaged, UK, compared with disadvantaged, 55
*Society and Democracy in
Germany* (Dahrendorf), 226
Southern Development Agency
(*Cassa per il Mezzogiorno*), 171
SPES Project, work done by, 196–
200, 203–4, 207, 208–9, 213,
216, 217, 218, 219, 220, 222,
223
Stark, T., 38
Statement of Intent, 129
Steenwijk, Alwine de Vos van, 94
Stoleru, Lionel, 96
structural explanation of inequality and poverty, 16–20
structurally unemployed, B, 74–5
subsistence, minimum level of, It,
161
subsistence, security of, B, 84
subsistence minimum, right to a
(RSM), B, 68, 69, 72, 75
supplementary benefit: Ir, 141;
UK, 38, 237–8, number relying
on, 43–4, 47, 49–50, 53, 54,
scales misleading, 36
Supplementary Welfare Allowances, Ir, 130